Leading under Duress

Leading under Duress

How Exceptional Teachers Thrive in the Global South

Jean-Pierre K. Bongila

LEXINGTON BOOKS

Lanham • Boulder • New York • London

Lexington Books
Bloomsbury Publishing Inc, 1385 Broadway, New York, NY 10018, USA
Bloomsbury Publishing Plc, 50 Bedford Square, London, WC1B 3DP, UK
Bloomsbury Publishing Ireland, 29 Earlsfort Terrace, Dublin 2, D02 AY28, Ireland
www.rowman.com

British Library Cataloguing in Publication Information Available

Library of Congress Cataloging-in-Publication Data

Names: Bongila, Jean-Pierre K., 1961- author.
Title: Leading under duress: how exceptional teachers thrive in the Global South/Jean-Pierre Bongila.
Description: Lanham: Lexington Books, [2024] | Includes bibliographical references and index.
Summary: "This comparative study of teacher attrition in the Global South and OE CD countries examines the exceptionality of twenty selected learning leaders in the D.R. Congo, Ghana, and Uganda who have stayed in the teaching profession"—Provided by publisher.
Identifiers: LCCN 2024034674 (print) | LCCN 2024034675 (ebook) | ISBN 9781793620576 (cloth) | ISBN 9781793620583 (ebook)
Subjects: LCSH: Teachers—Africa—Psychology. | Educational Leadership—Africa. | Teachers—Africa—Interviews. | Teacher Turnover—Africa. | Altruism—Africa.
Classification: LCC LB1775.4.A35 B364 2024 (print) | LCC LB1775.4.A35 (ebook) | DDC 371.10096—dc23/eng/20241009
LC record available at https://lccn.loc.gov/2024034674
LC ebook record available at https://lccn.loc.gov/2024034675

For product safety related questions contact productsafety@bloomsbury.com.

∞™ The paper used in this publication meets the minimum requirements of American National Standard for Information Sciences—Permanence of Paper for Printed Library Materials, ANSI/NISO Z39.48-1992.

To Fr. David Smith:
You exemplified teaching with integrity.
You inspired my building bridges of cultures with genuine grace.
Indeed, you scrutinized each sentence of my
publications with great humility.
Pray for exceptional learning leaders who endeavor for justice and peace.
May you rest in Christ's eternal peace.

To Senator David Durenberger:
You will always remain this irreplaceable friend.
With whom I crossed Africa studying and pondering leadership.
Who dreamed of a "Bilingual School of Leadership."
Pray that your dream and its reality soon blend.
May you rest in Christ's eternal peace.

Contents

Preface

The exceptional teachers who lead their classes and their profession with professional ethics in toxic environments constitute an endangered species in many countries, particularly those of the Global South involved in this study. My observation emerges from a whole sabbatical year of studying these ethical learning leaders in the African countries of the Democratic Republic of the Congo (D.R. Congo), Ghana, and Uganda. Although the study of these special learning leaders leans toward an end, my educated reminiscence of its outcomes abounds, mainly as I take some physical and temporal distance from the field investigation of the topic. Toward the conclusion of this study, I am left with the pleasurable task of writing a preface to the book, which I have begun on my flight back from Africa to the United States via Europe and Canada. Although the flight is filled, I experience a feeling of loneliness in the skies. I wanted to contribute to ethical and educational leadership by examining bright spots in leadership education whose example may compel others to follow suit. My contribution to the two fields of leadership research and practice would not explain my choice of this topic. Two rather unexhaustive rationales come to mind: my primary identity as a Catholic priest and my teaching ministry as a professor of ethical and educational leadership courses that involve a significant portion of leading study abroad courses in the Global South.

My identity as a Catholic priest compels me—on a personal and pastoral level—to seek the good in any human being. Although Christianity teaches that all people are sinners and undeserving of God's grace, Christians recognize the "spotless" lamb in Jesus Christ, both as human and God, who gives the entire humanity hope for sanctity and—ultimately—eternal life.

Moreover, I have taken the liberty to believe there always exist those bright "immaculate" spots in every human soul, even in that of the worst sinners. By the same token, various discourses on teachers' attrition and their low morale, particularly in the Global South, painted a bleak picture of the overall education profession that led me to posit that there should be something exceptional there to reckon with. As a learning leader, I believe in the sacrality and the ethics of the profession.

More importantly, I have been privileged enough to meet and acquaint myself with ethical learning leaders both in the Global North and the Global South who have performed their profession with utmost integrity and professionalism. To use the words of Michael Fullan (2018), those humans "are fundamentally motivated by two factors: doing things that are intrinsically meaningful to themselves, and working with others—peers, for example—in accomplishing worthwhile goals never before reached" (Fullan, 2018, p. 5). However, the exceptional teachers in this study find meaning in teaching, which most identify as their calling or vocation, and strive to educate their students to become leaders who work skillfully to advance the common good. In the ideal, Fullan states, "Ask teachers what school they would most like to teach in, or whether they want to stay in teaching at all, and you hear two criteria that top their lists: the quality of their colleagues and the quality of school leadership" (Fullan, 2018, p. 5). In practice, most exceptional learning leaders in this study did not work in an environment that fostered the above two ideals. In many instances, the reality surrounding their profession was marred with toxicity and systemic corruption. That they professionally and ethically excelled in less than favorable working conditions—to put it mildly—makes them even more exceptional and, therefore, worthy of being studied and praised.

One of those exceptional pearls who had agreed to participate in this study was Susan, happy memory. Unlike a few instructors who declined to participate in this study after being nominated by their school and academic community, Susan enthusiastically embraced my eagerness to give a voice to the voiceless learning leaders and agreed to receive the study survey and participate in it. About a week after she had received the survey and promised to respond in the following hours, I received a message of her passing. May she peacefully and eternally rest in the Pantheon of the exceptional learning leaders who distinguish themselves by their professional ethics and sustained integrity. Upon learning of her passing, I asked that one of the spotters who knew of Susan's exceptionality write a eulogy for the illustrious teacher. Here is what came up:

> In a career spanning 20 years, Susan was a Special Educational Needs (SEN) Facilitator and Counselor—10 years tutoring regular children and 10 years, children living with disabilities. Susan gladly accepted to participate as a community partner, representing Multikids Inclusive Academy in East Legon, Accra,

> in data collection in Ghana for the study on "Exceptional Teachers/Professors in the Global South." Susan's death was unexpected and, to be honest, unfair. She was full of life, generous of heart and would do anything for anyone; peaceful, and poignantly kind. Susan dedicated her life to improving and driving change in the SEN field. She had a fondness for people with special needs and her mentees. She was very focused on self-development and would always encourage people around her to make the best out of life no matter the circumstances. Susan was popular among students and well respected and thought of by colleagues. Her depth of knowledge in the field of SEN made her a good choice for recommendation by schools, parents, and other professionals within the area of education when there was a need for an educational assessment and interpretation or Continuous Professional Development (CPD) training for schools. As a counsellor, she brought her expertise and experience to bear on her dealings with colleagues and students. She had amazing conflict resolution skills; always helping parties involved to see things from the other's point of view. She was very professional with her approach to behaviour management in the classroom. Unfortunately, Susan is no longer with us physically, but we take consolation in the fact that she has left her footprints in the sands of time. For these reasons and many others, we are very proud of her and will forever remember her with affection.

The heart of the book concerns exceptional individuals like Susan. In essence, the purpose of this book is threefold:

First, this study examined the question of teacher attrition/retention common to both the countries selected (the D.R. Congo, Ghana, and Uganda) and the OECD countries, including the United States, through an investigation of the "exceptional" teachers in the Global South countries.

Although the contexts of teacher attrition and retention vary from country to country, this research has provided food for thought to US institutions, such as my own University of St. Thomas, that train teachers and encourage them to remain in their vocation. This book intends to bring contexts of teacher retention and the exceptionality of some exemplary teachers closer to institutions of higher learning in the United States to promote cultural interaction. In many ways, I used a constant comparison method (Charmaz, 2014) to provide a synoptic view of the phenomena as they appear in both the Global North and the Global South for cultural interconnectedness purposes. In fact, in my nineteen years of university teaching in the United States, I have frequently included a module on social justice at the global level, fostering cultural interconnectedness as well as the common good. My annual abroad program, Leadership in the International Contexts, explicitly aims to foster cultural dialogues as I expose US students to African cultures and vice versa. Therefore, investigating the steadfastness of Global South teachers who have remained in the profession when every condition would compel them to quit should equally puzzle educational systems in rich and developing nations.

Second, my study intends to give voice to those "exceptional" teachers and analyze the ethical rationale behind their unfailing commitment to their teaching vocation. They spoke of their teaching philosophies, which revealed altruistic impulses. Because altruism, both in theory and in practice, appeared to be the motive that propelled these exemplary teachers to actions for the common good, the book moved forward to present and discuss in more detail extraneous reasons, such as personal gains, that might have prompted them to find comfort in the conditions in which they worked and lived. To provide context, this book also depicts the professional and social conditions in which the learning leaders in this study operated. In their own words, participants in this study suggested that their teaching conditions were realistically inadequate to foster the ideal learning environment for students.

It followed that the exceptional teachers had alternative mechanisms to maintain themselves professionally and remained people of great integrity professionally and socially. Therefore, the book gives those teachers a platform to address the alternative strategies that helped them survive professional and social duress. It also endeavors to examine and bring to light those coping mechanisms, which other struggling teachers could use in the Global South and the Global North as applicable. Throughout the book, particularly in chapters 4 and 5, these heroic teachers expressed their wishes of how they hope their lived experience of teaching with integrity—despite all—would resonate in their institutions, the Global South and, why not, the Global North.

Third, this book is intended to analyze the voices of exceptional teachers and their altruistic actions through the lens of philanthropic and leadership ethics theories. It makes the point that leadership ethics can bring a unique and overdue contribution to the rationale beyond the professional integrity of the teachers in this study. The book dwells extensively on altruism as this concept permeates many ethical standards, particularly the ethics of care (Shapiro & Stefkovich, 2021) and virtue ethics (Ruggiero, 2024). Put in the context of Africa, altruism means and closely relates to the African virtue of *kimuntu*, also referred to as *Ubuntu* (Desmond Tutu, 2000). My interpretation of this concept meets Bujo's (2011) understanding that *kimuntu* relates to African altruism or generosity as far as communal love and community building are concerned. In "Grounding Ethical Leadership in African Diaspora and Election Rights" (2013), I wrote, "Whatever metaphor or taxonomy I might use to identify this virtue will make it look nonexhaustive so profound is this concept. In itself, *kimuntu* adequately presumes the presence of other virtues such as compassion, empathy, charity, and others" (Bongila, 2013). Bujo (2011) rightly calls it "this inalienable fundamental principle of African ethics," evoking the proverbial formula: "I am because we are and because we are, I am too." Notably, *kimuntu* or African solidarity does not mean the individual loses their identity because of the community.

Nevertheless, concerning the study in this book, I refrained from attributing to the exceptional teachers the epithet of altruism because their philanthropic actions demonstrated a level of self-benefit. Instead, I suggested that one of the significant reasons why exceptional teachers remained faithful to their teaching profession amounts to a kind of *kimuntu* that might well relate to the two-way asymmetric model of philanthropy (Grunig, 1992) and the warm glow giving theory (Mark Ottoni-Wilhelm, 2017). Looking from both the perspectives of philanthropic giving and ethical leadership theories, the altruistic *kimuntu* of the exceptional learning leaders appears edulcorated while remaining exemplary.

To my knowledge, no researcher has conducted a qualitative research study—through narrative inquiry—of the persistent teachers whom this inquiry calls "exceptional" to uncover the ethical reasons behind their persistence. This study's uniqueness lies in its analysis of untold stories of the voiceless teachers in the Global South countries of the D.R. Congo, Ghana, and Uganda. Uniquely, this study recognizes and brings to bear the heroism of those teachers, hoping that a new generation of teachers will benefit from the respect and adulation teachers receive in countries like South Korea (Pisa, 2011; Global Teacher Status Index, 2018).

What the reader would hopefully take away from this book is the emphasis on the importance of ethical leadership that comes in handy in wisely solving and analyzing issues of social importance, such as attrition and retention, with which both the Global South and the Global North grapple. More importantly, the altruistic mindset and behavior of the exceptional teachers in the Global South—whose conditions of life and work stand below those of the Global North—should be a source of great inspiration for all while protecting this endangered species from self-destruction. Likely, the narrative inquiry methodology applied with the exceptional teachers, doubled with some form of grounded theory's constant comparison, can be subject to adaptation and adoption across space, time, cultures, and academic disciplines. While the reader will get a glimpse of the less-than-ethical conditions that brought about the phenomenon of exceptional learning leaders in the Global South, they will ultimately appreciate the high level of those teachers' leadership ethics, which circle their altruistic actions, which in turn originate from their African *kimuntu*.

Acknowledgments

Many people directly or indirectly contributed to the development of this book. First, I would like to acknowledge the spotters who provided tremendous help with the identification and recommendation of exceptional teachers: Rev. Sister Elizabeth Nakayiza (RSCJ) and Sr. Elizabeth Nakku (IHMR), former and current deans of the School of Education at the University of Kisubi (Uganda); Dr. Francis Gbormittah (University of Accra Legon, Ghana); Rev. Fr. Jean Mboma (S.J.), dean of the School of Agronomic and Veterinarian Sciences at Loyola University (D.R. Congo); Rev. Brother Narcisse Mungeye (Fjk); Rev. Nicaise Mibatu of my illustrious cohort from the Minor Seminary of Kinzambi, also known as "La Cyzique" (D.R. Congo).

I can only be grateful to all the selected exceptional learning leaders who participated in this study for their availability and exemplary dedication to the teaching profession.

To my esteemed colleagues at the Department of Educational Leadership: Dr. Candace Chou, Dr. Jayne Sommers, and Dr. Aura Wharton-Beck, whose tremendous support has contributed to the materialization of this academic piece of work, I say thank you.

Special recognition goes to the Most Reverends Mununu Kasiala and Timothée Bodika, my late and current bishops, for supporting my academic ministry. A particular thank-you should be directed to Rev. Dennis Dease, president emeritus of the University of St. Thomas, who has always been at the forefront of global initiatives, and to our mutual great friend, the late former Minnesota Senator David Durenberger.

I sincerely thank the wonderful friends and family members who have painstakingly supported my quest for global and ethical leadership. May my friend Rev. Honore Kombo, *companion de lutte*, be recognized for his encouragement and counsel. To my great friends: Beverly and Toomas

Ruberg (Canada), Megan Doyle (USA), Theo Nana and family, Rev. Narcisse Mungeyi, Beatrice Kindembe, Patric Kabangu, Marcellin Mbwamboma, Rev. Francois X. Eale, Ms. Minette Tchokomeni, and the Mutombo family, Guy-Lucien and Mianda Whembolua, Laura Kapita and Marie-Christiane, and Belange and Francoise Kaba, I say thank you.

This list would be incomplete without mentioning my family members, Sandra Bongila, Patricia, and Paulin Buaka; Thierry Mbuluku, Armand Ntantu, and family, my sisters Ya Wivine Kulemfuka, Ya Fete Makyla, and Josee Milinta; Nina and Christelle Nganga, my uncle Olard, and Ya Therese in Canada.

Introduction

Value of Education in OECD vs. Global South

"Wealth, if you use it, comes to an end.
Learning, if you use it, increases."

(Swahili Proverb)

Exceptional teachers live and perform in an environment where education and the very essence of educational leadership have been undervalued. To give credence to this premise, I have endeavored to examine broadly in this chapter the status of education in general and the teaching profession in particular.

The chapter starts from a global perspective to examine the overall status of the teaching profession globally. Using statistical data from the United Nations Educational, Scientific and Cultural Organization (UNESCO), the Organization for Economic Cooperation and Development (OECD), and others, this section analyzes the importance that most countries in the world attribute to education, the teaching profession, and teachers as central leaders of learning. The underpinning question of this chapter consists of whether and how countries value education and teachers as learning leaders. What does research say about the consequences of that consideration (or lack thereof) to education and the teaching profession? To answer these questions regarding the status of the teaching profession, the book divides the countries into two significant groups.

The first group consists of OECD countries whose social and economic advances should translate into a high level of consideration for teachers as major contributors to learning, which in turn influences the social development of their countries. This group includes the highest-performing educational systems (Darling-Hammond & Rothman, 2015) and almost all OECD members. Studies after studies (UNESCO, 2021; UN, 2021; UNICEF, 2021) have shown that all people and all countries regard education as the primary engine of social development. They considerably recognize the value of education, which encompasses teachers' fair treatment and market compensation. However, a second group of countries has failed to advance the status of education as a whole practically.

Unfortunately, most of those countries generally belong to the Global South, particularly Sub-Saharan Africa (Guthrie, 2018). They are characterized by both the stagnation of their socioeconomic conditions and the decline in the social status of their lead learners, including school administrators and schoolteachers. For various reasons not within this study's scope, those countries fail to meet some critical benchmarks of the value of education. When educational institutions and systems fail to meet these aforementioned requirements mentioned above for the value of education, the consequences are multiple, including teaching absenteeism, teacher attrition, and a multifaceted corruption of the whole educational engine. From this chaotic environment emerge the exceptional teachers who resist any form of spoliation of their sacred pledge to education with integrity.

VALUE OF EDUCATION

Nelson Mandela made a timeless proclamation when he stated: "Education is the most powerful weapon we can use to change the world!" Exceptional educational leaders in this present book work tirelessly to make this proclamation a reality through their business of leading students' learning. As these leaders endeavor to maintain the value of education, they also hope society provides the necessary human, financial, and material capital to show their support for this unique endeavor. The United Nations (UN) understands the value of education for humankind that aspires to a brighter and prosperous future. In fact, in its document *Academic Impact*, the UN (2022) affirms that education is the basic building block of every society. It is the best investment countries can make to build prosperous, healthy, and equitable societies. Article 26 of the 1948 Universal Declaration of Human Rights states, "Everyone has the right to education." "Education is not only a right, but a passport to human development that opens doors and expands opportunities and freedoms" (UN, 2022). If the UN maintains that educational institutions are a source of formal education in society, it also recognizes the value of teachers as the prominent leaders of educational endeavors. As the UN underscores the importance of educational institutions as sources to disseminate education and its significance, it also subsumes the role of teachers as the disseminators of knowledge. Teachers are central to educational levels, which vary from country to country. Countries that invest more in their educational systems, including teachers, are likely to yield high-quality education (World Population Review, 2022). It is commonly accepted that developed nations tend to offer their citizens a higher quality of education than the Global South countries because the former invest sufficiently in both their students and their teachers.

Regarding the Global South countries of Africa, a Gallup Poll (2014) survey was conducted in 2013 on thirty-one African countries on the *value Africans place on education*. The main survey question—"which of the following is most valuable for someone (in your country) to have in order to succeed in life (education, family and friend connections, strong work ethic and intelligence)?"—showed that 41% of Africans see education as vital to success, 30% (family/friend connections), 17% (intelligence) and 12% (work ethic) (Gallup, 2014). However, the Gallup Poll survey yielded two major responses: personal connections and education. The results suggested that "Africans often perceive personal connections as more important to success." The choice of education as the most crucial factor for a successful life varied from Botswana (73%) to Ivory Coast (13%) among the countries surveyed.

In table 0.1, I reproduce only the results for the three countries in the study, with Ghana placing second after Botswana regarding education as the most essential factor for success (72%), the D.R. Congo (18%), and Uganda (42%). The central premise of this study holds that education has been undervalued, particularly in the Global South countries. The present Gallup Poll infers that people in the D.R. Congo see education as of less value than those in Uganda and Ghana. Because the value attributed to education goes along with the consideration given to teachers, it is safe to infer that those learning leaders do not benefit from the respect due to their profession. The exceptionality of the teachers in this book is a function of their challenges within their educational systems. The most chaotic educational systems are rarely likely to generate exceptional teachers. Nevertheless, should those teachers exist, they would appear resilient because they have resisted chaotic environments that entertain such unethical behaviors as rampant corruption, absenteeism, abuse of students, trafficking of grades, and the like. In other words, the people

Table 0.1 Value of Education in Africa

In your opinion, which of the following is MOST valuable for someone [in your country] to have in order to succeed in life?

	Education	*Family/Friend Connections*	*Strong Work Ethic*	*Intelligence*
D.R. Congo	18%	54%	8%	19%
Ghana	72%	12%	9%	7%
Uganda	42%	19%	15%	24%

Adapted from Gallup Poll (2014). See Appendix B.

whom school communities in the D.R. Congo, Uganda, and Ghana recognized as exceptional teachers must have distinguished themselves by their incredible resilience.

Gallup Poll (2014) reported that educated parents are crucial to African education. This conclusion emerged from a weeklong series that analyzed how education leaders, students, and teachers evaluated education in the United States and worldwide. As concerns Africa, Gallup Poll conducted face-to-face interviews in 2013 with a minimum of 1,000 adults in Angola, Benin, Botswana, Burkina Faso, Cameroon, Chad, Congo, Kinshasa, Ethiopia, Gabon, Ghana, Guinea, Ivory Coast, Kenya, Liberia, Madagascar, Malawi, Mali, Mauritania, Niger, Nigeria, Congo Brazzaville, Rwanda, Senegal, Sierra Leone, South Africa, Tanzania, Uganda, Zambia, and Zimbabwe. The study determined that the likelihood of an individual attending or graduating from secondary school was greater if both parents had completed primary education. In Africa, parents' education largely determines their children's schooling level. Therefore, in the Gallup Poll, when African parents value education and invest in it, they pave the way for future generations of professionals, including teachers. The Poll's bottom line held that the "'parent effect,' combined with a true understanding of the value of education, creates an environment where children are more likely to learn and achieve higher goals" (Gallup Poll, 2014). UNICEF (2022) echoes the same critical role African parents play in promoting the education of their children, as it states, "Most studies conducted in sub-Saharan Africa show that the higher the education level of the head of the household, or a child's parents/caregivers, the lower the risk of the child being out of school. Educated parents are more competent in mentoring their children in their studies, and they have higher academic and professional ambitions for them" (p. 11).

Recently, Azomahou and Yitbarek (2021) conducted a study on the intergenerational transmission of education in nine Sub-Saharan African countries, using nationally representative household survey data on parents of adult individuals. The nine countries examined included Comoros, Ghana, Guinea, Madagascar, Malawi, Nigeria, Rwanda, Tanzania, and Uganda. Results indicated that in Ghana, Nigeria, Uganda, and Malawi, children from parents with some level of education—as opposed to no education at all—were likely to complete a minimum of secondary education. Children from parents who completed more than a secondary education—as opposed to those from parents with no education—were likely to get a higher education. These results align with prior research by Gallup Poll (2014) and underscore the importance and value of education as a tool for change-making in society. More importantly, the above studies emphasize the "parent effect" in how the next generations value and embrace education.

One example is worth mentioning. The academic tenure of Professor Emeritus Dr. Jean Lubuma at the University of Pretoria illustrates the "parent effect" on their children in Africa. In 2019, Professor Lubuma was saying goodbye to the University of Pretoria, where he served as a professor of Mathematics and Applied Mathematics, chair of Mathematics Models and Methods in Bioengineering and Biosciences (2013–15), and dean of the Faculty of Natural and Agricultural Sciences from 2015 to 2019. Below is a short excerpt from Professor Lubuma's process of becoming a teacher/professor published by the University of Pretoria News (2019).

> What began as a dream for a 17-year-old Grade 11 pupil in Kikwit Sacré Cocur, Democratic Republic of Congo, has culminated in an illustrious career that he could only dream of. Professor Jean Lubuma retired from his position as Dean of the Faculty of Natural and Agricultural Sciences (NAS) at the end of September 2019. Being a dean is something, he said, he had never dreamt would ever happen. "When I was young, I wanted to be a math teacher. My father was one of my inspirations, being himself a primary school teacher, and I had an amazing math teacher in high school from Grade 11. By the end of my high school career, everyone knew that I would be a mathematics teacher," Prof. Lubuma said.

Professor Lubuma began his academic career in 1985 as a Lecturer and later Senior Lecturer at the University of Annaba, Algeria (University of Pretoria News, 2019). His father could have been a teacher in the 1970s when the teaching profession was well respected in his native D.R. Congo. One would argue that Professor Lubuma might have had second thoughts following in his father's footsteps had he been a teacher in the 1990s and 2000s when the deterioration of this profession became acute. Notwithstanding this hypothetical, Professor Lubuma's pathway to the teaching profession exemplifies the finding by Azomahou and Yitbarek (2021) that children are likely to pursue a focused educational dream if their parents hold a minimum of a secondary education level. The University of Pretoria News (2019) further narrates Professor Lubuma's persistence to solely embrace his father's profession to be a learning leader:

> The plan, however, changed slightly. His [Professor Lubuma's] formal admission to the University of Kinshasa saw him land in the Bachelor of Engineering program, as opposed to mathematics. "I refused to attend Engineering lectures and went straight to attend lectures of the Bachelor of Mathematics programme in the Science Faculty for about five months, without being registered there. Then, we had to write mid-term tests that would determine whether we stayed in these courses or not. I wrote the Analysis and Algebra tests and got 90% for each of them. It was at this point that I realised, after a little encouragement

from a friend, that I needed to sort out the issue of registration," Prof. Lubuma said. He ended up standing in the registrar's office, asking to be transferred from Engineering to Mathematics, something unheard of, mainly because everyone else was moving in the opposite direction. "He told me it would be straightforward for him to sign and allow me to make that change. He just had a warning for me that I was making this change at my own risk. I had never heard this phrase he used before. After learning what it meant, it fuelled me to work hard for my dream. I have not looked back since," he said. Prof Lubuma also learned that there were teachers at the university. It's what kept him in academia and his dream alive.

HONORING TEACHERS

Imagine visiting a country like South Korea, where teachers are highly esteemed. As you sit on the balcony of your hotel, you notice a severe commotion on the main street leading to the main stadium of Seoul, the capital city of Korea. You hear loudspeakers announcing a repeating message with very rhythmic music. Although there is almost always a traffic jam in the city, this is not usually the case on Sundays when people prefer to take other directions for religious services or stay home. But this Sunday is unusual because a parade of luxurious cars follows the heavy traffic, most surrounded by police-like escorts on flashing motorcycles. Then, toward the end of the escort, you see a series of limousines moving toward the stadium; the last limousine appears to be that of a famous celebrity or a national dignitary adorned with flowers and surrounded by a huge number of police-like motorcycles accompanied by a piece of ceremonial music. You take an Uber ride toward the stadium because that is where everyone is going. Once in the stadium, you are in front of the innumerable crowd of students in uniform, parents, bystanders, the minister of education, and other people looking like dignitaries. As the last limousine with a movie star standing in the back of the vehicle enters the stadium, the crowd of over 80,000 people stands up and rises in jubilation. The limousine with its famous person drives around the stadium while music is playing, and the crowd becomes frenetic with louder and louder applause while the limousine stops. The famous person is escorted to the podium with flowers. You finally manage to ask a person standing next to you what the occasion was all about and who the celebrity is that people acclaimed loudly as the president or a highly rated movie star. The person looks at you with a bit of surprise that you are so ignorant of the event and the person who was so dignified. He nicely responds that the day, May 15, was Teachers' Day in South Korea, and the person receiving the honors is the teacher of the year.

This anecdotal account illustrates, however, the value some countries akin to South Korea attach to teachers in particular and education in general, which culminates in teachers' recognition on World Teachers' Day. UNESCO's 1994 establishment of World Teachers' Day has given tremendous impetus to countries like the D.R. Congo, Ghana, Uganda, and Korea to recognize the irreplaceable role teachers play in the multifaceted development of a society.

Although World Teachers' Day falls on October 5, South Korea celebrates its own teachers on May 15, a tradition this country started in 1963 (Koreabridge, 2011). Whether Teachers' Day occurs on May 15 or the closest school day before that date, current and former students head to their classrooms to present their favorite teachers with carnations. On the same date, the Ministry of Education issues a merit award to the most outstanding teacher in the nation. The nation rewards the merit educator for three skills: the teacher's ideal methodology, influence on students, and leadership toward improving society. However, in the provinces and all over the country, alumni groups organize special ceremonies or "gratitude-showing ceremonies" at their local schools to express their gratitude to their former teachers. Those alumni believe they all spent about two decades of their youth in school, and honoring their favorite teachers reminds them of their youth and brings them back together with their past classmates (Koreabridge, 2011).

A member of the Organization for Economic Cooperation and Development (OECD) along with thirty-seven other countries, including Finland, Germany, and the United States, South Korea is known for its high value on education, particularly its teachers (Deepti Mani, 2018). Its spending on education for 2018 was 4.46% of its GDP (YCharts, 2019). The world knows South Korea particularly for its high standards of education, which has been nicknamed "education fever" (Lee, 2006). The value South Korea attaches to education pays off as it ranks among the top-performing OECD countries in terms of reading literacy, mathematics, and sciences. Korea's average student score in the Program for International Student Assessment (PISA) averages 519, while the overall OECD average stands around 493 (OECD, 2018). This nation consistently ranks among the top for global education.

Compared to the OECD countries in general and South Korea in particular, Sub-Saharan Africa had—to a certain degree—honored its extraordinary teachers, most of whom belong to the independence epoch of the 1960s. However, there is a gap in the literature on how Africa might have consistently given reverence to its leaders of knowledge, except for a few educational and charismatic leaders such as Nyerere of Tanzania and Kwame Nkrumah of Ghana. Official actions to honor them have timidly appeared since UNESCO's establishment of World Teachers' Day, also known as International Teachers' Day, in 1994, is held annually on October 5. For memory, World Teachers' Day commemorates the 1966 signing of the UNESCO Recommendation on the Status of Teachers to address the status and conditions of teachers worldwide (UNESCO, 2017). It is not apparent that most students, particularly school alums, have ever heard of or celebrated that day in commemoration of their past and present teachers. More recently, some timidly visible events in some countries, including those in this study, have been mentioned and are encouraging.

In the D.R. Congo, Teachers' Day has not gotten significant media attention. It is safe to assume that students and parents knew little about sporadic events surrounding this day. Media Terre Education (2019), a news website, had published a summary of events mainly organized by Workers and Teachers Unions under the theme "the right to education is also the right to qualified teachers." The DRC trade unions affiliated with Education International, CSC-*Enseignement*, FENECO/UNTC, and SYECO gathered hundreds of their members at the CSC headquarters for the occasion. A theatrical group paid tribute to the Congolese Teacher through several songs and sketches followed by addresses from the Secretary Generals of the aforementioned Unions. They stigmatized the fact that teacher training structures are increasingly emptying today because the teaching profession no longer attracts; rather, it opens the way to job insecurity. The best students, those who have distinguished themselves, no longer stay in the profession. Continuing training is sporadic and has remained the domain of pilot projects that are extinguished with the end of partner funding; even for the recent reforms on basic education, teacher training is taking place in inhumane conditions, the speakers insisted.

On a positive note, there is a remembrance of World Teachers' Day; all the presenters and participants in the above events rightly represent past students who have been taught by learning leaders. However, the visible and intentional presence of current and past and current students and a representation of teachers, seems greatly absent. More importantly, the events highlight the plights of teachers in the D.R. Congo under which exceptional teachers live but thrive.

In Uganda, the celebration of World Teachers' Day occurred on October 12, 2021, rather than the official October 5 because President Yoweri Museveni wanted to attend the commemoration. He was unavailable on October 5 (UNESCO, 2021). Under the drive "Appreciate a Teacher," the Ugandan Ministry of Education and Sports, the Ugandan National Union (UNATU), UNESCO, together with UNICEF and other partners, organized a week's initiative called "Teacher Appreciation Week." The main objective of the drive was to incentivize parents, students, and other stakeholders to take an opportunity to appreciate teachers and recognize their contribution to the development of Uganda. Concretely, the initiative mobilized people to send "Thank you, Teacher" messages, gifts, offers, discounts, and other tokens of appreciation to teachers to make teachers feel valued, loved, and appreciated. This resulted in a state of happiness, joy, and good health for teachers, which is a very good motivation for an attempt to avert the increasing level of demotivation caused by COVID-19 (UNESCO, 2021). Government leaders, as well as teachers' unions and other organizations, assembled to honor the work of teachers, illustrating that African countries in general and Uganda in particular are making positive inroads in honoring the very leaders of learning. The above proclamations do not specify whether the very leaders of learning received recognition from their former or current students.

However, from my study of exceptional teachers in Uganda, many of the details in the accounts below corroborate the participants' stories in this research. Andalou Agency, a news website, published a World Teachers' Day story titled "Teachers in Uganda Despair Over Not Being Paid for Over a Year and Bogus Policies" (Olukya, 2021). The author reported issues that plague the Ugandan educational system as they surfaced on the days surrounding World Teachers' Day. I summarize those issues in three categories: unbalanced teachers' salaries, teachers' coping mechanisms, and privileged sciences teachers versus second-class arts teachers.

Regarding unbalanced salaries, the Ugandan educational system includes three categories of schools: (a) the government fully funds government schools; (b) government-aided schools run like private schools that receive some government subvention, mainly in the form of salaries for qualified teachers; and (c) private schools, which do not receive any assistance whatsoever from the government. During the COVID-19 lockdown, when most schools were closed, public school teachers continued to receive their salaries while their counterparts in private schools were left to their fate. This was the case with Flavia and many more (Olukya, 2021).

Flavia, a primary three teacher at a private school in Idudi village in eastern Uganda, Bugiri district, told Anadolu Agency that she sees no sense in this year's, 2021, World Teachers' Day because she lives in "a sorry state."

> I am a single mother with three children. I teach at a private primary school. Since COVID-19 hit the country early last year and schools were closed under a lockdown, I have not been earning a salary. I was last paid in April last year. . . . Teachers at government schools have continued to receive their salaries throughout the COVID-19 lockdown, but it is far from enough. Our salaries are not a big deal. We are underpaid. Can you imagine a teacher earning only 500,000 [Ugandan] shillings [around $142] per month? (Olukya, 2021)

To survive, teachers must resort to alternative means of subsistence. Only private school teachers who do not receive compensation from the government look for means to make ends meet. Other teachers do the same because their salaries do not cover their households' primary necessities.

Flavia said she started making pancakes and selling them all over the village to make ends meet. She said that among the embarrassing situations she experiences is being stopped by her students to buy pancakes. Nevertheless, she is not alone in such a dilemma. Thousands of teachers in the county are in a similar situation. Among them are teachers in central Uganda's Lwengo district, where many teachers who have long gone without pay have resorted to making bricks. "We do not have anything to celebrate about on World Teachers' Day. Can you imagine we now make bricks for a living?" said their leader, John Kagulire (Olukya, 2021).

Throughout this research, I have encountered the outcry of teachers from elementary to university levels regarding the Ugandan government bias toward science teachers and against arts instructors at all levels. The tension between science teachers and their arts counterparts seems palpable from elementary to university levels. It all began in 2010 when the Uganda government developed a policy giving science teachers a top allowance of 30%. The policy went into effect in 2012 and later became part of teachers' payroll in 2014, causing arts teachers to go on strike in June 2022 (Barigaba, 2022). "I am a graduate geography teacher at a government secondary school who earns 700,000 shillings ($198) working with science teachers in government schools [who] are being paid 1,200,000 shillings [$340] per month, yet we spend the same time in training, and I even have a bigger workload," he said. He said recently, the president became obsessed with issues related to science and treats science teachers like "small gods." "Can you imagine that starting next year, science teachers are to be paid 4 million shillings ($1,132) per month, and we will remain to earn the same? That is a bogus policy," he added. "That will do more harm than good. Paying a higher salary to science teachers than other teachers, headmasters, and district education officers creates a situation that is not conducive to a good education environment" (Olukya, 2021).

However, the way ahead is still long in Uganda, particularly with issues of unfair salaries, teachers' coping mechanisms outside of or on top of teaching, and the preferential treatment of science teachers compared to arts teachers. "Tony William Muganga, a teacher at a government secondary school, said many teachers in Uganda do not take World Teachers' Day seriously because they are not happy about 'unrealistic government policies'" (Olukya, 2021). The exceptional teachers in this study emerged from the above contexts of a complex educational system.

As Ghana celebrated the 2021 World Teachers' Day, I was fascinated by the uplifting messages students from the African Institute for Mathematical Sciences (AIMS, 2021) posted online for their teachers. The hope is that the messages convey a national sentiment about honoring teachers even beyond the designated day of October 5. Students praised their teachers for their transformative roles in improving the world. Students enthusiastically addressed their teachers as transformative leaders who behaved at once like friends and disciplinarians, mentors and cheerleaders, star makers, and light for the unborn generation. Students saw the role of their teachers as commanders of the world as opposed to generals who command armies and presidents who head nations. They wished their teachers fun on World Teachers' Day because they hold the privilege of transforming students' minds and the reason why some children aspire to become extraordinary people in the world.

As a teacher, I have been looking forward to the 2022 World Teacher's Day celebrations in Uganda, specifically in Entebbe, where I have been stationed for the last three months. The theme for the 2022 World Teachers was "the transformation of education begins with teachers" (UNESCO, 2022). In 2021, Uganda celebrated World Teachers' Day on October 12 at the special request of the country's president. However, there was no change of day in 2022. October 5 came and went without any significant events that caught my attention. I confess to the extreme limit of my knowledge of the settings of events in the country. I relied only on major media outlets such as cable news, online publications, and social media to garner information I filtered for my intellectual curiosity. However, some publications in this regard could be in the making in the three countries of the D.R. Congo, Ghana, and Uganda, which would not be available on October 5. On October 6, I had to leave Uganda for my next destination with a small disappointment that not much had happened, probably throughout Sub-Saharan Africa, in honor of teachers. As I was waiting to board the plane at Entebbe airport, my friend sent me a song written in honor of teachers in Africa, which, according to him, originated from Cameroon. The song had gone viral. It turned my disappointment into a delight, making my flight to the D.R. Congo even more enjoyable. The song, "Tribute to the Teachers" by Heatwaves Cameroon (2022), appears to embody the rationale behind the steadfastness of the learning learners in this study. Here are the song's lyrics:

> Tribute to the Teachers
> It is a pride to be a teacher

The above two lines bear truthfulness in several OECD countries like South Korea, Norway, and Sweden, to cite only a few, where the teaching profession is reserved for a selected few (Darling-Hammond, 2010). However, the exceptional teachers in this book live and work in environments where the teaching profession has become a last resort for those who otherwise could not secure an education in medical school, engineering, or law school (UNESCO, 2021).

> Oh yes, more than a pride
> It is a passion to be a teacher

No matter how different societies perceive the role of their learning leaders, the exceptional teachers in this study noticeably feel a sense of pride in what they do. They are proud of their role in society when, once in a while, some past students remind them about the change they caused in their lives. They are still in the teaching profession because they feel passionate about it.

> All that we need is better treatment
> It is with love we build a nation

Whether in the Global South or Global North countries, the cries of teachers are heard who reclaim their right to fair compensation as they dedicate themselves to the construction of the human capital of each country (Barnes, 2016; Alexander et al., 2020; Chiong et al., 2017).

> All that we need is better treatment
> A teacher is the nation-builder

Since colonial times, the U.S. government and people have counted on educators to build a fair and democratic society, instill the fundamentals of its society, straighten behaviors, and impart the notion of the common good while accommodating the mosaic of its culture. Nevertheless, the majority of the teachers in the United States, and more acutely in the Global South countries in this study, claim their plow goes unattended.

> Who spent sleepless nights preparing his lesson
> Transformation of Education begins with the teacher

In the United States, in particular, study after study (OECD, 2011; Jotkoff, 2022; Cachero, 2019) has shown how teachers are both overworked and often overwhelmed, some of them on the verge of depression and other mental illnesses that come with work pressure.

> They build doctors, pilots, engineers, and all great people
> Oh no with meager salary

The songwriter rightly echoes common knowledge that there would not be presidents, pilots, engineers, and thus human capital to build nations without the indispensable work of teachers. Yet, that common knowledge does not translate into fair treatment of those dedicated learning leaders (Kelchtermans, 2017).

We plead on the parents to stop negative intervention
Instead assist them to their work

Not only does the songwriter frame the ills society inflicts on the learning leaders, but they also reframe (Bolman & Deal, 2021) the educational enterprise by inviting parents to shift their minds and positively view the education profession. Ultimately, toward the end of the lyrics, the songwriter is merely calling for the respect of the learning leader, as in these two other lines:

I'm building your future, you kill me
Oh why? respect the teacher

RESPECT FOR TEACHERS

A country that values education also shows great respect for its teachers. Scholars agree that it is hard to measure the influence of teacher status, that is, the social and cultural forces that determine how much we respect teachers (Dolton, 2013). However, it is imperative to assess the respect given to teachers to improve this area and attract future professionals. Dolton (2013) states that, "Governments that are serious about attracting the best people into teaching must look seriously at the status of teachers—alongside other factors such as their salaries." More importantly, examining the respect given to teachers might help determine the level of consideration the exceptional teachers in this study receive from their communities due to their steadfastness in the leading learning profession.

In her article "Where in the World Are Teachers Most Respected? Not in the U.S., a New Survey Shows," Washington Post's analyst Valerie Strauss (2018) summarizes a report from the Global Teacher Status Index (2018). The report resulted from a survey of people in thirty-five countries. Survey questions included teachers' social standing, comparison between the respect due to teachers and to other professions, how teachers should be paid, and whether parents are likely to encourage their children to consider becoming teachers. The Index shows that China and Malaysia are the countries that most respected their teachers. These two countries see teaching professions as on par with medical doctors. The top countries on the Index of 100 are China (100), Malaysia (93.3), Taiwan (70.2), Russia (65), Indonesia (62.1), and Korea (61.2). While the United States ranks sixteenth in terms of the respect it pays to the teaching profession, the following countries are at the bottom of the scale: Argentina (23.6), Ghana (18.9), Italy (13.6), Israel (6.6), and Brazil (1) (Global Teacher Status Index, 2018).

Participants in the survey were also asked to rank by order of respect fourteen professions, including doctor, nurse, lawyer, librarian, local government manager, social worker, accountant, police officer, engineer, management consultant, and website engineer. Respect given to teachers ranked seventh out of fourteen across the thirty-five nations surveyed. In most countries, the social status of teachers was comparable to that of social workers. China and Malaysia see teachers as equal to doctors in social status. (See Appendix A: 2018 Global Teacher Status Index.) It is worth noting that American teachers think their profession's status is lower at 37.1 out of 100 than the general public places it (at 48.7 out of 100). As concerns the encouragement parents would give their children to become teachers, significant contrasts exist among the thirty-five countries surveyed. More than 50% of parents in China, India, Ghana, and Malaysia incentivize younger generations to become teachers. Although Americans think teachers are underpaid, the survey indicated that 42% of parents would encourage their children to embrace the teaching profession.

As opposed to families in countries that encourage their children to consider teaching a rewarding profession, many African countries—with a handful of exceptions like Ghana—are unlikely to incentivize future generations to join the teaching profession. My experience teaching "Leadership in the International Contexts" has led me to travel to a dozen Global South countries with graduate students from the University of St. Thomas, MN. The course emphasizes the education systems of the countries I visit with students because most of them major in educational leadership. When visiting classrooms and interacting with students, whether in their classrooms or informal settings, UST students or I in a foreign country always ask, "What would you want to become after your education?" It is always a happy surprise when, by any chance, one of the students out of the hundreds shows the courage to state publicly or privately that they want to become a teacher.

Conversely, it is always typical for younger students to wish to become doctors, lawyers, pilots, and businesspeople. Almost none of them want to be a teacher. That current generations of students show aversion to the profession that prepares them to become leaders of tomorrow reveals the lack of incentive they receive from their society. This lack of interest in the teaching profession manifests the lack of consideration and respect that most African societies, specifically those I visited with my students, attach to teaching and teachers as the leaders of learning.

Not to mislead the reader, Africa has had an indefectible veneration for teachers, particularly during the waves of independence in the 1960s. It was very dignifying to bear the title of teacher rendered by "Mwalimu" in Swahili, "Musomesa" in Luganda, "Longi" in Kikongo, and "Molakisi" in Lingala. Of the dignitaries who bore this venerable title of teacher during the wave of African independence from colonial powers, a few names are worth mentioning, such as Julius Nyerere (1922–99) of Tanzania, Kwame Nkrumah (1909–72) of Ghana, Léopold Sédar Senghor (1906–2001) of Senegal, Robert Mugabe (1924–2019) of Zimbabwe, Ali Mazrui from Tanzania, Ngugi wa Thiong'o from Kenya, Wole Soyinka from Nigeria and many others who have, at some point in their illustrious lives, been teachers.

The above story of Professor Jean Lubuma, who endeavored to become a math teacher and professor because of his father's influence, who taught math at a primary school, and his high school grade 11 teacher, shows respect for teachers. Nowadays, that consideration, however, belongs to the realm of exceptionality. Even more exceptional is the story of Teacher Peter Tabichi from Kenya, who won the 2019 Global Teacher Prize, making him the best teacher in the world. Father Tabichi was born in rural Kenya and was inspired to become a teacher because of his family, whose impact on making a difference in society he admired (Chebet, 2019).

Pleading for "giving teachers the respect they deserve" in South Africa, Mofokeng (2020) writes: "When a university published a list of careers for which a sizeable number of its first-year students had applied and none saw teaching as their preferred career, I knew we were in trouble as a country (. . .)." With few exceptions, Mofokeng's observation reflects a common trend throughout African educational systems. As in the case of Dr. Lubuma, choosing a career in education at the start of the university program seems to be a last resort in Africa. The Teaching and Learning International Survey (TALIS) makes the point that only about 49% of the current workforce in South Africa had education as their first choice, which represents the lowest among countries that participated in the survey (OECD, 2018). For memory, the OECD (2018) explains that the TALIS is a study that compares teachers' working conditions and school learning environments worldwide to inform education policy. Through its survey, TALIS collects data using teacher and principal questionnaires. Those questionnaires include questions on various topics such as school leadership, professional development, school climate, teaching practices, and job satisfaction.

Unlike in Africa, countries like Singapore understood Nelson Mandela's words that education can propel a country to become a superpower. Singapore attained this goal by recruiting its excellent students into teaching (Darling-Hammond, 2018). It selected prospective teachers from the top one-third of students graduating from secondary education. To my knowledge, such requirements of excellence in selecting future teachers hardly exist in Africa.

On the contrary, African society considers those who choose a degree in education as intellectually weak and incapable of succeeding in other disciplines that require more intellectual abilities. Additionally, said Mofokeng (2020), it is disappointing that many schools of education in South Africa have lowered the recruitment standards to allow academically weaker candidates to get in. Worse, experience has it that African teachers do not receive the credit they deserve. In many countries, like South Africa, there have been reports of violent incidents and disrespect against teachers perpetrated by students and parents. Most of the latter fault teachers for not teaching their children discipline and respect for others, which parents themselves should teach at home. In the next section, I examine how teachers in the OECD countries compare to those in the Global South of Africa concerning job satisfaction.

TEACHER SATISFACTION

To value education also means attending to teachers' job satisfaction. This concept needs particular attention, especially in this study on exceptional teachers who might not receive such satisfaction but remain in the profession. Definitions of job satisfaction are numerous, but they culminate in some commonalities. Researchers define *job satisfaction* as how people feel about various aspects of their jobs (Spector, 1997). Some have seen job satisfaction as related to demographic characteristics, work, pay, relations with coworkers, promotion, or a combination of different factors such as education, experience, supervision, work, and coworkers (Monyatsi, 2012). Some researchers, including Saiti and Papadopoulos (2015), see job satisfaction as an essential feature closely linked to working behaviors such as productivity and efficiency. They concede that job (professional) satisfaction is a complicated and dynamic social phenomenon. However, it boils down to factors that enhance quality performance, people's cohesion, and morale and encompasses a positive influence on an educational organization.

According to the OECD (2018) TALIS, job satisfaction includes "the sense of fulfillment and gratification that teachers get from their work." Moreover, TALIS maintains that job satisfaction may positively be associated with how teachers behave and perform on the job. A teacher's job satisfaction can reflect the value a country, in general, and teachers, in particular, give to its educational system. Education Week (2014) surveyed teachers in several countries in Europe, North America, and Latin America. The survey report indicated that teachers enjoy high job satisfaction despite some cracks. The report cites an international study of school working conditions, which indicated that a global teaching force faces the dilemma of being caught between idealism and frustration. Specifically, the report highlighted the reality that educators worldwide love teaching. However, teachers do not believe that their communities support and value their work. OECD (2022) released a survey on the TALIS, asking teachers and school leaders about the appropriateness of their working conditions and learning environments. The survey was meant to help countries face various educational challenges. Over 100,000 teachers in 7–9 grades from 6,500 schools in 34 countries took the survey. The results found that teachers with high education levels in OECD countries value continuing training. They can identify instructional strategies that increase student learning and value peer collaboration. The study also indicated that teachers found great satisfaction due to their collaboration with colleagues. Additionally, the survey noted that women represented 68% of the teaching force, comprised of overwhelmingly college-educated personnel. These personnel engage in a minimum of one service professional development per year.

However, on the other hand, OECD teachers find their professional development intermittent and only sometimes relevant to their day-to-day teaching activities. They need more time and support to implement new instructional strategies. Although educators in countries like the United States and Singapore value collaboration with colleagues, they still feel isolated in their classrooms. Commenting on the report by TALIS, Melinda G. George, president of the Washington-based National Commission on Teaching and America's Future, which collaborated with the OECD on the United States, had this to say: "We think this is a critical analysis of what is going on for teachers" (OECD, 2022).

Although 90% of teachers are satisfied with their jobs and 91% do not regret becoming a teacher in OECD countries, 74% think society does not value their jobs (OECD, 2022). The majority of veteran teachers also reported that the teaching profession is undervalued. They experience a degree of disillusionment with teaching as they progress along their career path. Additionally, about 14% of teachers under fifty said they wish to leave the profession before retirement or five years after signing up for the career. Acute stress and too much administrative work were the primary reasons behind the early attrition of most participants in the above study. In addition to job stress, it is common knowledge that teachers do not receive compensation equal to the amount of work they produce.

The subject of teachers' job satisfaction seems to have benefited from more studies in OECD countries than in Sub-Saharan Africa. However, there has been research in individual countries such as South Africa, Ghana (Shabe et al., 2019), and Tanzania (Nyamubi, 2017; Ngwale, 2021) that can allow for some educated generalization. In his research article "Determinants of Secondary School Teachers' Job Satisfaction in Tanzania," Nyamubi (2017) used focus group discussions to address the factors determining secondary school job satisfaction in Tanzania. The results showed that teachers found satisfaction with monetary and nonmonetary incentives, including support from the school community, opportunities for career development, a well-defined individual appraisal system, timely promotion, and requisite workplace conditions. The study also found that teachers' collegiality and cooperation with coworkers and students and the respect of community members can foster teachers' job satisfaction.

Like in OECD countries, most African learning institutions see job satisfaction as a phenomenon that explains individual feelings toward the job (Aliakbari, 2013). However, Genelyn, Baluyos, Rivera, and Baluyos (2019) add nuances to the above understanding of job satisfaction. They include employees' feelings about their work, which interrelate with several personal factors, including age, sex, education, and job-related factors, namely payment level, opportunity for upward mobility, and working conditions. Concretely, teachers attain high-job satisfaction when fulfilling their job expectations. Such fulfillment can also include additional benefits to make teachers happy and satisfied with their job (Akinlolu et al., 2019). Most studies identify pay and workloads as core factors affecting teacher job satisfaction in South Africa (Nganzi, 2014), Tanzania, and most educational institutions in Sub-Saharan Africa. Nganzi's study in South Africa concluded that teachers meet job satisfaction with market and stable salaries. Additionally, Lumadi (2008) showed that poor salaries have caused many teachers to tender their resignation letters. Irregularities and insufficient salaries have compelled many teachers to find alternative means to make ends meet. At institutions where teachers raise the excessive workload issue, they find themselves compelled to work overtime in the evenings and on weekends. Besides the core issues of insufficient pay and excessive workload, other issues that cut through teachers' job satisfaction include safety and security risks in rural and township schools (in South Africa) (Gina & White, 2014), poor facilities, including a lack of library and science and computer laboratories, in addition to learners' discipline issues (Shabe et al., Xaba, 2020).

Further, Ngwale (2021) conducted a study on the contribution of teachers' job satisfaction on their job performance in Tanzanian secondary schools. The results indicated a significant contribution of teachers' job satisfaction to their job performance. For teachers' job fulfillment to contribute to their performance, the core factors of proportional workload and market salary, as well as the factors mentioned above, are of the utmost importance.

TEACHERS' SALARY

Table 0.2 presents the average salary of a teacher per each OECD country. The highest-paid teachers are in Luxembourg ($101,000), Germany ($80,000), and Canada ($72,000), while the least-paid teachers can be found in Hungary ($20,000) and the Slovak Republic ($19,000). PayScale's (2021) report, *The Most and Least Meaningful Jobs,* draws a comparative distinction between job salary, job meaning, and job satisfaction in the United States.

Table 0.2 Teacher Average Salary in OECD Countries

Australia	65,657.9
Austria	55,141.7
Canada	71,663.6
Chile	37,823.6
Colombia	39,960.9
Costa Rica	33,143.9
Czech Republic	28,181.6
Denmark	60,185.3
Finland	44,179.8
France	39,048.9
Germany	80,407.4
Greece	27,335.5
Hungary	19,891.1
Iceland	42,024.1
Ireland	62,312.8
Israel	33,163.0
Italy	38,983.7
Japan	49,497.5
Korea	59,103.3
Lithuania	33,667.2
Luxembourg	101,360.1
Mexico	33,906.5
Netherlands	71,023.8
New Zealand	53,246.8
Norway	51,351.8
Poland	30,768.2
Portugal	44,801.7
Slovak Republic	19,294.7
Slovenia	45,857.1
Spain	49,897.7
Sweden	47,664.0
Türkiye	30,811.9
United States	62,101.9

Source: OECD (2022), Teachers' salaries (indicator). doi: 10.1787/f689fb91-en

The report shows that teachers at all levels report consistently high levels of job meaning. Meanwhile, they also report consistently low rates of pay. For example, clergy's median pay is $46,600, but they hold the highest job meaning (98%) with 95% satisfaction.

Interestingly, post-secondary English language and literature teachers come next to clergy. They reported a job satisfaction of 74%. Despite a median salary of $43,600, teachers posted the second highest job satisfaction rate (96%), only after clergy. More than 80% of kindergarten, middle school, and secondary school teachers who earn less than $45,000 per year in the United States maintain that their job betters the world. Despite the common understanding that teachers are low-paid workers, it is worth noting that teachers' careers offer many intangible benefits, including the strong feeling that their work makes the world a better place, at least as far as the United States and OECD countries are concerned.

The above discussion runs the risk of painting too quickly a rosy picture of teachers' overall satisfaction with their jobs because of its meaningfulness. It, however, should beg the question, "Why do teachers leave?" and whether most of them share the same assessment as presented by OECD's (2022) data and PayScale's (2021) report. Among countless reasons for "why teachers leave," this report cites the demands and low pay of the teaching profession, which does not make it easy to stay even for veteran teachers who have dedicated several years to the profession. The report quotes some steadfast teachers who eventually became disillusioned with their beloved vocation.

For example, an educational content writer and consultant who taught for over a decade said, "I loved teaching. . . . I feel more present, more 'myself' when I'm teaching than when I'm doing anything else." Another one enjoyed any opportunity to teach because it provided them with continued learning, involvement in the school community, and the opportunity to build a family-like bond with students and their parents. This particular teacher claimed they did not enjoy taking summers off as they looked forward to returning to the classroom. Despite holding such a selfless love for their calling, the PayScale Report (2021) indicated that the teachers' profession took a significant toll because their salaries could not afford them any luxuries. They felt that a middle-class lifestyle was permanently out of their reach. Low salaries combined with increasing responsibilities outside the classroom often made teachers decide to "leave the party while I was still having fun." The report quoted one teacher as saying, "I don't regret leaving teaching. . . . I only regret that even though it was so hard to leave, the profession, the culture made it feel like it would've been even harder to stay."

Perhaps it is cautious to nuance the OECD's (2022) contention that 90% of its teachers are satisfied with their jobs. That teachers are leaving their positions in great numbers gives educational leadership researchers pause and encourages them to listen to other voices that exist even in the United States. PayScale Report (2021) reproduces the following account of a teacher in North Carolina:

> As an educator in NC I've seen many a great teacher rushing out the door to head to second and sometimes third jobs just to provide a reasonable salary to support their families. . . . Teachers don't get in this business to get rich; they get in it to make a difference in the lives of students. Take money off the table as a hurdle and teachers will pour themselves into their passions to teach. Right now—if you can retire you do so. There is no incentive to get into teaching even with the funding shift to the least experienced teachers that was sold as a

> raise—which was not. There are good young teachers but no replacement for experience and having mentor master teachers. Education is the basis of any economy. I wish that was valued as well as teachers! (PayScale, 2021)

Will (2022) published an article titled "Teacher Job Satisfaction Hits an All-Time Low" in *Education Week*. The author cited a recent survey by the Merrimack College Teacher Survey, a nationally representative poll of more than 1,300 teachers conducted by the EdWeek Research Center. Results showed that about 50% are satisfied with their jobs, and only 12% of teachers said they would be delighted with their job in 2022 as opposed to 32% in 2012 in the United States alone. More than 50% of the teachers interviewed said they would not advise their younger selves to pursue a teaching profession. Although participants said they still love teaching, they also confessed they have had enough of the growing workload, the inadequacy of their salaries, and particularly the lack of respect for their profession. Massachusetts' 2020 teacher of the year, Takeru Nagayoshi, thirty, exemplifies this erosion in the workforce by leaving the teaching profession in 2021. Award-winning Advanced Placement English for seven years, the teacher found the frustrations of teaching unsustainable. Those included, among other motives, the impossibility of the work-life balance with the guilt and fatigue that go with it, the exacerbation of students' needs during and after the pandemic, and the disconnect between students and their learning. Above all, says the survey: "Teachers don't feel respected." Twenty-five percent of teachers feel their students' parents and guardians do not respect them. Parents have become increasingly combative and demanding, paying attention to teachers' professional expertise.

Teachers' Salary in Africa

Regarding teachers' salaries in Africa, scholars concede the limited documentation of this policy-relevant topic in Sub-Saharan Africa, partly due to the lack of systematic teacher salary data across African countries (Evans et al., 2020). As Blanc (2019) contended, the last few years have seen unprecedented numbers of teacher strikes over teacher salaries in the world in general, and in Africa in particular. However, teachers' market salaries constitute a tool to attract, retain, and motivate high-quality teachers to deliver quality education in Africa. Studies have established the role of salary in attracting quality candidates to public sectors, including education. For example, Ferraz and Finan (2011) document that increasing politicians' salaries improved political performance in Brazil. It is safe to imply that when salaries increase, more able applicants will apply for professions in education and other public sectors (Dal et al., 2013). Some studies have gone so far as to correlate teacher salary and student performance in OECD countries (Dolton et al., 2011). Regarding Africa, UNESCO estimated that Sub-Saharan African countries need 17 million additional teachers to achieve universal primary and secondary education (UNESCO, 2016). Teacher market pay should be a key ingredient in achieving this goal.

Evans, Yuan, and Filmer (2020) conducted a survey titled "Are teachers in Africa poorly paid? Evidence from 15 countries." They presented data on teacher pay in fifteen African countries and compared it with five middle-income countries from other regions. They concluded that teachers in seven African countries receive less compensation than in the other comparator countries. However, teachers in all the countries reported working fewer hours than other workers. Additionally, the authors found that teachers' monthly salaries were lower than those of other comparable paid workers. Rekindling the value of education in the Global South also means paying teachers a decent salary to ensure their job satisfaction.

In his study of the determinants of secondary school teachers' job satisfaction in Tanzania, Nyamubi (2017) found that monetary compensation was a critical incentive for the participants. Participants in this study wished that their income corresponded to their workload. They noted missing or insufficient benefits such as monthly salaries, periodic salary adjustments, paid leaves of absence, etc. The author argues that teachers' job satisfaction would improve if streamlining salary structures and remuneration packages were aligned with other professions. Participants raised other compensation issues, such as inequitable salary scales for teachers with the same qualifications and work experience in the same schools.

Moreover, the irregularities of those salaries were a significant concern for teachers who participated in this study. The government determines teachers' salaries in public schools, leaving little room for negotiation (Nguni, 2005). It is somewhat ironic that, on the one hand, governments recognize the insufficiency of teachers' salaries; on the other hand, they encourage teachers to commit themselves to the school while denying them opportunities to seek other income-generating activities (Naymubi, 2017).

OECD Investment in Education

A country that values education contributes a substantial GDP to support this critically important sector of its social development. The OECD countries invest heavily in educational institutions for several reasons, including fostering economic growth, enhancing productivity, contributing to personal and social development, and reducing social inequality. As shown in figure 0.1, each country determines the allocation of the expenditure based on the size of the country's school population, enrollment rates, teachers' salaries, and the complexity of instructional materials. In 2018, all thirty-eight OECD countries spent an average of 4.9% of their gross domestic product (GDP) on educational institutions, including primary and college levels (OECD, 2021). These countries devote about 3.4% of their GDP to elementary and secondary education while allocating 1.4% to university education. Overall, public sectors remain the primary source of educational funding in OECD countries (4.1% of GDP). Not all countries invest the exact size of their GDP in education. For example, some countries like Ireland, Japan, Lithuania, and the Russian Federation invest less than 3.5% of their GDP, whereas Costa Rica and Norway fund education for over 6%. In its "Education at a Glance 2021" report, the OECD revealed that Norway is among the countries that spend the largest portion of their GDP—6.7%— on education, including the college level. The report also indicated that Russia, with an investment of 3.4% of its GDP, is among the OECD countries that invest the least in education. In most OECD countries, at the kindergarten and primary levels (broadly representing

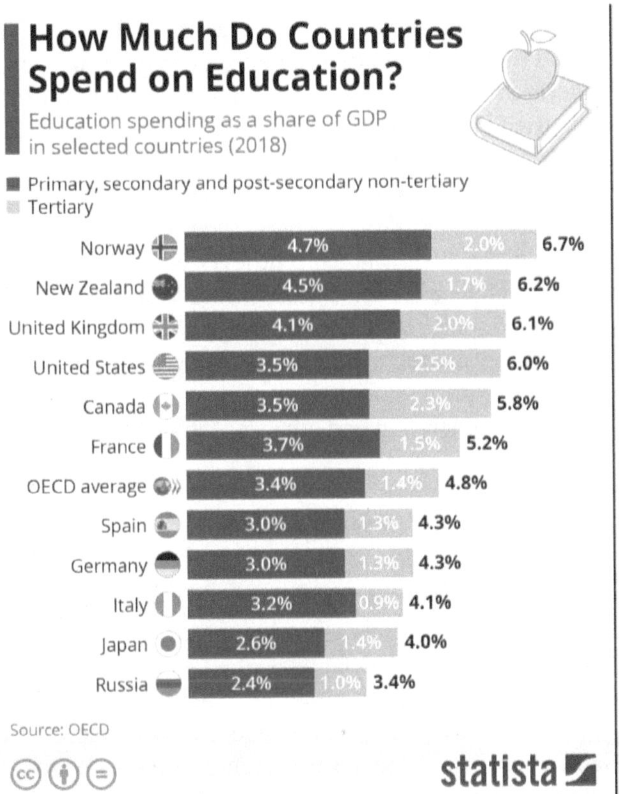

Figure 0.1 How Much Do Countries Spend on Education? Source: Armstrong, M. (2021). Statistica, September 16. Reproduced from OECD.

the population from six to fourteen years of age), enrollment rates average 100%. The portion of the nation's wealth invested in educational institutions and the support to its learning population demonstrates the country's priority to education.

A country that values education also invests in the learning of each student. The National Center on Education and the Economy NCEE (2018) presents the annual spending of member countries per student in its comparative data for top-performing countries in education. Regarding the spending per student of selected OECD countries, the United States comes on top with almost $15,000 per student per year, followed by Canada ($13,000) and South Korea ($12,000).

Unlike the OECD countries that invest heavily in education, about 4.9% of GDP, African countries spend 4.1% of their GDP on education, just above the lower end of the benchmark (African Union, 2022). Africa's spending average of 4.1% is close to the global average of 4.3%. According to UNICEF, cited by African Union (2022), education spending figures across the regions vary from 3.1% in Central Africa to 5.9% in Southern Africa (African Union, 2022). Compared to OECD countries, country disparities, as far as education funding is concerned, are more significant in Africa, ranging from 1% in the Central African Republic to 8% in Sierra Leone (African Union, 2022). Overall, the percentage of education funding is less than 4% in 50% of the African countries. To achieve universal primary and secondary education by 2030, Africa will need about 17 million teachers, according to the UN. This number is unlikely to be met with the current level of investment in education. In addition to the challenges posed by low investment in education, UNICEF identifies teachers' administrative and pedagogical management, which needs to be improved. Those shortcomings include inadequate career management, poor teacher training, professional development, pedagogical support, and particularly scarce remuneration and other incentives (African Union, 2022).

CONCLUSION

At the inception of this study, I posited that exceptional teachers live and work in an educational context that has lost much of its value. Throughout this chapter, I have presented the elements of educational value that emerged from scholarly works, including honoring teachers, respect for teachers, teachers' satisfaction, teachers' salaries, and country investment in education. Sub-Saharan Africa is noticeably lagging compared to how OECD countries engage with those elements. Although the continent has honored extraordinary teachers of the past, today, most teachers complain that they are overworked, underpaid, and hardly or inadequately recognized for their knowledge and worth in society. The practice of recruiting teachers from the not-so-brilliant cohorts of students in many African countries—among other factors—continues to play into the lack of respect some parents and students show toward the leading learners. This situation and the irregularity and/or lack of appropriate income those learners receive contribute to the lack of satisfaction teachers feel about their rather transformative work of imparting knowledge. Individual countries' low investment in education in general and in teachers as the leading figures of that education contributes to maintaining this critical area of social development in a precarious status. Suppose the educational value has declined in many parts of the world. In that case, the decline seems even more acute in countries such as the D.R. Congo, Ghana, and Uganda, where the exceptional teachers in this study live and endeavor to lead learning. To this already complex education environment in these three countries, scholars often add the rampant corruption of educational systems, causing teachers' absenteeism, disinterest, and attrition. However, exceptional teachers have remained indefectibly committed to the teaching profession. The next chapter examines the reasons that cause other, but exceptional teachers to move on.

Chapter 1

Teacher Retention and Attrition in OECD and Africa

"Where there are experts, there will be no lack of learners."

(Swahili Proverb)

This chapter examines teacher retention and attrition due to the value a given society attaches to learning leaders, particularly teachers. Studies have shown that countries that hold their teachers in high esteem will likely experience excellent retention and low attrition (Scherer, 2009; Stewart, 2010; Stewart, 2011). On the contrary, countries that struggle to retain teachers are likely to pay less attention to their teachers' social wellness (Global Teacher Status Index, 2018). This chapter tackles several key questions that apply to both OECD and Sub-Saharan countries regarding the retention of learning leaders. For example, what factors motivate these leaders to remain in their institutions despite challenges that have caused some to find greener pastures elsewhere? What is the significance of retention and attrition in maintaining an educational institution's structural and human resource stability? Furthermore, what factors may have motivated a handful of learning leaders, including the exceptional teachers in this study, to persist in their profession? This chapter examines the phenomena of retention and attrition in the two groups of countries identified in the preceding chapter: OECD countries and Global South countries of Sub-Saharan Africa. In particular, the chapter analyzes factors that can affect both the value of educational systems and the retention and, conversely, the attrition of teachers. These factors include financial compensation, social and professional awards, social status related to professions of the same level of education, and social benefits such as vacation, maternity leave, retirement or pension, and so on. I posit that despite the contingency of the above retention and attrition factors, the exceptional learning leaders have remained unfazed and solely focused on their ethics of professionalism.

I had hoped to begin this chapter on a positive note, describing how learning leaders remain everlastingly in their teaching profession, calling to mind the concept of teachers' retention. However, as I further researched this topic, I found more studies on attrition than retention. Most scholars have focused on the reasons that have caused countless teachers to leave their profession every year to look for better pastures. Literature on retention seems scarce because scholars do not focus as much on the rationale behind the decision of many learning leaders to persevere. In reality, teacher attrition permeates almost every institution of learning, from elementary to higher education, and affects even the most valued educators. Take the example of LéAnn Cassidy, fifty-seven, a middle school classroom teacher in Connecticut, the 2018 Connecticut History Teacher of the Year, and the 2018 Connecticut Teacher of the Year finalist. She has been a classroom teacher for thirty-four years but is considering retiring early (Will, 2022). In the Introduction, I reported the story of Takeru Nagayoshi, thirty, the 2020 Massachusetts Teacher of the Year, who made the long list of outstanding learning leaders to leave the classroom in 2021. The study by Will (2022) in the United States also highlighted participants' warnings that they and their colleagues would not stay in the profession long-term for several reasons. One U.S. learning leader who participated in Will's study rightly extrapolated that the experiences that led them to consider leaving their profession were universal. However, it sounded like they were complaining. They were not complaining but felt hurt because they truly loved their jobs, and it was sad to see how many were disillusioned with it all (Will, 2022).

Like any learning leaders, the exceptional teachers in this study must have lived the challenges and pressures brought about by the tension between the phenomena of attrition and retention in their midst. While many of those leaders have succumbed to the pressure of attrition, the exemplary learning leaders have stood victorious amid conflicting tensions. It pays to examine these two notions in the light of prior literature while focusing on retention because it stands as one of the pillar criteria of the steadfastness of exemplary teachers. By examining the two concepts, I hope to be mindful of my focus on the exemplary learning leaders who have not been personally involved in attrition as a voluntary or involuntary process of leaving one's profession. What is attrition in educational leadership?

ATTRITION IN EDUCATIONAL LEADERSHIP

Teacher retention and attrition is a timely and complex subject, given its impact on the U.S. educational system and other developed and developing countries, particularly Sub-Saharan Africa. Many countries report a loss of enthusiasm in teaching, with 44% of new teachers leaving their positions within the first five years and 10% deserting in year one in the United States alone (National School Board Association, 2019). Mugizi et al. (2019) reported that the attrition rate has reached 44% in Sub-Saharan Africa and could average the same level in the D.R. Congo, Ghana, and Uganda, creating shortages of teachers, particularly in primary education.

Two decades ago, Xaba (2003) posited that turnover and attrition were phenomena of global concern. The author indicated that educator attrition was reported as a national crisis in Britain, while the situation worsened in Sweden, Germany, and New Zealand. More recently, TALIS (2020) reported that England was still facing a shortage of teachers, suggesting that the quality of working conditions in their schools caused teachers to leave teaching. In the United States, attrition is still trending high. Twenty years ago, many states in the United States had already reported teacher shortages due to turnover (Markley, 2001; Santiago, 2001). According to a National Education Association (NEA, 2021) survey, 32% of the respondents said they would leave the profession sooner than planned because of the pandemic. This number represents a slight increase compared to 2019 when about 28% of NEA members said they would leave the profession sooner.

Interestingly, Bilikpe and Tengzuyele (2018) claimed, "In most African countries, the phenomenon of teacher turnover is accepted as 'normal,' especially in Sub-Saharan countries like Zambia, Kenya, Nigeria, the Central African Republic and South Africa . . . maybe because Africa has lived with it for so long" (p. 376). This view does not explain educational leaders' efforts in Sub-Saharan Africa; their governments and scholars have dedicated themselves to solving the issue of attrition. On the contrary, most educational leaders in the Global South, particularly in the countries in this study, have largely blamed the collapse of their educational systems on the phenomenon of attrition. The exceptional learning leaders in this study would hardly consider attrition an accepted or normalized condition of the school systems in which they operate.

Commonly, people see attrition as a reduction in the educational workforce when the learning leaders leave their educational institutions without replacement. As in the above examples of teachers leaving or planning to leave their profession, attrition occurs gradually. However, experts in educational leadership and policy (Darling-Hammond & Podolsky, 2019) distinguish attrition from turnover, though other educational leadership experts use the two terms interchangeably. Conversely, teacher turnover happens when learning leaders leave their teaching jobs and are replaced within a time. According to scholars, the taxonomy of the reasons for teachers leaving their teaching institutions may include the following: personal reasons, retirement, resignation, workplace issues, lack of benefits, poor management, professional goals, layoffs, and transfers (UNESCO, 2022; Pisa, 2017). Literature advancing personal reasons for teachers leaving the profession is scant because most studies on teacher attrition indicate that professional motives often cause learning leaders to leave the job they dearly love. For example, in response to a 2019 blog by Elizabeth Mulvahill (2020) titled "Why teachers quit?" April McCarthy had this to say:

> As a teacher for 38 years in Special Ed. Sees that students and parents have more rights than teachers. Students and parents can accuse teachers of stuff (which was NOT true) and then tell admin that: The Teacher will not discuss what they said happen with their child). I felt as if I was never given the opportunity to speak with parents and students. I was never heard. The districts will take the parents/students word over the Teacher without doing an investigation. I asked for an investigation to be held in my case, but none was held. I loved teaching and I know that there are a few students/parents out there that do respect the teaching profession. It's my time to step down and pray for all teachers. The saying "one bad apple can spoil the whole bunch" is true. My love for teaching has been spoiled!! (Mulvahill, 2019)

DISTINGUISHING VOLUNTARY AND INVOLUNTARY TURNOVER

Using interchangeably the terms attrition and turnover, Tanova and Holtom (2008) distinguished voluntary and involuntary turnover as well as avoidable and unavoidable turnover. Voluntary attrition occurs when learning leaders leave their educational organizations voluntarily through retirement or other pre-arranged means. Some educational leaders (Tanova & Holtom, 2008) have argued that the educational institution reserves the right to refrain from replacing learning leaders who leave the institution through voluntary turnover. Harman et al. (2007) specified that scholars researching voluntary turnover usually look at predicting, preventing, and effectively managing turnover. They tend to view voluntary or involuntary turnover as a negative phenomenon that prevents the organization from remaining effective. In contrast, scholars agree that voluntary turnover (including retirement and sick leave) occurs as a result of the free will of the employee. On the contrary, involuntary attrition occurs when such undesired actions as layoffs and terminations—often due to poor performance—force the learning leader to leave the institution involuntarily.

Both voluntary and involuntary attrition (such as termination) differ in their causes and consequences. Educational leadership scholars (Fullan, 2018) warn that failure to correctly manage poorly performing learning leaders can result in the voluntary resignation of top-performing teachers. As discussed above, poorly performing employees who shirk their work responsibilities can unduly place an unfair burden on top-performing learning leaders such as exemplary teachers. An educational environment that shows complacency toward such educators may cause resentment, accumulated dissatisfaction, and eventual resignation of highly performing learning leaders. Despite the educational plethora of attrition causes, the general view is that learning leaders resign when they feel stagnant in a job and wish to move to a better professional environment. This sentiment of stagnation occurs when educators feel there is no scope for progress at their current educational institution.

DISTINGUISHING AVOIDABLE AND UNAVOIDABLE TURNOVER

Morrell and Arnold (2007) maintain that turnover can be regarded as avoidable if an educational institution could have done something to prevent the learning leader from leaving. Most of the time, the institution could not prevent a specific educator from leaving. However, gathering information about the reasons for resignations may constitute a key identifier of avoidable turnover and help implement interventions that could prevent future voluntary attrition. The school can identify retrospectively avoidable turnover by sampling resigned educators and developing interventions for those learning leaders still teaching. Some educational leaders advise paying attention to avoidable turnover whenever educators intend to move on but are still making up their minds. Conversely, unavoidable voluntary turnover happens for reasons beyond the educational institution's control. Most reasons, such as getting a more lucrative and remunerative job, may not even be job-related. Regarding predicting educators' intentions to leave based on intention-to-quit figures, Tanova and Holtom (2008) warn that actual turnover figures provide a more accurate representation of teachers' outcomes.

Whether avoidable, unavoidable, voluntary, or involuntary, the attrition of learning leaders, be it in the United States, other OECD countries, or Sub-Saharan Africa, negatively impacts the functioning of educational institutions. The burden on the rest of the school community, particularly the remaining teachers, including the exceptional ones, is hard to measure.

Attrition in OECD

In their research paper, "What makes teachers stay? A cross-sectional exploration of the individual and contextual factors associated with teacher retention in Sweden," (Casely-Hayford et al., 2022) did not escape the unavoidable process of discussing attrition before they could tackle the topic of retention. As explained in prior pages, literature on retention seems inextricably tied to turnover and attrition. In Sweden, an OECD country itself, the Swedish National Agency for Education projected that the country would need 227,000 teachers by 2031, representing a shortfall of more than 80,000 teachers (Casely-Hayford, J. et al., 2022). These authors maintain that the teacher shortage crisis is mainly driven by the inability to retain teachers, as indicated by teachers' turnover and attrition rates. Like in other OECD countries, there has been a 10% gradual decline in the proportion of qualified teachers working in the profession between 2000 and 2016 in Sweden. This same year, Sweden retained about 80% of its nurses and 70% of its police officers but only 60% of its teachers (Casely-Hayford, J. et al., 2022). Although Casely-Hayford et al. are concerned with retention in Sweden, they also had to overview attrition in all OECD countries and beyond.

Educational leaders agree that teacher attrition rates vary from one country to another and sometimes from one district to another within the same country. A decade ago, OECD countries reported teacher attrition rates between 2% and 14% per year. Korea held the lowest rate, while the United States had the highest rates. Individual countries also experienced changes in attrition rates over time. To give only the example of New Zealand and the United States, the attrition rates in those two countries rose from 8.5% to 10.4% between 1996 and 2000 in New Zealand while it went from 5.6% to 8.4% between 1988 and 2005 in the United States (Wallace & Sartono, 2010).

In a 2011 review of their document titled "Teachers Matter: Attracting, Developing and Retaining Effective Teachers: Pointers for policy," OECD (2011) presents general pointers for policy development based on a prior edition of the same document (OECD, 2005). In the 2011 document, the OECD raised the common attrition concerns participating countries identified. Most of those primary concerns, which the OECD identifies as the impasses to attracting and retaining learning leaders in its member countries, also align closely with the causes of attrition in OECD countries. For example, the document cites the erosion of the image and status of teaching and the fact that "teachers often feel that their work is undervalued" (OECD, 2011, p. 1). It also addresses "the impact of high workloads, stress, and poor working environments on job satisfaction, and teaching effectiveness, limited means in most countries to recognize and reward teachers' work" (OECD, 2011, p. 1).

Additionally, these concerns at the origin of turnovers included how school systems often respond to teacher shortages in the short term. School systems would endeavor to have teachers in classrooms by using detrimental measures. For example, they would lower the requirements for qualification for entry to the teaching profession; they would assign teachers subject matters in which they are not qualified; they would increase the number of classes allocated to each teacher; they would increase class sizes. These documents first recognize the ongoing reality of the scarcity of teachers in the OECD due to turnover or attrition. They then propose concrete policy-making steps to improve the learning leaders' working conditions, attract candidates to the profession, and retain effective ones. Figure 1.1 represents the policy summary OECD proposed to put in place to circumvent teacher attrition by attracting, recruiting, retaining, and developing qualified learning leaders. To attract qualified teachers, OECD suggests making teaching an attractive career choice. To do so, educational institutions should improve the image and status of learning leadership. They should allocate learning leadership's salary competitiveness. They should improve teaching employment conditions. Additionally, OECD recommends that educational institutions make reward mechanisms more flexible. Finally, they should rethink "the trade-off between student-teacher ratio and average teacher salary" (OECD, 2011).

Attrition in the United States

In February 2022, the NEA published its press release survey NEA survey: "Massive staff shortages in schools leading to educator burnout; alarming number of educators indicating they plan to leave profession" (Jotkoff, 2022). Notably, as the largest union in the United States, the NEA represents about 3 million learning leaders. It unveiled one of its most extensive surveys of members' opinions on critical public education issues during the pandemic.

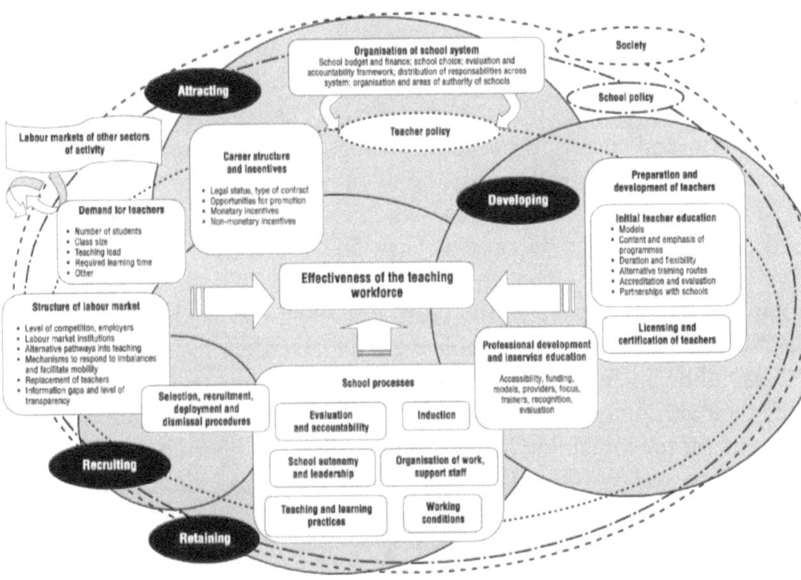

Figure 1.1 Teachers Matter: Pointers for Policy Development. Source: OECD (2011).

To begin with, the NEA praised the commitment of the teachers during the pandemic, quoting the NEA president Becky Pringle as saying, "Throughout this pandemic, America's educators have shown us how committed they are to helping their students thrive. In every community across America, our educators are partnering with parents and families to ensure all students have the freedom to achieve their dreams." A Yahoo Lifestyle (2019) survey of more than fifty teachers also resulted in the same praiseful message of the heroic work leading learners perform in the United States. Those who value teachers are likely to recognize that, nowadays, leading learning also means heroism. Social media, political stages, and news sites hail teachers as unfaltering public servants. They have owned that reputation, given their many roles as therapists, parents, first responders, counselors, etc. Learning leaders have been praised for donating kidneys to their learners, fostering their students, and even taking bullets while trying to tackle school shooters. Beyond those praises of learning leaders, there appears to be a feeling that society has misused their generosity and heroism by undervaluing and mistreating them throughout the United States.

Yet, the NEA's survey (Jotkoff, 2022) revealed that a massive staff shortage in America's public schools was resulting in educators feeling increasingly burned out. Fifty-five percent of learning leaders indicated they are ready to leave the teaching profession they love earlier than they had planned. Says Pringle, "This is a five-alarm crisis. We are facing an exodus as more than half of our nation's teachers, and other school staff are now indicating they will be leaving education sooner than planned. If we're serious about getting every child the support they need to thrive, our elected leaders across the nation need to address this crisis now" (Jotkoff, 2022).

Teachers' perseverance throughout the most challenging school years led to exhaustion and lingering burnout, preventing the learning leaders from giving their learners much-needed one-on-one attention. Joktoff (2022) cited the Bureau of Labor Statistics, which estimated that the pandemic has caused America's public schools to have 567,000 fewer educators than in the pre-pandemic eras. Although the attrition trend existed pre-pandemic, it was noticeably exacerbated in the years following the pandemic, according to the NEA survey. In 2022, schools were understaffed, resulting in 74% of members filling in for colleagues, learning leaders, or taking other duties beyond their attributions. As a result of the attrition, there was more work and obligations for the remaining leaders of education, as reported by 80% of the members surveyed by NEA. Educators also experienced burnout, according to 90% of those who participated in this survey.

In Yahoo Lifestyle's (2019) survey, a minimum of fifty teachers shared that they had enough of budget cuts, classroom violence, low salaries, and the need for extra jobs to make ends meet. Teachers confessed they were fed up with standardized tests because they stifled their creativity. They were tired of a job demanding every waking moment, including sick days. In her resignation letter, former South Carolina teacher Sariah McCall wrote, "The only things keeping me from resigning until now were the love I have for my students, the love I have for the act of teaching, and the heavy guilt I feel for my children being negatively impacted by this in any way, emotionally or academically" (Cachero, 2019). The University of Massachusetts (2022) states that turnover contributing to teacher shortages may cause schools to resort to increasing the sizes of classes or cutting some of their offerings. They also list potential adverse side effects of attrition that can result in hiring less-experienced classroom teachers. Less experienced staff in itself can come with additional side effects. For example, schools can reduce the time teachers spend with their students; schools might need to repeat professional development experiences for teachers; the remaining staff can experience a drain on energy and burnout.

In response to learning leaders' revendications for better living and working conditions, the NEA suggested the following:

> To address educator burnout, raising educator salaries receives the strongest support (96% support, 81% strongly support), followed by providing additional mental health support for students (94% support), hiring more teachers (93%), hiring more support staff (92%), and less paperwork (90%). 91% say that pandemic-related stress is a severe educator problem. (Jotkoff, 2022, n.p.)

Attrition in Africa

While the reality of attrition is rampant throughout Sub-Saharan educational systems, Wallace and Sartono (2010) warn that data collection regarding this issue can be poor. Their study revealed that some of the responses they obtained from participants in their research could have been based on assumptions or anecdotal reports. These scholars recommended that by using existing instruments such as annual school surveys and human resources databases, school systems would likely produce more reliable, policy-driven, relevant data on the pattern of loss of learning leaders. In a document released on Sustainable Development Goals, UNESCO (2022) published a list of teacher attrition rates per education level from 2015 to 2021. The list did not contain any data related to Sub-Saharan Africa as a sub-region, nor did it have data from the three countries in this study, the D.R. Congo, Ghana, and Uganda.

However, Pitsoe and Machaisa (2012) noted that attrition rates increase when a country's economy weakens. Low-income countries, particularly those in Sub-Saharan Africa, have the highest loss of learning leaders due to attrition. Rural areas in Africa have mainly reported increased challenges with attrition. For example, in a study of South African schools, Mafora (2013) [See OPUKU] interviewed fifteen school principals about challenges teachers faced and strategies to manage teacher attrition. The author identified factors such as lack of policy and poor working conditions as barriers to teacher attrition in rural schools. The above section showed that the strongest economies in the world (OECD countries) have been suffering from teacher attrition despite all the financial means at their disposal. Therefore, one would agree with the conclusion by Pitsoe and Machaisa (2012) that in Sub-Saharan Africa, attrition is a catastrophe despite dubious data in this area. Ng'ethe et al. (2012) opined that despite acknowledging these educational management challenges, empirical research on attrition and retention in developing countries still needs to be expanded. Such research could explain this phenomenon and identify measures capable of diagnosing and preventing the turnover of learning leaders who leave a void in their educational institutions.

Perhaps the attrition formula UNESCO has recommended could yield more reliable results, although it would depend on individual countries to apply it accurately. This institution defines *attrition* as the "Percentage of teachers at a given level of education leaving the profession in a given school year." UNESCO believes in the importance of assessing and monitoring teacher attrition to ensure "a sufficient supply of qualified and well-trained teachers as well as to their effective deployment, support and management" (UNESCO, 2017).

The attrition rate represents the number of teachers who have left the institution (leavers), expressed as a percentage of the total number of teachers from the year before (year t–1). To calculate the number of instructors who have left the school (leavers) in a given year (year t), one should do the following according to Wallace and Sartono (2010):

1. Number of instructors in the preceding year (year t–1)
2. Minus the number of instructors in the current year (year t)
3. Plus, the number of new instructors teaching in year t
4. Percentage of the total

The results of the attrition rate obtained through the above formula would not explain why those educators (leavers) left the classrooms. To analyze the factors that lead to the learning leaders' departure, a school would have to collect detailed data using surveys of instructors who left the profession, annual censuses, and other means, as previously recommended by Wallace and Sartono (2010).

Like in OECD countries, teacher attrition rates vary from one country and from one era to another in Sub-Saharan Africa. Wallace and Sartono (2010) stated two significant sources of attrition in Africa: retirement and voluntary resignation. While attrition through retirement is relatively predictable, resignation remains tributary to labor market opportunities. In 2010, many African countries reported low and unsustainable teacher attrition rates. These authors posited that an education system should expect a 3%–4% attrition rate annually had there not been voluntary attrition, usually brought about by retirement, illness, and death. They recommend that policymakers consider a threshold of 5% attrition as the lowest sustainable rate in Sub-Saharan Africa.

In their study of the factors influencing the choice of a teaching career in Ghana, Abotsi et al. (2020) state that teacher attrition remains a lingering problem despite significant efforts to cure this challenge. Before the outbreak of COVID-19, it was estimated that about 10,000 teachers left the classroom yearly, according to the Ghana National Association of Teachers (GNAT). A study by Cobbold (2010) found that about 70% of Ghanaian teachers who further their education to obtain higher university degrees never return to the classroom at the end of their studies.

This study reports a shortage of 40,000 trained teachers in basic schools. UNESCO's Task Force on Teachers for Education 2030 (UNESCO, 2021) states that in Ghana, teachers with higher levels of education are more likely to drop out to pursue other opportunities. To curtail the current shortage of teachers, UNESCO projects that Ghana will need 23,500 teachers in primary education and 130,000 in secondary education by 2030.

Whether in OECD or Sub-Saharan countries like Ghana, top-performing educators leave a void when they exit the school. Quite often, that exit remains costly to fill and challenging to manage (Robison, 2008). According to Somaya and Williamson (2008), it is estimated that replacing an existing learning leader in Sub-Saharan Africa could cost 100% to 150% of the annual salary of such a learning leader. Additionally, several studies have discussed the psychological and tangible consequences of voluntary resignations of educators on the school community and the educational institution as an organization. When an effective learning leader leaves a school, the latter could experience the loss of the knowledge, skills, and experience of the departing teacher, disruption of subject matter delivery, declining student and teammate morale, disruptions in the performance of classes and the school, and departmental stress (Pienaar & Bester, 2008; Pinkowitz, Moskal & Green, 2009).

The above data on attrition and its consequences might also call for the examination of those teachers who have stayed in their teaching profession. For example, a study of fourteen teachers conducted by Chiong et al. (2017) in UK schools found that intrinsic factors (enjoyment in the process of teaching), professional mastery (belief in their teaching expertise), and altruistic factors (finding teaching socially meaningful) motivated the longest-serving teachers to stay in the profession.

RETENTION

To qualify as an exceptional learning leader for this study, teachers should have retained their teaching profession for at least five years. Yet, educational institutions—from OECD to the Sub-Saharan countries—have struggled with retaining their most valuable teachers. As noted in the above section, retention always takes a back seat in analyzing school human capital because attrition seems more prevalent in educational institutions. Teacher retention refers to keeping qualified teachers in the profession and is the inverse of teacher attrition, which refers to qualified teachers making premature exits from the profession (Kelchtermans, 2017). However, various schools of thought have used retention in different ways. For example, Merriam-Webster Dictionary (2022) describes retention “as the act or ability to keep or retain something or someone.” In the context of educational leadership, teacher retention has to do with the capability of educational leaders to put in place mechanisms to sustain the teaching workforce from recruitment to retirement. Educational leaders would ensure that those retention mechanisms include such elements as training, deploying, and ensuring the stability of the teaching human capital. In areas of the world where the deployment of teachers by the local or national ministry of education remains the norm (such as in Uganda and Ghana), teacher stability should exclude the unnecessary transfer of teachers from rural to urban schools or from one teaching field to another (Acheampong & Fosua Gyasi, 2019).

The success and advancement of an educational organization largely depend on the retention of existing learning leaders and the ability to entice a team of new teachers. Experts regard retaining effective teachers and instructors as a critical human resources strategy (Tanova & Holtom, 2008). One reason most researchers give precedence to attrition over retention stems from the premise that once they have identified the reasons behind attrition, they should be able to reveal why learning leaders stay in the profession (Harman et al., 2007). The assumption is that if a variable relates negatively to attrition through empirical research, then one would assume the existence of a positive impact on retention (Steel, 2002). For example, suppose research indicates that teachers do not resign when regularly paid a fair market salary. In that case, one will conclude that a fair market salary contributes to teachers’ retention. This reasoning might appear sound, but in reality, there might be other factors besides outstanding salaries that incentivize teachers to stay in their posts. Furthermore, researchers often measured teacher intention to quit or voluntary turnover to identify the retention level. They would then report an association with constructs that relate to retention.

The fact remains that research on teacher retention has long depended on teacher attrition due to the scarcity of studies on persisting learning leaders.

Such studies would monitor teachers' teams over time, as Waldman and Arora (2004) suggested. Ng'ethe et al. (2012) maintain that no definitive academic answers exist regarding how to study retention independently from attrition. These authors imply that turnover and retention remain an exciting research topic because the retention of effective learning leaders constitutes a critical component of the effectiveness of an educational institution. To a certain measure, educational institutions can use turnover to measure organizational effectiveness with the implicit assumption that the more stable the organization, the less attrition. To ensure a complete view of the phenomenon, researchers in educational leadership can also endeavor to obtain data from teachers who have left and those who have remained in the institution. Still, regarding attrition, data at the organizational level can yield results about remaining educators. Data could include such factors as identifying those who have left, their new professional destination, the skills they have taken with them, and the cost of their leaving the educational organization.

In contrast to the plethora of data researchers could garner on attrition in educational institutions, there seems to be limited data available on the rationale behind retaining learning leaders (Smither, 2003, p. 20). To assess their productivity and fulfillment, scholars recommend "routine diagnostic checks" on top-performing employees, including teachers. Such an assessment would have the merit of obtaining data from educators who have chosen to stay and identifying the factors that have caused the stayers to remain in their teaching positions. Fortunately, the current study of exceptional teachers in the Global South, who have contributed to the teacher retention of their educational institutions because they have persisted for over ten years, can add knowledge to the quest for teacher retention from within rather than from the attrition perspective.

Why Do Teachers Stay? Retention in OECD

In my quest for the rationale behind the retention of exceptional learning leaders in this study, it behooves me to examine the phenomenon of retention in the OECD countries and Sub-Saharan Africa. Research on learning leaders reveals several reasons behind the retention of teachers in OECD countries. Those reasons are complex and part of teachers' continuous negotiation process (Lindqvist & Nordanger, 2016).

Individual Factors

Some studies conducted in OECD countries, particularly in Sweden, suggested that individual and contextual factors contributed to teacher retention. For example, Caseley, Hayford et al. (2022) led a study on "What makes teachers stay? A cross-sectional exploration of the individual and contextual factors associated with teacher retention in Sweden." The authors intended to contribute to the knowledge of contributive factors to facilitate teacher retention in Sweden. In other studies, individual factors, including "intrinsic motivation" and "efficacy," facilitated the retention of learning leaders (Alexander et al., 2020; Chiong et al., 2017). Research saw motivation as a significant reason behind recruitment and retention. Additional studies explored how long-serving learning leaders sustained their motivation and persistence in educational institutions. For example, Chiong et al. (2017) investigated the motivation of teachers who remained in their profession for more than ten years. The researchers used rich interview data from over 900 teachers and 14 in-depth interviews with teachers throughout Sweden. Results showed two leading individual-level retention factors: intrinsic motivation and professional mastery. Still, other studies indicated that a sense of efficacy, meaning teacher instructional and student capability to interact, contributed to learning leaders' retention. Other studies have suggested that, compared to teachers who leave the profession, those who stay report high-performance levels in instruction, student engagement, and class management (De Neve & Devos, 2016). Hong (2012) conducted a comparative study of fourteen teachers, seven of whom had left the profession and seven who had stayed. Results indicated that both groups reported "the same level of motivation for teaching and identifying similar difficulties in classroom management and instruction." However, teachers who did not leave the profession indicated they had higher self-efficacy beliefs in addition to supportive contextual factors. These contextual factors fostered their motivation, efficacy, occupational health, and retention intention (Hong, 2012). Naomi's blog story below illustrates the motivation that prompted her to remain in her school in Australia, another OECD country, instead of quitting her job. Her story was so compelling that one of her followers commented along these lines:

> The one paragraph that caught my eye and summed up the situation was
>
> "Suddenly, I realized that teaching could not be about the subject I was teaching but it had to be about the students. I gave myself an ultimatum. I needed to be there for the students or leave." . . . I applaud your honesty and soul searching and HOPE you stay in the profession. We need more people like you!!!! (Barnes, 2016)

Why I Stayed in Teaching

> I'm not sure I ever really committed to teaching because I felt uncomfortable with the teaching bit all the way through my degree and for the first five years on the job (I loved the History and Social Science bit). But I was brought up to honour my commitments. It was embedded. "You always finish what you start, Naomi." I can still hear my father's Protestant Work Ethic in my ear. I

> also couldn't think of anything else I could do that would allow me to be paid for working with History. One day I remember having a Year 10 class brutally destroy my love for History. I walked away from work that day at a crossroad. I stick to the profession or find a new one. If I was to stay, I needed another reason to be there. The situation in the classroom was pretty bleak but as the weeks went on, evidence came to light that the key perpetrators of my disillusionment were in a pretty bad place. In fact, one of the most difficult students was being online bullied by the other culprits. It was pretty sophisticated bullying as well. Both the police and Microsoft got involved. Suddenly, I realised that teaching could not be about the subject I was teaching but it had to be about the students. I gave myself an ultimatum. I needed to be there for the students or leave. I stayed for eight more years. (Barnes, 2016)

Contextual Factors

Besides individual factors leading teachers to stay in their professions, research has also identified contextual factors as causes of teacher retention in OECD countries. McKay (2019) examined the factors influencing teachers' decisions to retain their positions in a Title I middle school in the United States. The results indicated that self-efficacy, support of colleagues, and administrative support, all contextual factors, contributed to the learning leaders' decision to stay in their jobs. Self-efficacy implies one's confidence in one's ability to do one's job well; support of colleagues included teacher induction, orientation, or mentor programs; administration support inferred the confidence the principal had in learning leaders' expertise and the respect the principal gave to individual teachers. Hong (2012) also found that efficacy and supportive contextual factors that enhanced motivation and occupational health increased teacher retention intention. Casely-Hayford et al. (2022) also mentioned that teachers are likely stay teaching when they experience contextual factors such as a professional sense of autonomy, job control, and authority about curriculum, student discipline, and instruction.

However, compared to other studies that showed that the work environment fosters teachers' intention to retain their jobs, Casely-Hayford et al. (2022) did not find a correlation between work-related factors and teachers' intention to stay in their jobs. Instead, their findings showed that individual factors, particularly teachers' perceived health state, explain the learning leaders' intention to retain their teaching profession.

Despite this slight difference in the findings, there is a common trend in all the above studies on retention in the OECD countries. The results suggest that positive work support and work-related resources can significantly contribute to learning leaders' willingness to stay in the profession. Supportive colleagues can facilitate retention; they constitute some form of buffer against toxic work conditions and professional stress. A study by Miller and Youngs

(2021) even has argued that a collegial environment coupled with social connectedness, support, and trust can foster teacher retention. More explicitly, the support of colleagues, in addition to positive professional relations and instructional support, brings about a sense of collective teaching efficacy. In turn, teaching efficacy further empowers learning leaders and increases the chances of staying in the teaching profession.

Based upon the individual and contextual factors perceived as the engine of teacher retention, the OECD (2011) elaborated on policies to curtail attrition and incentivize learning leaders to stay in their profession. In addition, the OECD goes several steps further by creating policies that attract and retain effective teachers, recruit competent people into the profession, and provide support and incentives for professional development. More importantly, the OECD acknowledges that teachers would reach their potential only when settings provide appropriate support, challenges, and awards. The OECD recommends improving status and labor market competitiveness, teacher development, and schoolwork contexts to increase retention chances further. Another recommendation concerns the focus on attracting and retaining particular learning leaders. Below are some of the policies suggested by the OECD for making teaching an attractive career where stakeholders choose to stay.

> Making teaching an attractive career choice by:
> Improving the image and status of teaching; teaching's salary competitiveness; employment conditions; and capitalizing on an over-supply of teachers
> Expanding the supply pool of potential teachers; making reward mechanisms more flexible; improving entrance conditions for new teachers; and rethinking the trade-off between student-teacher ratio and average teacher salary
>
> Retaining effective teachers in schools by:
> Evaluating and rewarding effective teaching; providing more opportunities for career variety and diversification; improving leadership and school climate; and improving working conditions
> Responding to ineffective teachers; providing more support for beginning teachers; and providing more flexible working hours and conditions

Teacher Retention in Sub-Saharan Africa

In addition to the precautions and policies the OECD established to curb teacher attrition and improve retention, developed countries such as the United States spend billions of dollars to retain influential learning leaders in their educational institutions (Acheampong & Fosua Gyasi, 2019). Nevertheless, Sub-Saharan Africa deals with its own form of teacher retention, considering that this poor region might not allocate the same resources as developed countries to keep teachers in the profession.

Why Do Teachers in Poverty-Stricken Countries Stay?

The overall context surrounding education in Sub-Saharan Africa appear bleak compared to OECD countries that benefit from their economic strengths to increase the presence of dedicated teachers in their schools. Regardless of their financial and social struggles and the overall erosion of the educational fabric in the Global South, which includes corruption and undervaluing of education, some Sub-Saharan learning leaders have stayed in their jobs. Their persistence should prompt any thinker to ask, "Why do teachers remain in the profession if they cannot even make ends meet or attend to the basic needs of their families?" Several researchers before us have attempted to respond to this question. For example, Gomba (2015) conducted a study to identify factors that influenced veteran teachers (those who have taught for more than ten years) in Zimbabwe to stay in teaching, whereas some left for economic reasons. Results showed that the following reasons contributed to teachers' decision to stay for decades in the same school: self-sacrificing school leader/principal (one who uses personal resources to better the conditions of teachers and the school); family support; fear of the unknown (if they decide to leave); job security, unmarketable because of age; and favorable leadership and support from colleagues.

Addressing retention in South African schools, Van der Vyver et al.'s (2020) study determined that the school principal's leadership, which directly influences teachers' experience of professional well-being, affects their retention. These authors posited that certain behaviors contribute to the poor retention rate of teachers in South Africa. Principals who displayed caring behavior in their leadership were more likely to enhance the well-being of their teachers and, therefore, their retention. Conversely, principals who lacked care led teachers to experience a reduction in the quality of their working experience and well-being. They argued that the uniqueness of their study lay in the linkage of the two variables of principal leadership and teacher well-being. Their main goal was to explore the relationship between principal leadership behavior and the well-being of teachers, which, in turn improves their retention. More specifically, these authors found that transformational and transactional dimensions of leadership likely contributed to teachers' professional well-being and, therefore, to their retention. However, the dimension of transformational leadership contributed more to teachers' wellness and desire to stay. On the contrary, a principal's laissez-faire leadership behavior negatively affected the well-being of teachers.

To give further context to the leadership theories Van der Vyver et al. (2020) used in their study, which supported and explained their findings, I reproduce their theoretical framework titled full-range leadership theory

(FRLT) in table 1.1. According to Antonakis et al. (2002), "In its current form, the FRLT represents nine single-order factors comprised of five transformational leadership factors, three transactional leadership factors, and one nontransactional laissez-faire leadership" (p. 264). Leadership experts routinely use the survey instrument in the Multifactor Leadership Questionnaire (MLQ) to measure the nine factors in the FRLT (Northouse, 2021). While transformational leadership requires leaders to raise the followers' awareness of transcendent collective interests, in transactional leadership, leaders set objectives and monitor outcomes in a contractual exchange with the followers (Van der Vyver et al., 2020). Laissez-faire leadership represents

Table 1.1 The Nine Factors of the Framework Titled Full-Range Leadership Theory (FRLT)

Dimension of leadership behavior	*Factors*	*Meaning*
Transformational	(a) Idealized influence (attributed)	The ability to influence followers as a role model in values and morals.
	(b) Idealized influence (behavior)	The ability to motivate and inspire followers to accomplish objectives through extra effort.
	(c) Inspirational motivation	Communicating the leader's vision and mission and finding the means to realize these objectives.
	(d) Intellectual stimulation	The ability to stimulate followers to think creatively, challenge others, and be innovative in problem-solving.
	(e) Individualized consideration	The ability to meet followers' unique needs and develop them to realize their full potential.
Dimension of leadership behavior	*Factors*	*Meaning*
Transactional	(a) Contingent reward	Leaders who clearly define obligations, objectives, and tasks for followers and stipulate rewards associated with the contractual commitments being met.
	(f) Management by exception (active)	Leaders who actively check that work standards are met.
Laissez-faire	(a) Management by exception (passive)	Leaders who passively check that work standards are met.
	(g) Passive avoidant	Leaders who do not take responsibility avoid making decisions and do not use authority.

Source: Adapted from Luo et al. (2013).

a non-contractual engagement between the leader and the follower, a lack of authority, and an avoidance of making leadership decisions.

The article by Opuku et al. (2020), "Exploring the Factors that Enhance Teacher Retention in Rural Schools in Ghana," gives an adequate illustration of factors that might lead to teacher retention in Ghana in particular and in Sub-Saharan Africa in general. Using a quantitative survey, the authors based their study on a conceptual framework known as the "four-capital model to assess teacher retention" (Opuku et al., 2020, p. 204). The model includes four significant tenets: human capital, social capital, structural capital, and positive psychological capital. Human capital involves continuing professional development with its corollary of quality pre-service education and professional knowledge. Social capital includes the following: a culture that nurtures common goals, equality of members, teamwork, interested and caring leaders, and a favorable working environment. While structural capital refers to the existence of basic facilities in schools, financial perks, and opportunities for professional upward mobility, positive psychological capital has to do with factors that can impact retention, such as commitment, "resilience, and the desire to work as a teacher" (Opuku et al., p. 205). However, because of the peculiarity of the Ghana educational contexts, these authors focused only on the social and structural capital, hypothesizing that teachers' decision to stay or not to stay in a school could be socially or structurally motivated. The results suggested the following: (a) collegial relationships play an important role in teacher retention; (b) there are significant differences between older and younger teachers, with the former being more likely to retain their posts than the latter; (c) both social capital and structural capital are critical for the retention of teachers.

Putting it all together, the studies by Van der Vyver et al. (2020) in South Africa and Okpuku (2020) in Ghana, and others throughout Africa have revealed probable reasons why some learning leaders in the Sub-Saharan Global South have retained their profession. The common themes among these retention reasons include caring leadership (transformational or transactional), supportive social capital, and structural solid capital. First, a caring educational leadership style—transformational or transactional—matters significantly in teachers' decisions to keep working for the same institution. Although not explicitly evoked by Opuku et al. (2020), their social capital (as one of the reasons for teacher retention) infers the presence of a caring leader who fosters a culture that nurtures common goals, supportive collegiality, and a favorable working environment. Since some studies have indicated that older teachers are likely to retain their posts because they are deeply involved in their educational community's environment and culture, it appears that caring and mentoring leadership can engage and retain younger teachers.

Second, supportive social capital, including supportive colleagues and mentors, a friendly working environment characterized by mutual respect, equal treatment, and an uplifting school community, appears to have compelled some learning leaders to retain their posts. Third, the presence of solid structural capital, meaning the existence of fair market remuneration, basic facilities in schools, and opportunities for professional upward mobility, has also added to the list of reasons behind the retention of learning leaders in Sub-Saharan Africa. A study by Gomba (2015) in Zimbabwean schools supports social and structural capital as teacher retention incentives. This researcher interviewed six teachers from three Zimbabwean schools regarding their decisions to remain in their posts. Results showed that learning leaders retained their positions thanks to job security, family assistance, and colleague support. More explicitly, factors of teacher retention, such as decent working conditions, including bonuses, recognition, and prospects for professional development (Gomba, 2015), fall under the realm of structural capital. In contrast, teachers' retention is caused by a school environment that fosters a culture of togetherness and collegial support concerning social structure. Likewise, the results of a study by Theron et al. (2014) indicate the critical importance of social and structural capital. In their quest for the factors influencing the retention of instructors in South African higher education institutions, Theron et al. (2014) suggested that "compensation and recognition, and management support were . . . possible factors that could encourage respondents to stay in their institution" (p. 10).

Retention Strategies

Unlike the OECD countries that designed a cohesive set of policies meant to foster the level of attrition in their schools, Sub-Saharan Africa does not present such coordinated measures. However, the above and similar studies have provided food for thought for practitioners and policymakers in educational leadership and beyond to develop appropriate measures to foster teacher retention in the Sub-Saharan Africa region. For example, the government of Ghana has packaged some incentives to attract and retain teachers in rural schools. They have distributed solar lamps, bicycles, and motorcycles to entice invaluable learning leaders to accept postings and transfers to rural areas (MOE, 2015). The government also instituted some form of district sponsorship for teachers in training to attract and retain them in rural areas. Because of this policy, new teachers who benefited from this sponsorship had to accept posting in rural areas for at least three years. The policy also mandated that new teachers reimburse the sponsorship should they decline government postings. In effect, the policy promoted a balanced distribution of teachers in both rural and urban schools.

Acheampong et al. (2019) saw the policy as a government's promotion of a balanced distribution of teachers throughout the country. Because caring leadership plays an incredible role in enticing teachers to retain their positions, Van de Vyver et al. (2020) have suggested instructing teachers and prospective principals on the characteristics and impacts of transformational, transactional, and laissez-faire leadership behaviors. I agree that workshops and in-service sessions should constitute important forums for learning leaders to brush up on and discuss theories and practices of educational leadership overall.

CONCLUSION

In this chapter, I discussed why learning leaders throughout the world, particularly in the Global South countries of Sub-Saharan Africa, retain their jobs. However, I could not address the retention phenomenon without discussing the more challenging issue (the elephant in the room, so to speak) of attrition that has plagued both the OECD and the Global South education systems, although to different degrees. On the one hand, it is evident that the exceptional teachers in this study, those who have remained steadfast in their jobs for a minimum of five years, have witnessed and experienced attrition occurrences due to several reasons, some personal and others professional. However, other reasons will remain unknown despite the efforts of experienced researchers trying to understand them. On the other hand, it is also evident that those chosen to participate in this study have resisted attrition because they have remained working in the same schools. Like their colleagues who left, the exceptional teachers might have been pressured by corruption, uncaring leadership, unfair financial and social treatments, a toxic educational environment, and all the other attrition reasons discussed in this chapter that have contributed to the loss of value of the very educational fabric of Sub-Saharan Africa. They have resisted. They have held some essential secrets that have kept them "immune" to the corruption of education and the fragility of their colleagues who could no longer stay in the profession, some of whom genuinely loved the profession. I intend not to blame those who found that education could no longer serve their purposes because I could have behaved similarly depending on the circumstances. However, my point remains to praise the heroic learning leaders for whom this chapter's "retention" portion and its multifaceted reasons have borne more meaning than attrition. I posit that their reasons for staying in the profession might be beyond the taxonomy of the rationales covered in the chapter. Whatever their reasons, it pays to hear their voices, know their reasons for staying, and analyze those reasons with selected ethical theoretical frameworks.

The assessment of blogger Kellie about the movie *Queen of Katwe* as "The Story of the African Teacher" could not be further from the accurate picture of an exceptional teacher. For memory, *Queen of Katwe* (Wheeler, 2016) is a movie based on the true story of a Ugandan girl from the famous slum of Katwe who became a chess prodigy and won several trophies thanks to the resilience of her schoolteacher and principal. Kellie's analysis brings to the surface many of my preconceived attributes of exceptional teachers in this study. I have pictured them as unselfish because they dream for their students more than they dream for themselves; fooled by their governments that do not adequately value their abnegation; incorruptible in a systemic environment of corruption; supportive of their colleagues to maintain their professional ethics; serene even in overcrowded classes; and unfazed in the most toxic educational environment.

Below, I reproduce some excerpts from Kellie's blog about the persistence of "The African Teacher."

> For me, *Queen of Katwe* was the story of Phiona (the child who breaks out), a story of many more that do not make it out of poverty, but also the story of the African Teacher. The African Teacher who dares to dream for the students more than he ever dreamed for himself. The Teacher who desires for the children she teaches, the success she has only read of in books, but was not privileged enough to pursue it. She lives the dream in her students. The African Teacher who has repeatedly been failed by the government but chooses not to get jaded and believes that hard work, determination and discipline are the keys to success, despite repeated evidence in her country that corruption is really how people get ahead. . . . A story of a group of teachers in a slum in Kahawa West setting aside their meager resources to fund a porridge program for the kindergarten kids, after noticing that most did not have breakfast coming to school. It is the story of a teacher who does not let a flooded class that does not have windows get in the way of learning. It is the story of that head Teacher who escorted a girl to Loreto High School Limuru with nothing but her school admission letter, the primary school uniform she was wearing, and much faith that a teacher at Loreto would figure out something so that the girl could get an education. It is the story of a Teacher we all know and have been inspired by, to be where we are today. For me, A Child of an African Teacher, *Queen of Katwe*, was about a Teacher who dares to dream for the kids. (Kellie, 2016)

Chapter 2

Exceptional Teachers under Duress

"You can learn a lot about someone by observing him when he is hungry."

(African Proverb)

My study aimed to investigate how and why exceptional teachers in the Global South countries of the D.R. Congo, Ghana, and Uganda show unfailing commitment to their teaching despite the lack of appreciation for the teaching profession in their respective countries. Research after research have indicated that the teaching profession has been undervalued in most parts of the world, particularly in Global South countries such as the D.R. Congo, Ghana, and Uganda, to mention a few (Scherer, 2009; Rinke, 2014; Darling-Hammond & Rothman, 2019; Etshim, 2017; Wabule, 2017). The rationale behind teachers' social, financial, and cultural negligence includes several reasons depending on the country and context (Etshim, 2017). While many countries are reporting a loss of enthusiasm for the teaching profession, with 50% of new teachers leaving their positions within the first five years in the United States alone (Scherer, 2003; Rinke, 2014), it is important to rationalize those teachers who bravely remain on the job. This decrease in enthusiasm for teaching is even more acutely chronic in selected developing countries where social, financial, and cultural incentives remain either scarce or nonexistent.

Unlike studies examining the causes and effects of teacher attrition in the D.R. Congo, Ghana, and Uganda, my research is built on two premises. First, teacher attrition is an acute and timely phenomenon that poses an educational and ethical problem in the educational systems of Global South countries, as evidenced by UNICEF (2021), Oboko and Wassa (2020), Teacher Initiative in Sub-Saharan Africa (TISSA) (2014), and other sources, including the Ugandan National Teachers' Union (UNATU) (TISSA, 2014). Second, schoolteachers have remained steadfast in their profession in the three selected countries despite the lack of adequate accommodation, fair salaries, and social benefits, as indicated by TISSA (2013).

My study intends to give voice to those "exceptional" teachers and analyze the ethical rationale behind their unfailing commitment to their teaching vocation. In this time of globalization, where information is interchangeable and interconnected, educational leaders may also learn from the experiences of these exceptional Global South teachers to incentivize those like them. However, the ultimate goal will be to improve their social conditions to allow them a decent life, as in South Korea, Finland, and Norway (Hanushek, 2011; Pisa, 2017). The untold or under-told stories of the teachers who make a difference in the lives of children in Global South countries are likely to resonate with many other educators worldwide.

The premise of this study on the exceptionality of some learning leaders in the Sub-Saharan countries of Africa aligns well with the preoccupation of Gomba (2015), who researched teacher retention in Zimbabwe. This author noted that primary and secondary school teachers swapped their teaching profession for other more lucrative, higher-paying jobs. However, Gomba continues, research has also found that some learning leaders have remained. Why have they remained? This author cites studies that came up with several findings, three of which offered views relatively dissimilar to those I presented in the previous chapter.

The first finding holds that some learning leaders have stayed in their profession "because they care and love kids, enjoyed the job, genuine colleague support, and the feeling that they were making a difference" (Gomba, 2015, p. 57). A second finding says that some teachers have stayed because they have benefitted from a sense of autonomy and control and enjoyed the ability to function independently in classrooms. The third discovery, and most controversial, states that people would enter and stay in the teaching profession because they see it as more attractive than other professions (Guirano et al., 2006). Put differently, this finding maintains that learning leaders would stay in their teaching profession no matter what because it helps them to put food on the table. On the contrary, I argue that the exceptional learning leaders in this study would not stay on the job at all costs, as this chapter is likely to show. Instead, I designed this study against the backdrop notion that exceptional teachers work unselfishly for the betterment of their students even when they face hardships, including delays or lack of salaries. I would continue to argue that exceptional teachers are in the profession because it fits their calling and ethics.

In this chapter, I intend to delve more into the phenomenon of retention I covered in the previous chapter to examine the reasons that have motivated exceptional learning leaders in this study to stay in their profession. To my knowledge, no researcher has conducted qualitative research—through narrative inquiry—of the persistent teachers whom this study calls "exceptional" to uncover the reasons behind their perseverance. The uniqueness of this study mainly lies in its analysis of the untold stories of the voiceless teachers in the Global South countries of the D.R. Congo, Ghana, and Uganda. Uniquely, this study recognizes and brings to bear the heroism of those teachers, hoping that a new generation of teachers will benefit from the respect and adulation teachers receive in countries like South Korea (Pisa, 2017; Global et al., 2018).

Basically, the chapter seeks to respond to the significant research questions and sub-questions that guide this study, namely, "Why do the exceptional teachers in the select Global South countries remain in the job despite the overall lack of consideration attributed to their profession?" Why have the twenty selected teachers in this study remained steadfast in their moral conduct of their students' learning in a precarious environment that has little or no regard for their value as professionals and educators of future generations? How do these heroic teachers hope their lived experiences resonate throughout on behalf of other teachers in similar social and cultural environments? What are the ethical leadership implications of the selected teachers' steadfastness for educational leaders in the Global South and beyond?

The chapter purports to describe the persistence of the teachers whose communities have identified them as exceptional. In their own words, twenty selected teachers tell their lived experiences and highlight why they remain in their positions and lead their students' learning ethically, which captivates the admiration of their institutions and communities. Finally, this chapter discusses the data analysis and presents the common themes that emerged from the data.

A WORD ON METHODOLOGY

To answer the above research question, it is suitable to present the methodology, including the data collection strategies that led to the results of this investigation. Concretely, this chapter presents the data collection methods and the results of the field study I conducted in the three countries: of D.R. Congo, Uganda, and Ghana. I chose narrative inquiry (Vera et al., 2020) within the qualitative research tradition (Merrian & Tisdell, 2016) to capture the stories of those exceptional learning leaders.

Narrative Inquiry

This study used narrative inquiry to examine the rationale behind the persistence of exceptional teachers in their teaching profession. It sought to capture the meaning the selected learning leaders attached to their exceptionality through their lived stories. For Sub-Saharan Africans, storytelling (narrative) has always been a powerful tool to communicate wisdom and knowledge. Narrative inquiry or narrative analysis does justice to the exceptional educators of Africa because it belongs to the domain of "storytelling," which the exceptional learning leaders are used to, given the importance their cultures place on conveying their wisdom from one generation to another. This qualitative method aims at "illocutionary" intentions and the desire to communicate meaning (Bruner, 1990). Scholars use a narrative approach to capture the moment's emotion and render stories in an active rather than passive voice. In the same way, the exceptional teachers told their stories as they lived them in the past and relived them at the time of this study (which was the present). Le Goff (1992) tied these two phenomena of memory (past events) and notions of time (rendering in the present) to storytelling. Using a narrative method means the following: (a) the learning leaders in this study have held in stories the knowledge of their perseverance in the teaching profession; (b) that knowledge "can be relayed, stored and retrieved" (Fry, 2002, p. 166). Clandinin and Connelly (2000) conceptualized narrative inquiry from a Deweyan theory of experience and developed a metaphor of a three-dimensional narrative inquiry space. The three-dimensional space includes temporality or a simultaneous look into the past, present, and future of people, places, things, and events under study; sociality or focus on the personal and social conditions of the participants in a balance appropriate to the inquiry; and place or occurrence in specific places or sequences of places where personal events occurred.

As far as temporality is concerned, the stories of the learning leaders in this study date back to before they joined their current place of employment, address their present, and extend to the future of their leadership education. Sociality comes into play given that the personal conditions of the teachers in this study occur in and interact with the societies in which they live and work. The specific place at the center of the participants' stories consists of the schools or institutions of higher learning where they work.

Institutional Review Board and Spotters

A study of this magnitude required the approval of the Institutional Review Board of the University of St. Thomas, which I obtained after securing the collaboration and permission of three institutions of higher learning that I chose as spotters of potential participants in this study (see Appendix A). The selection of the spotter institutions occurred through the relations I have established with the three institutions over the years. One was the University of Kikwit in my hometown in the D.R. Congo; the other was the University of Kisubi, which hosted me and my students for a study abroad course on "Leadership in the International Context of Uganda" in July of 2022. In contrast, the University of Accra–Legon in Ghana hosted the same course with a different group of students before the pandemic in July 2018.

These three institutions made this study possible as they agreed to collaborate with school communities in their areas to identify each of the twelve potential exceptional educators who met the criteria to participate in my study. The criteria for learning leaders, regardless of the level at which they teach, to be considered exceptional included the following:

- Being native of and working in one of the three countries of D.R. Congo, Ghana, and Uganda
- Having taught at any level, elementary, secondary, or higher education in the same institution for at least five consecutive years
- Being recognized by their communities as steadfast in their teaching, professional, and social life, including particularly dedication to teaching, excellent reputation, and integrity
- Being nominated for the study by their school communities
- In some cases, being vetted by their own past or present students

Initially, this study targeted a total sample of thirty-six teachers in the three identified countries. I intended to select an eligible population of exceptional teachers who have been recognized as such by their communities and have had impeccable working experience of at least five years. Despite the lack of appreciation for the teaching profession, the participants have shown steadfastness and unfailing commitment to their teaching jobs in their respective schools.

When it became challenging for some of the spotters to reach out to their school communities and provide educators they believed qualified for this study, I opened up the spotter field to include academic professionals and communities who referred additional potential candidates to me. All along, I made sure to vet each candidate by requesting additional information from those candidates' past or present students to ascertain their eligibility for the study.

Procedural Focus Group

Merrian and Tisdell (2017) contend that "a focus group is an interview in a topic such as a group of people who know about the topic. . . . Perhaps the most unique characteristic of focus group research is the interactive discussion through which data are generated, which leads to a different type of data not accessible through individual interviews" (p. 114). Likewise, to develop a comparative list of qualifying criteria for exceptional teachers or instructors, I organized two procedural focus groups of six students each from purposefully selected institutions of higher learning. The focus groups are deemed procedural because their results only led to selecting participants for this study and understanding the contexts of education in the Sub-Saharan region. The study concerned a specific category of teachers instead of students, and inputs from the latter were added to the selection criteria. The two focus groups took place in private locations in the two countries I physically visited for this study (Uganda and the D.R. Congo). Attendants to the two focus groups were three female and three male undergraduates (per country) with an average of two to four years of college education. The attendants also teamed up in data analysis using a critical concept analytical framework (Krueger & Casey, 2009) consisting of identifying factors of central importance and discovering the core ideas. Students who attended the procedural focus groups discussed, responded to, and analyzed the following questions:

Question 1: What are the qualities of an exceptional or ideal/moral lecturer/professor?

Word Cloud #1 (figure 2.1.) represents responses to this question, which include passion to share knowledge; ability to go the extra mile to teach; great humility; unfailing commitment; excellent punctuality in responding to students' queries and assignments; academically skilled and competent; up-to-date researcher; well-mannered and considerate; excellent punctuality in responding to students' queries and assignments; good communication skills; capability to motivate students; ability to be a professional advisor; ethical leadership; skills of a counselor; ability to align theory with practice; approachability and selflessness.

Figure 2.1 Word Cloud 1: Qualities of an Exceptional or Ideal Lecturer or Professor.

Question 2: What are the characteristics of your least preferred professor?

Word Cloud #2 (figure 2.2) contains responses to question 2, including the following: a person with attitude; an instructor who delays correcting papers and students have to run after him/her; a male instructor who is biased toward female students; a womanizer; a sodomizer; a tribalist; a female instructor biased against female students; an instructor who creates competition between her and female students; an instructor who shows favoritism (e.g., female teachers toward male students); who shows lack of commitment in marking (grading students); who befriends students for personal pleasure and incentivizes biases and favoritism; who fails students for not bribing them; who fails female students for not consenting to sleep with them; an arrogant instructor who dictates all the knowledge; for example, a teacher who impregnated a student and was never terminated because he was the best math teacher in the school district.

Each criterion about the exceptional teacher and the least preferred instructor included comments and stories that could make up an entire chapter. For the sake of this study, I reproduced some discussion lines and short stories that came as a surprise to me. Those details show the depth of corruption in educational systems and the heroism of the exceptional teachers who strive to avoid the ethical collapse of educational systems. Students in this focus group hated "male or female instructors who befriend students for personal pleasures and encourage biases and favoritism with their behavior." Worse, they were horrified and disgusted when referring to "a teacher who impregnated a

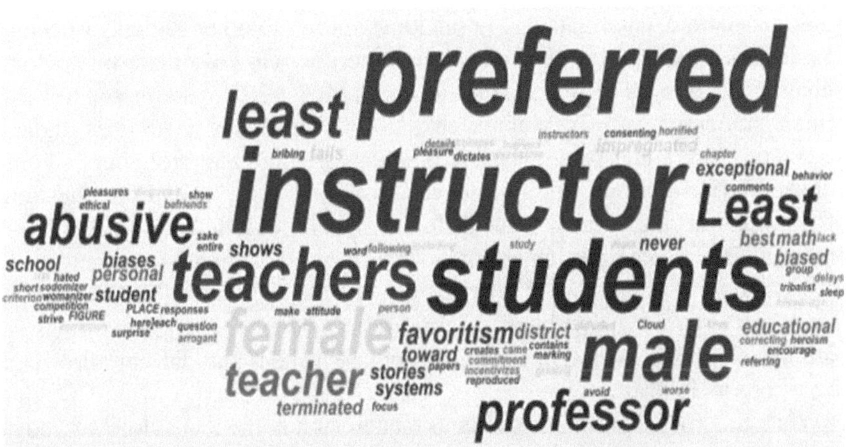

Figure 2.2 Word Cloud 2: Characteristics of a Least Preferred Instructor.

student and was never terminated because he was the best math teacher in the school district." A participant told this story:

> We had a female teacher who gave us a group assignment, and I was assigned a boy to work with. The teacher instructed us to contact her directly in case we had challenges or questions, and we could set individual meetings with her. I was not clear with one of the exercises we had to do on my team and tried in vain to request an appointment with the instructor. My teammate, however, informed me that he was able to reach out to the instructor and he immediately received an appointment for the same day, and asked whether I would wish to join him. The female instructor did not expect me. Upon our arrival at her office, I could sense the warmness with which she welcomed my man teammate before realizing that I was standing behind the young man. I was surprised at her brisk mood swing when she saw me. She immediately asked, "Why are you here today?" I said, "I have tried to meet with you for the same questions because the two of us are working together, and. . . ." Before I even finished talking, she yelled: "Get out of my office and go wait until I'm done with him. . . ." Although I knew all the way from experience that some female instructors take sexual advantage of their students, I did not think anything was happening with the particular instructor I had known for taking some prior courses with her. To keep a long story short, when we departed the professor's office, I bluntly asked my colleague whether he entertained another form of relationship with the instructor. He laughed and said, "What can I tell you? We have been all over. . . . I am having good grades, and sometimes I am being paid financially for. . . . Do you get it?"

As a researcher, I had to get my head straight, but I was so horrified that I decided to probe participants' thoughts about the story. They all agreed it was unacademic, unethical, and perniciously unfair to other students working to get good marks. My other question came up: "How do male instructors behave?" They said: "Same . . . or worse. . . . Most of them are biased toward female students whom they abuse sexually as well." These students underscored the reality that "these abusive practices are rampant throughout all our educational institutions, and no one can stop it. . . ." I pursued the question of how private institutions were different in this regard. They said: "They are not." One female participant then said: "I go to a private university. . . . Please allow me to call one of my male instructors, and you will hear the dirty language the two of us will use. . . . Additionally, he has tried many times to date me. . . . I am so sick of it. . . ." I stopped it there and did not allow her to call her male instructor.

What the focus group participants stated about the behaviors of most male lecturers provided credence to the BBC documentary *Sex for Grades: Undercover in West African Universities* in West Africa. The video alleges that sexual harassment of female students by male lecturers is said to be not only endemic but also normalized (BBC, 2019).

Selection of Participants

This study used a non-probabilistic maximum variation sampling (Creswell & Poth, 2018; Merriam & Tisdell, 2016) because I intended the sample to include various participants. Specifically, this purposive sample included learning leaders from elementary schools to higher education, from rural to urban areas, and from public and private educational institutions. I purposely intended the sample to be as representative as possible to represent the average participant (Creswell & Creswell, 2018), and I wanted to understand how those different groups of teachers viewed the leadership ethics behind their steadfastness to their teaching profession.

This study combined two sets of criteria—one provided by the school communities who chose their own exceptional teachers and the other emanating from the two procedural focus groups described above. The two sources provided precious details that became the ultimate criteria for qualifying a given teacher as an exceptional learning leader in this study. Combining the two sets of criteria helped to rule out any chance of getting into the pool of the selected participating teachers who would otherwise not meet the conditions for exceptionality. Additionally, the procedural focus group results provided an essential list of disqualifiers in the characteristics of the least preferred teachers or instructors. In the end, participant eligibility included being nominated by the school community, dedication to teaching, an excellent reputation, integrity, learning leader and counselor, and a minimum of 5 years of working experience in the same institution (table 2.1).

Twenty learning leaders (nine females and eleven males) participated in this study (eight in the D.R. Congo, two in Ghana, and ten in Uganda) (see table 2.1). I selected this population because they are eligible exceptional teachers who have been recognized as such by their communities and have had impeccable working experience of at least five years. Despite the lack of appreciation for the teaching profession, the participants have shown steadfastness and unfailing commitment to their teaching jobs in their respective schools. Although I have assigned participants pseudonyms to abide by the Institutional Review Board of my university's policy on confidentiality, I have left the non-identifiers such as their countries of origin, educational level, and teaching experiences. The twenty learning leaders hold an average teaching experience of twenty-three years. Ten participants are university professors (assistants, associate professors, and full professors) in various schools of higher education, including education, psychology, law, and public administration. Eight participants teach in secondary schools, and two are elementary school teachers. Fifty percent of the participants teach in public schools or universities, and the other 50% work in private educational institutions, whereas 60% of the institutions were in urban areas (cities and towns), and 40% were in rural areas. This maximum variation sample (Patton, 2002)

Table 2.1 Eligibility Criteria for Exceptional Learning Leaders

Default Criteria of Eligibility	*Specifics*
Native of D.R Congo, Ghana, or Uganda	
Nomination by the school community	Or nomination by institutional spotters
Dedication to teaching	Passion to share knowledge; ability to go the extra mile to teach; unfailing commitment
Excellent reputation for integrity	Great humility; great punctuality in responding to students' queries and assignments; good communication skills; capability to motivate students
Learning leader and counselor	Ability to be a professional advisor; ethical leader; skillful counselor; ability to align theory with practice; approachability and selflessness
Persistence	5+ years in the same institution

had many features in common: They teach in the background of dysfunctional educational systems in Sub-Saharan Africa. Their countries and cultures do not appropriately value or reward their teaching profession. They function in undervalued conditions.

Nevertheless, they hold the tacit esteem and recognition of their communities because they have remained undeterred and resilient. It is worth noting that two nominated candidates did not return the survey questionnaire, nor did they participate in the interview sessions; one participant died before the interviews. Additionally, I eliminated two other potential participants who did not meet all the selection criteria listed above, although credible spotters recommended them. Table 2.2 gives the profiles of the twenty selected teachers/professors who participated in this study.

Data collection, processing, and analysis began upon my travels to Uganda and the D.R. Congo in the summer of 2022. I spent more than a month traveling throughout each country, except Ghana, to meet research participants. The study intentionally used five data collection strategies, including (a) a Qualtrics survey administered to selected educators in the D.R. Congo, Ghana, and Uganda; (b) a forty- to sixty-minute interview either on the phone, via WhatsApp or Zoom video conference; (c) educators' artifacts such as photos, prayers, and diaries; (d) researcher's comments; and (e) a student procedural focus group. The interview questions were identical to the survey queries (see appendix A). Except for the questions that required factual data, the other questions were open-ended enough to allow for probes and follow-up explanations.

Table 2.2 List of Selected Learning Leaders Participating in the Study

No.	Name	Country	Gender	*Educational Institution*	*Age range (years)*	*Years of Teaching*
1	Antie	Uganda	F	Higher Ed.	36–50	11–30
2	Bill	Uganda	M	Sec. School	36–50	11–30
3	Chantal	Uganda	F	Sec. School	36–50	7
4	Dindo	Uganda	M	Sec. School	25–35	7
5	Eliza	Uganda	F	Elem. School	20–35	5
6	Felix	Uganda	M	Higher Ed.	36–50	11–30
7	Georg	Uganda	M	Sec. School	36–50	10
8	Henry	Uganda	M	Sec. School	36–50	10
9	Innos	Uganda	M	Elem. School	25–30	5
10	John	Uganda	M	Sec. School	36–50	11–30
11	Kalunga	D.R. Congo	M	Higher Ed	51–65	11–30
12	Linda	D.R. Congo	F	Higher Ed.	51–65	11–30
13	Maria	D.R. Congo	F	Second Ed.	36–50	11–30
14	Oscar	D.R. Congo	M	Higher Ed.	51–65	11–30
15	Pat	D.R. Congo	F	Second Ed.	51–60	11–30
16	Quella	D.R. Congo	F	Higher Ed.	36–50	11–30
17	Roger	D.R. Congo	M	Higher Ed.	66–75	30+
18	Simon	D.R. Congo	M	Higher Ed.	36–50	5
19	Tata	Ghana	F	Higher Ed.	51–65	6–10
20	Ursula	Ghana	F	Higher Ed.	36–50	6–10

Using the same tool for both the survey and the interviews had the benefit of engaging participants in in-depth narratives of their survey responses (Bongila, 2003). Since the inception of this study, I did not plan to travel to Ghana. Instead, I forwarded the survey to participants, awaited their responses via email, and then administered the interview over the phone or via Zoom. The survey's return rate was around 90%. As mentioned in the book introduction, one recruited participant (Suzan) responded to the survey but passed on afterward before a scheduled interview. I discarded the survey because of the inability to cross-compare it with interview data. I audio-recorded and transcribed the interviews to prepare the data for detailed analysis.

To analyze the data collected, I used a form of narrative analysis. Caulfield's (2022) six steps of narrative analysis, namely familiarization, coding, generating themes, reviewing themes, defining and naming themes, and writing up, provided a basis for designing an analysis process suitable for this study. The narrative analysis I adopted for this study boiled down to four steps. Before analyzing the data, I transcribed the interviews after administering them. In the D.R. Congo, I administered all the surveys and interviews in French. Then, I translated the transcriptions and transcribed all the data in English. To begin the data analysis process, I proceeded in the following fashion. First, I reread the transcripts several times to familiarize myself with the participants' narratives (Weaver-Hightower, 2019).

Second, I used deductive coding, which is concept-driven coding (Miles et al., 2014), because it involves predefining analytical bits to analyze the data I transcribed. As recommended by these scholars, I drew twenty-two deductive codes from the study's survey and interview questions before administering them to the participants. In addition, I discovered eight inductive codes from the transcripts, which I included in the analytical bits. These codes emerged progressively during data collection. "These [codes] are better grounded empirically and are especially satisfying to the researcher who uncovered an important local factor" (Miles et al., 2014, p. 81). Combining the deductive and inductive codes resulted in the thirty analytical codes in table 2.3.

I found the deductive coding approach advantageous because it helped guarantee that I have coded my areas of interest surrounding the rationale behind the leadership ethics of the exceptional learning leaders in this study. However, I kept in check a potential bias consisting of predetermining participants' answers. To minimize that specific risk (Merriam & Tisdell, 2016), I ensured I got all the essential codes and themes emerging from the data, as indicated above.

Third, I generated themes from transcripts, which I then wrote up. The generation of themes also followed a deductive technique because, as a

Table 2.3 Deductive and Inductive Codes

	Deductive Codes		*Inductive Codes*
1	Professional integrity	1	Religious background
2	Duress/hardship	2	Coach/counselor
3	Passion for teaching	3	Transforming life
4	Resisting challenges	4	Family culture
5	Devaluation of education	5	Farming/gardening
6	Threats (emotional, physical, verbal)	6	Prayer as artifact
7	Lack of appreciation	7	Happiness/joy
8	Teaching motivation	8	Parental resistance
9	Teaching philosophy		
10	Coping mechanisms		
11	Self-gratification		
12	Verbal abuses		
13	Degradation (of education)		
14	Financial incentives		
15	Lack of opportunity		
16	Corruption		
17	Physical abuses		
18	Emotional abuses		
19	Calling/vocation		
20	Moral integrity		
21	Professional regrets		
22	Emotional satisfaction		

researcher, I could drive the data analysis to my interest to uncover the benefit exceptional learning leaders received from their steadfastness in the teaching profession.

Fourth, I went one step further to analyze the emerging themes through the lens of leadership ethics theories (ethical egoism and psychological egoism) (Gotthelf, 2016) and public communication models (press agentry, public information, two-way asymmetric, two-way symmetric) as applied to philanthropy (Grunig, 1992). To analyze artifacts, such as photos and other physical tools, I relied on the descriptive narrative and the meaning participants ascribed to their objects (Merrian & Tisdell, 2016). In turn, I included those narratives as an integral part of the data I collected, which I codified and merged into the themes that formed the results of this study.

Data Security and Confidentiality

For data security and confidentiality, I abided by the University of St. Thomas' I.R.B.'s policy. Before collecting data through surveys and interview, I took the necessary time to review the consent form with participants, especially their rights to discontinue participation at any point during the study. I used pseudonyms for the participants and their institutions, keeping all personal information, recordings, and transcriptions confidential. I kept all identifiable data, such as audio recordings, consent forms, and transcripts, on my computer with a password known only to me. I deleted audio recordings after I finished transcribing and analyzing them. Regarding survey data, I stored them on Qualtrics and intend to destroy them twelve months after the study's completion.

Trustworthiness and Reliability

As shown above, this study used several data collection methods to ascertain a saturated collection of data and an in-depth analysis of the phenomenon of learning leaders' retention and the ethical motives behind their stay. Besides my own researcher's notes and comments, the collection of artifacts such as pictures and prayers, which kept participants going during hardships, added tremendously to the quality and quantity of the data I collected. Participants took the survey and forwarded it to me a minimum of two weeks prior to participating in the interview sessions. Participants used the same questions for both the survey and the interviews. This technique allowed me to gather more detailed data from the interviews than from the written survey, where participants tend to rush through questions that require narrative responses (Bongila, 2003). I mainly noticed participants' discrepant responses to the same narrative questions from the survey and the interview sessions.

Those discrepancies led to insightful follow-up questions and probes, which enriched the data in a targeted manner.

Asking the same questions in different ways also accounts for the reliability of this data process and analysis. Brink (1991) specifically outlined one method of qualitative reliability within the interview by asking the same question in different ways and at different times (Weather-Hightower, 2019). The data process generated two themes in response to the research question of why the exceptional teachers in the Global South remained in the classrooms in otherwise least attractive contexts of education degradation and uncertainties. The learning leaders (a) kept motivation; they resisted challenges and threats, and they held a unique altruistic teaching philosophy; (b) they held alternative coping mechanisms, and they found personal benefit in teaching. In the remaining chapter, I will present only the first theme. The second theme will be developed in chapter 3.

PROFESSIONAL MOTIVATION AND ALTRUISTIC TEACHING PHILOSOPHY

Whether in the survey or interview responses, the exceptional learning leaders in this study revealed that their motivation and passion for the teaching profession accounted for their persistence in the job. Their resolve to teach compelled them to resist the multifaceted challenges and threats they incurred because of their indefectible professionalism in learning leadership. First, reporting on motivation and passion as the foundations of their integrity is suitable.

These two factors (motivation and passion) constituted the foundation of their ethical integrity. Most participants told stories of events or circumstances that enhanced their motivation to remain in teaching. Among other events that evidenced his motivation for the profession, Innos told how one of his students followed his guidance to become a Catholic priest. He had this to say:

> The learner, who later became Fr. Sebastien (pseudonym), was a stubborn student. He often dodged classes, pretend he was sick, and engage in undisciplined practices. But after sitting him down and guiding him, he chose to take on the priesthood. Then he came back to me, and we sat down. . . . I understood that he was on the move between school and home. Whenever he would run out of money, he would forge sickness then asks for permission to go back home. . . . After sitting him down, I showed him that he isn't studying for anyone, but for himself. . . . Within the private talks we used to have, and after counselling him

> here and there we become closer friends. Then he said he desired to become a priest and needed my support and recommendation. So, I told him if that's what your desire is, I've gotten no problem to recommend you go on with what your desires are. He decided to join the seminary. He had some forms to fill. Okay. And, among them, on the forms, they needed one to recommend him who had more information, who knew him better for the previous two, three years in his education background. So, I took a risk, but within the two years I spent with him, he changed. So, as I was recommending him, I did, I told him that I'm doing this and I hope you have made up your mind, and through the counselling, I hope you'll be a better person. The opportunity to change this formerly stubborn student gave me peace of mind. The very day of the ordination confirmed me in my drive for teaching. It was an emotional moment. Each time I see Fr. Sebastian—now our parish priest—I thank God for confirming me in my teaching profession.

In his way, Felix, although not an ordained minister, also referred to the priesthood as a source of motivation in the teaching profession. "I wanted to be a priest; that was that I think on the forefront, I made this [teaching] to relate to the priest [I did not become]." He thinks of his teaching as an extension of the Bishop's assignments when he was still in the seminary, where he even received the nickname "teacher." He remembered that once he was walking in a village distant from his home, and someone yelled at him, although very gently, "Teacher, teacher." He turned around and waved at the person he did not recognize. These events and others have increased his motivation to lead learning in higher education. Felix concluded the question about his deep motivations for remaining in the teaching profession by stating, "However, the opportunity is not there," prompting me to probe him further. So would you say that you remain a teacher here because there's no other opportunity for you in Uganda?

"What would you do if there was an opportunity for you outside of teaching?"

> Of course, I have to leave if it is more lucrative, but I would not be more relevant there. I have done a lot for charity. But I think I've not been so much recognized. . . . And if I get an opportunity, I need to take my children to good schools also. I need to develop myself. Yeah. So, if I get an opportunity, then I have to embrace the opportunity. (Felix)

A handful of participants in this study held a shaky view regarding whether they would run away from teaching if offered opportunities for a better salary or an excellent benefits package. Notably, participants would not easily express this view in the survey they took because they would feel limited by the space and time to complete the questions.

Neither would a simple interview without probes. Regardless, I did not consider this hypothetical as a criterion for disqualification because he had been at that school for over five years at the time of this study and was recommended by reliable spotters. Regarding the reasons that motivated Felix to remain steadfast in his profession, he reported that his family upbringing and his priesthood training in the seminary played an important role.

Likewise, Georg's motivation also alludes to the priesthood. He indicated that teaching has been his leitmotif: "I feel it is vocational. I couldn't be a priest. I couldn't be one, but at least I'm a teacher." This participant believes that priesthood allows one to make a difference in people's lives. For this reason, he stated, "I love making a difference in the lives of students. . . . It gives me a lot of pleasure when I stay with the students." He takes pleasure in receiving the young students when they are younger and seeing them grow into responsible human beings. "It gives me a lot of happiness, but I also love teaching."

Results also revealed that learning leaders' motivation to maintain their position as teachers was challenged by temptations to abandon it altogether as they faced multiple challenges. However, that motivation was so deeply ingrained in them that some learner leaders had to default to their love for teaching after somehow deciding to leave it. Henry's narrative was not uncommon. To the question of what cemented your resolution to remain in the teaching position, he had this to say:

> I had decided to leave teaching because of the uncertainty of payments. I attended a job camp. . . . I was going take a "boda-boda" (motorcycle) to Zambia when I met a woman. . . . She says, "Teacher." I turned around and saw that the woman was calling from a vehicle. "Do you remember me?" I said, "No." She said, "I was among the first students you taught in 2002." And she said, "Thank you so much. . . . You taught me things that helped me. Currently, I live in Germany and there is a program that can help you to grow younger people . . . we shall meet." She gave me a card. She said, "Where are you going?" I said, "I'm going to Zambia." She drove me up to Zambia. Then we met after some time. She's the one who connected me to a group in Germany. Now we are working on an exchange program with a youth ministry Institute Guard in Germany. So, when she told me that information, it toted me. She repeated, "Thank you for helping me being what I am." And I thought, but when I run away, what else do I need? That has kept ringing in my head. That event reminded me that my place was in teaching. The program she linked me to is producing fruits because as I speak now, they're around seven youth from my school who have benefited from it. They go for a volunteer service during their high school in Germany. They do four years. Then return to Uganda. All have returned except one who has got a sponsor. He is studying from there. . . . That really touched me. So,

> I did not get the job in Zambia, but found myself here. I have since gained so much with my teaching as I see students grow. (Henry)

Henry's narrative highlights the notion of making a difference in students' lives as one of the significant reasons that encouraged learning leaders to persist in their teaching. He made an impact in the life of the "forgotten" student who used the emotionally charged word "teacher" to mean a person who makes change happen for the best in other people. While Henry realized later that he had made a change in the life of a former student, Antie enjoyed the process of making that change, turning her into a learning leader/counselor, which confirmed her resolve to keep working in education. Antie's narration follows.

> This is a period in that school where I was teaching in Divine University (pseudonym), I got a group of six. They were three girls and three boys who were addicted to drugs and one of these girls was like a wild one. I was given that chance of serving as a matron and interacted with many of them. And the parents' kids told me, "You know, Madam, these children are addicted to drugs." I was able to talk to them. They told me their family backgrounds. We went to their homes. I got the school's director, and we visited the homes of the children, and we helped them out of that drug addiction. They became responsible people. One showed me that really, I have that talent of transforming life. That one girl student has helped me working with the learners not only as a teacher but even as a counselor. That is why I don't regret it. I have seen this is my call to a service I have to give, not in monetary terms, but it is something that you feel like doing. So, I have to do abcd. You find yourself committed that you don't even miss either a lecture or a lesson because you have that gift. You have to feel there are people waiting, there are souls that need you around. (Antie)

As Chantal would confess, making a difference in students' lives also comes with some personal rewards. She feels happy seeing her students excel academically and even in their lifestyles after their education. She recounted coming across one of her former students who became a doctor. When her child fell ill, it was that doctor, that former student of hers, who "immediately came to my rescue at that time of crisis." She enjoyed both the life success of her student and the benefit she obtained from that student's success, adding, "I like it so when I see them [my students] prosper. I feel great, and it makes me at least maintain that spirit." Indeed, benefitting from services and tokens of appreciation—although not major motivational factors—had gone a long way to encourage these exceptional learning leaders to keep going. For example, Chantal mentioned that her school had a provision for an award for teachers whose students would get a distinction in one of the selected subjects they taught. There was an award of 10,000 Ugandan Shillings (roughly $2.50) for every distinction. Chantal was among the English teachers in that school. "So that year, English language in the school had about 85 distinctions out of the students who registered, so that money was distributed among us. Generally, it was a kind of motivation. So, it was also that celebration of the joy there that motivated me" (Chantal).

The outlier perspective was brought by Eliza, who also stated that they love making a difference in students' lives. They benefited from being with the little children they enjoyed as much as the children enjoyed them. However, they were adamant about persisting in the job because "it is hard to get another way to go." They argued that when you have studied for the profession you have sought, "you have to keep that position and plan it very well. . . . I have no other job, so I remain here."

This view represents the reality that there do not exist many jobs in the Global South waiting for people with a background in education. Again, we could argue that Eliza and others like them would not make the list of exceptional learning leaders as defined in this study. However, despite these views, the school community that recommended her for the study might have considered her persistence in the job (more than five years), his steadfastness, and his professional and ethical integrity. Rightfully, Kalunga meant those core attributes of learning leadership when he concluded, "What motivates me is the beauty of the profession."

Besides being strongly motivated for the job, the exceptional learning leaders in this study reported that they stand out because of their ability to resist socio-professional duress. This second sub-theme—resisting challenges and threats—presents a snapshot of the hardship the participants face in the daily exercise of their teaching leadership while it also paints a picture of the spoiled side of education in the Global South countries involved in this study. In the survey and interview questions about this section, participants were requested to address the most significant challenges and threats they have encountered since joining their educational institutions.

Degradation of Education

The majority of participants reported that their most significant challenge has come from the devaluation of education, lack of social consideration, unfair salaries, and insufficient instructional materials. For Kalunga, the mother of all challenges stems from "the general degradation of education followed by the lack of instructional materials." Linda made an emotional observation about the degradation of education in her institution of higher learning:

> The most important challenges for me is this degradation of education, it is really for me a scourge, a catastrophe when I see how already in our time we

> talked about degradation But it was not at a glaring level like the one we are experiencing today. In our time, we thought that the problem was isolated, and we had the hope that with time, this problem would be solved, but on the contrary, we are witnessing a generalization. Even in the areas where things were getting better and better it has deteriorated so that corruption is generalized. And this is how it affects all aspects of teaching, starting with the teachers themselves, who should be role models. They have allowed themselves to be negatively influenced. Parents also are negatively influenced. Students are even worse. What disgusts me even more is how society has been affected. (Linda)

Most participants—especially those in rural areas—reported that parents had lost faith in better education outcomes for their children. They argue that parents do not respect their children's education, nor do they give enough time for students to learn exactly what the school requires. For example, Henry reported, "Like recently we had a case where the children were supposed to be in school. But the parents kept them home. Not because of tuition, but because they feel they should do some gardening." Another parent said, "My child does not go for that because he may be contracted with diseases," or, "My child cannot associate with this low person of low income," reported another participant. "You know, that's the kind of some of the parents we have. . . . It is not that they are protecting their children," Henry claimed they are only against the children's education. Other parents would say, "I don't want my child in any other activity." "It is only class, not in music, games, or anything," argued another participant. "So, it takes time to talk to these parents that education must be holistic to prepare a child morally and socially," says Henry.

Parents showing low regard for their children's education pose another challenge for the learning leaders, which is the demotivation of parents and students. Unfortunately, says Innos, some of those parents should know better the significance of education because they hold degrees or awards from institutions of higher learning. However, they became demoralized because they might have failed to find jobs. "So, the only solution they have is to come back to the village, and then they become nuisance to the society. So, parents or some people in the area prefer to undermine the education system. They keep referring to them" (Innos).

When you ask some parents why they don't bring their children to this school to have a bright future through education, they will tell you: "But so and so has studied higher levels, but he is doing ordinary jobs. . . . Why should I waste money paying for my daughter and son, but afterward, they will return to do the ordinary jobs?" As opposed to their counterparts in urban settings, the exceptional teachers in rural areas reported they dealt more acutely with the lack of perceived education value. For Innos, "this means we are in a community that does not value education much. Because based in the rural area . . . we have that challenge of learners dropping out drastically because they may lack role models in their lifestyle." Worse, Innos and others asserted that it was not uncommon for parents to pull their children out of school. Again, "they feel like education does not bring anything in the future, so you may not study and have life" (Innos).

Likewise, Bill rated the challenge of overall degradation of the value attached to education as their second major challenge. They explained that "this [the challenge] comes in the sense that in the community where we're serving, being a well-to-do, you find, there are people who have [means] from out of education." There seem to be no incentives for such parents to encourage their students to either work hard or attend private schools that depend solely on tuition from parents like them. Teachers are always on edge regarding their salaries and instructional materials, which the school can cut off anytime depending on how students pay. Worse, teachers at these institutions live without expecting any private or government promotion. "Government doesn't come to private institutions to call on promotions because they have limited control over them."

Addressing demotivation issues at the higher education level, Antie stated that "people look at education and feel like maybe education and particularly higher education is no longer important. Now they look at you in society and say ah even those who are less educated are better than these people." This participant pursued that people judge one's social status according to how much money they make rather than how much education they accomplish. They point to people who did not go to school but are doing fairly well in society. He added that when people learned he was studying to earn a PhD degree, they reacted by saying things similar to: "This person started PhD. Now, why you are wasting money you would have used for these other things. . . . You see so there is a general devaluing of education" (Antie). All participants in this study agreed that education has lost its place as the favorite tool of training individuals to become morally responsible leaders. But they also maintained that the current duress does not deter them from leading learning with professionalism and ethics.

Lack of Social Appreciation and Financial Incentives

Besides facing the challenge brought about by the overall loss of value of education in their respective countries, participants in this study also indicated that they were subjected to a lack of social appreciation. Fifty percent of participants in this study ranked the lack of social appreciation of teachers as either first or second in the levels of challenges they face. They included such factors as a lack of respect from students, parents, and educational officials.

The third and most significant challenge that exceptional learning leaders have reported is the absence of appropriate financial incentives. More than 90% of participants reported the challenge of irregularity of salaries. Although teachers in most public education institutions indicated that they receive financial compensation on a regular basis, they were quick to point out that they earn below the market value and other professions with the same level of education. Private institutions, which depend solely on student tuition and parent financial contributions, reported more drastic financial challenges in some areas. For example, Innos had this to say:

> You find that being a private institution that isn't even under the category of government aid, we get salaries depending on the time we spend at school. So, like a term must go three months. So, it means you be paid for three months. Holidays, you go without payment. So, you've got to find your way out, how to survive with the family members you're looking after. (Innos)

Furthermore, Innos also advanced a conflicting argument backed by a couple of other learning leaders in this study. The argument goes as follows: You have not received any salary as a teacher. You keep asking yourself: "How am I going to teach other people's children when my own is still at home?" (Innos). "So then comes the source of corruption because some students or parents are well-to-do whose earnings are a little bit higher. You know it because their children can come with pocket money to corrupt a junior teacher" (Innos). Sadly, this form of corruption is rampant in schools, particularly in institutions of higher learning, as evidenced by both the interview responses and the informal data from focus groups with college students. Like other exceptional leaders in this study, Innos's argument only shows how easy it must be for teachers without adequate salaries to fall prey to corruption. Almost all learning leaders at private institutions reported lower salaries than their counterparts in public institutions. More importantly, they complained about the constant delay in their payment. Some have gone without hope of getting paid for five to six months. Whenever possible, institutions can allocate transportation money on a need basis. Sometimes, institutions would invite them back to campus for important meetings, but the former could not reinforce attendance because teachers could be too penniless to afford transportation. Fortunately, despite all the above factors that could invite corruption, the learning leaders in this study have put emphatic resistance against any external factors that might tarnish the purity of their profession.

Henry expressed the view that the financial element was an essential right of teachers, and everyone should make sure that they own it. He acknowledged that they would not go without it. However, the challenge of late payment or lack of adequate payment would not prevent them from doing their job in a professionally ethical manner. "Yes, I need the survival. I need the health care. I need all this. Can I work with the leader [school principal] to have the needed minimum so I can continue to work properly? I believe so" (Henry).

Instructional Materials and Beyond

Next to the challenges of degradation of education and financial irregularities, participants identified a lack of instructional materials as a genuine hurdle to good learning leadership. The lack of instructional materials stood out as another challenge the learning leaders in this study faced daily. With a few exceptions, all participants—from elementary school to higher education—indicated that it was challenging to complete their jobs under the current circumstances. Some schools did not have basic libraries, let alone computer laboratories for students and staff. Private institutions that do not receive government support have budgets that do not leave any wriggle room for anything other than teacher salaries. "We tend . . . to budget depending on the kind of school fees they [students] pay, where the school fees are the source of income," says Henry. Bill adds, "So, school fees get us for payment of salaries. And then it's the same money that we use to run the school and to buy instructional materials" (Bill). Amazingly, each exceptional learning leader found their strategy to go around this critical issue and provide an education that captivated the parents and communities that recommended them for this study.

Besides the above significant challenges, some participants identified others worth mentioning. One stems from the challenge of finding time for family. Most participants who work in rural boarding elementary and secondary schools entered into a contract that required them to live in the compound of the school. They would spend at least five days a week in what they called the "staff quarter." Except on rare occasions, the staff quarter could accommodate only the teacher, while his family stayed in another village or a central city. My researcher's notes indicated that these teachers were super busy, waking up early in the morning before students, usually around 5:00. They would ring the bell for students to wake up. They would oversee them coming out of their dorms and supervise their shower, morning prayer (for religiously affiliated schools), lunch, and dinner. Playing the role of disciplinarians, they would make sure that students are all in class. After the morning labor, they can go to classrooms and teach. There is no significant break time for them as they would spend their time supervising students whenever needed. After class, they would oversee students' extracurricular activities, study time, and bedtime. To the question of when they had time to prepare their courses, they reported they would juggle between student activities. During the weekend, they would afford some time to take public transportation such as a motorcycle or a bus to divide their time between their family and lucrative activities such as farming and gardening. Bill counted among those heroic learning leaders at the time of data collection. He hoped to share his tiny room in the staff quarter with his family shortly to afford enough time to stay with them.

In addition, some participants referred to emotional challenges. For example, Felix opined about that challenge when he stated, "and I cannot sit down to begin marking when my children are going hungry." Some participants also denounced the demands of their institutions to attend compulsory meetings on campus without offering them transportation money. It is worth noting that this practice occurs often at private institutions, most of which pay their learning leaders with significant delays. "That's what I call emotional challenge" (Felix). In Uganda, the government has decided to privilege science teachers over their arts-related counterparts by paying them higher salaries, among other emoluments. Some of the arts learning leaders who participated in this study felt professionally undervalued and emotionally distressed. Despite their faithfulness to their profession, these exceptional teachers remain human beings with regrets and emotions, which should challenge their leadership of learning.

Surviving Threats

The exceptional learning leaders in this study have survived more than the above and other unspecified challenges. They also revealed occurrences of threats to their reputation, their profession, and their lives because they did not ascribe to unprofessional, rampant behaviors and practices in their institutions. To the question of whether they faced any form of threats for behaving differently, the majority of them responded positively. Among the many threats they have faced because of their unfailing commitment to teaching, the exceptional teachers indicated corruption, and physical, verbal, and emotional abuses.

Corruption

Kalunga made it short by stating, "my threat involves corruption, and it comes from colleagues" (Kalunga). For the participants, corruption could become a threat in two fashions. First, as an integrity-targeting threat, corruption is an irresistible temptation to professional integrity. This integrity-targeting threat often occurred when students, their parents, or even other colleagues brandished money or valuables in exchange for a better grade when the initial one was low. This form of corruption also happens in the complete absence of students' final grades or projects. It would require the recipient of such a gift to do the job they required students to perform as an assessment tool for the class.

However, many participants indicated that the students or their parents could no longer approach them with compromising gifts because they knew their reputation for rectitude. They had earned their integrity reputation when they rejected the first attempt to corrupt them with money or other in-kind items. This was Linda's specific case when she first began teaching at the university. She received a call from a student's parent whose son had not received a passing grade in her class. "Yes, for example, I was stunned when one of the parents called me to say, 'the child did not succeed. It seems that you are difficult, you are very hard. As a parent, can you really reconsider this situation?' I assure you that this call was among the worst calls I have received in my life. I can't imagine how a parent would have to come and plead for his child who has failed. Maybe they avoided making pecuniary corruption out of fear. That's how parents have used moral corruption," Linda said.

Second, participants also described corruption as a normalized systemic maneuver to compel instructors or teachers to engage in favoritism toward students that might have been recommended by colleagues or persons with authority in the educational system.

> My major threats come from academic officials and colleagues who criticize you and disdain you. Even the clergy: Fathers, religious brothers, religious sisters, you have no idea. No idea. So, from time to time, you say to yourself, "Everything is rotten. You question yourself whether it is you or them. I am alone and they are too many. It could be that they are right. When, after deliberations and the publications the final exams, when you have priests, religious brothers, religious sisters coming after you: this one is my niece, the other one is my nephew. He/she failed your class. How could that be?" Now, I ask any of them: Do you cater to them? "No." Do you wish to read their final papers to have an idea? "No, no. Not that. But give him/her grades. So, they could pass your class." Then, I ask myself whether I am wrong, or if they are wrong. And that's what it is. But I do not lose hope. There are still people who are fighting and holding their ground. (Oscar)

Emotional and Verbal Abuses

Some participants identified the various emotional cases of abuse they have faced from colleagues, school communities, and the government as a threat. For example, Georg reported that colleagues "see you doing your job, the job you're supposed to do, some of them get so comfortable and bully." This participant argued that their colleagues believed they were so straight because they received some extra emolument from the administration. "So, and sometimes you come to learn about. So emotionally you get disturbed. Nevertheless . . . you know what you want, you continue performing your duties" (Georg).

Colleagues' emotional threats also came in the form of verbal abuse. For example, "When students show too much liking for my subjects and for what I do, then there is that verbal exchange. . . . One of my colleagues said that I look for cheap popularity from the learners," said Georg. Most of the Ugandan participants thought they underwent emotional abuse on the part of their government leaders. Some exceptional learning leaders agreed that they were victims of physical and verbal threats due to their steadfastness on the job. Antie narrated their story as follows:

> When people saw how I was working, some colleagues here started the battle talking here and there and somebody really physically assaulted me, and this person was a religion leader and a colleague. But I forgave her. She was a religion leader, and she was also my teacher during my regime of studying. Because of the quality of work I was given, the administrators were always talking about me, but I didn't know. So [one day] when I greeted her, she was not responding. I was like, what did I do to this leader? She was like, "This girl who just came is taking our jobs. What are we going to do?" Another . . . time, I met her in the town. She had suitcases taking her daughter [her niece] to school. Because I know them, I went nearby to help. I said, "Big sister, good afternoon. May I help you?" She looked at me, kept quiet and looked at me. I said again, "Big sister, may I help you? Where are you heading to?" Because they were near the taxi park. I said can I help you? She kept quiet; she didn't say anything. I felt so small, and I said [to myself] this big sister hates me to this extent. I went home and told people at home they told me to ignore her. So, after that event, I came and told my supervisor who told me, "I'm sorry because of the other experience." I said, "No problem, we push on life but here we are even afraid to go to the dining room to eat because the hatred was too much from my colleague, that religion leader, or from those particular colleagues. . . . I was afraid to go to the dining room because you never know." (Antie)

At first, Antie's careful course of action may sound like an extreme measure or an extrapolation. However, in this study's context of the Global South countries, exceptional teachers can be perceived as annoying moralizers to ill-intentioned colleagues. Philosopher Nietzsche (2021) would advise an exceptional teacher like Antie to look after themselves when standing out to "monsters." Antie concludes their precautionary reaction to the colleague's threat with the following words: "For us, we take a greeting as something [very meaningful]. For example, if I greet you and you keep quiet, it's almost like poisoning in my culture" (Antie).

Keeping Ethical Values

As concerns maintaining sanity and integrity amid all the above challenges and threats, Antie realistically argued that "there are so many people who can lose their integrity when it comes to hardships." Echoing the views of many participants, they pursued that the ways they were trained cannot allow them to falter. As to why they maintain their integrity, this specific participant said it all:

> Otherwise, you feel you are cheating. You feel there is something you must fulfill to get a better society. Suppose you cheat for the student, but how would that student judge you the following day? You ask [yourself] those questions and feel you need to maintain professionalism. (Antie)

This reasoning sounds as if the ethical values all exceptional leaders have acquired throughout their upbringing and training have prepared them to uphold professional integrity and altruistic impulses. Figure 2.3 summarizes the exceptional learning leaders' reports of why they have kept working in the current circumstances of their profession.

Exceptional Learning Leaders: Altruistic Teaching Philosophy

A careful analysis of the teaching philosophies of the learning leaders in this study revealed an altruistic approach. As a researcher, I quickly reached saturation . . . because participants' accounts of their teaching philosophies repeated themselves and culminated in their benevolence and selflessness. In response to the research question of what factors participants perceived as an enhancement of their ethical drive to stay in their profession, all study learning leaders' combined responses boiled down to the second theme that emerged from the data, which is their altruistic philosophies of teaching. This second central finding/theme dovetails logically with the first theme, according to which *individual motivation and professional integrity amid duress*

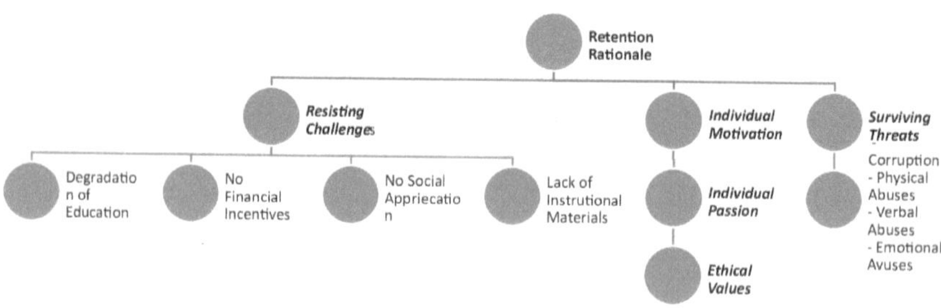

Figure 2.3 Retention of Exceptional Teachers' Rationale.

also accounted for the exceptional learning leaders' steadfastness. The importance of this relatively short theme on altruistic philosophies stems from the quasi-unanimity of participants about the perception of their roles as parents, learning leaders of excellence, and caring mentors, coaches, and counselors. A study by Wu et al. (2020) on *The Genetic Mechanism of Selfishness and Altruism in Parent-Offspring Coadaptation* suggested that parental care is an altruistic behavior broadly observed in nature. Exceptional learning leaders using parental care to deal with their learners means they provide them with food-like and protective care. These authors see those behaviors that benefit the development and survival of offspring, in this case, students, as costly for parents.

Almost 60% of the learning leaders in this study reported that they approach their overall work in education as caring parents. Sometimes, during the interview sessions, it was unclear whether some participants were referring to their children or students because they called them all "their children." After probing this seeming confusion, Henry clarified this when they explained, "I call them [my students] my children because I feel I'm a parent to them. My teaching makes me a parent and therefore I need to mentor these children. That makes me unique." Ursula echoed the same parental belief when dealing with students. He said, "I treat my students like they are my children and so in my teaching I seek to help students to discover their voice through understanding, evaluation, and expression." (Ursula). Further, they claimed that before teaching their children (students) every day, they must know the mental status of each of them. They keenly eye each learner or child "to see that this is what he wants to be. . . . I question whether I can make each child become what they want in life." Henry added that keeping track of their students made them unique. "I think is in my teaching philosophy. I believe the continuous tracking—having a forecast education of the child—is what I am striving to do" (Henry). Eliza added a nuance to their parental approach to their profession by indicating that they are friendly to their students. "I handle them in a parental way. . . . No, I do not spoil them. Rather, I guide them, counsel them and help them and model them to become better citizens" (Eliza).

Caring for students came next. Another significant common ground for this study's learning leaders is their roles as caring mentors, counselors, and even coaches. Experts in educational leadership and leadership ethics agree that caring for students constitutes an essential component of altruistic behaviors (Gilligan, 1982). Said Chantal:

> I do care about my learners. . . . I can just come to class because I know all of them. I can just see Rose is not around. Why is Rose not around today? It makes you follow up. I can even go an extra mile to reach the home where one is a

> day scholar. I talk to the parents. Why is this one not in school today? What is the problem? How can we help this person? And for sure, at times, I have been successful in bringing these learners back to school. In fact, you could find that some have been given up but when you come closer to them, you talk to the parents, you build a rapport you bring them back to school. (Chantal)

This participant opined that their philosophical approach to teaching is unique because other teachers might go to school to teach and leave. Others might need to determine whether students attended class at a particular time. The above and subsequent behaviors of the exceptional learning leaders in this study set them apart from the other teachers. In all likelihood, the exceptional teachers could exclaim like Chantal: "There are people who have admired me . . . and there are students who have become teachers saying, 'you inspired us'" (Chantal).

In addition to leading their students in parental and caring ways, most participants came across as leaders of educational excellence. Kalunga encapsulated this view by proclaiming, "What is unique in my teaching philosophy is the search for excellence" (Kalunga). Joining the bandwagon of those learning leaders who shared this view, Linda said, "I teach for rigor and perfectionism." They pursued that when they teach, they assess their objectives, and pause for self-evaluation. This process compels them to improve in ways that fulfill them and those who learn science from them (Linda).

It's worth noting at this point that endeavoring for students' excellence and success accounts for altruism on the part of the teachers. Kraut (2020) would argue that these factors constitute benefits and advantages to students; in other words, they involve altruism because they are good for someone and foster other goods.

Antie fosters student excellence by considering their uniqueness. "To me I see all students unique and people with different goals who need my assistance. You welcome them the way they are." They see their students as individuals who come with goals that they need to achieve "and so you help them in that line" (Antie). Helping each unique student achieve their goals also means treating them with equity and fairness, according to Quella. "I commit to treating my students on an equal footing, without any distinction or discrimination of any kind" (Quella). This exceptional learning leader has selflessly placed their knowledge at the service of the whole community in the hopes of remaining a model for African women. They hope to lead their students to the love of African cultural values in ways that combine academic life, religious life, and married life.

Some participants saw the above search for excellence and success for their students as the result of the service they rendered to their learners. For example, Felix stated, "My philosophy is giving all my effort to see to it that a student, irrespective of his or her background, this student receives education." They perceive education as a student's entitlement irrespective of the social status of their parents. Felix concluded with this very self-giving statement: "So to me, I am there to give that service to anyone who comes into my hands. I must make sure that this person succeeds" (Felix). Quella enriched this understanding by defining their teaching philosophy as "the will to excel in my job, to impart knowledge at the maximum level that benefits future generations" (Quella).

Service with altruistic integrity characterizes Henry's teaching philosophy, which they also expressed practically:

> And I always tell my students, "don't make me become a thief . . . because when you pay school fees, the tuition . . . and you don't get anything. There's no change in you. Me who am paid out of your tuition. I'm a thief. I've taken the tuition, but you've gained nothing. So, I become a thief. . . ." I believe that's what makes me unique because of that follow up and making a child realize I'm in school. (Henry)

Figure 2.4 represents an altruistic view that emerged as a common characteristic of exceptional learning leaders' teaching philosophies. Most of them

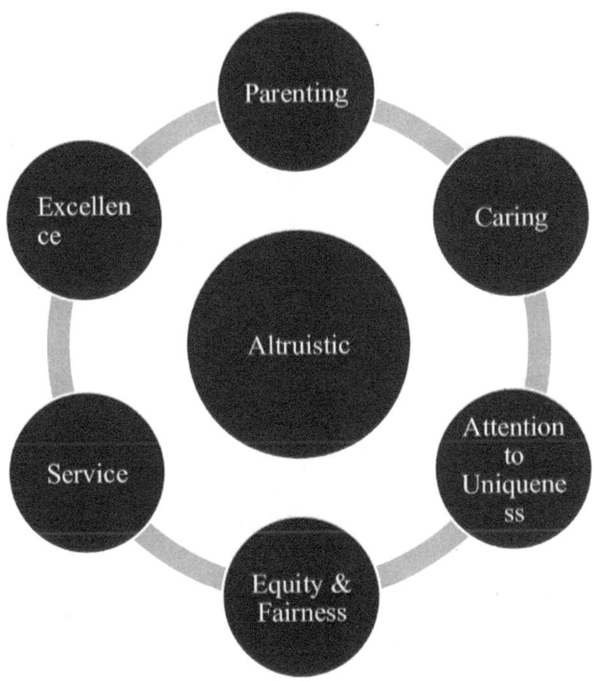

Figure 2.4 Exceptional Teachers' Altruistic Teaching Philosophy.

regarded their work with students as parenting, which involves caring for their students/children and paying attention to their uniqueness with all fairness. Their altruistic philosophies also involved rendering students a service that propels them to the life and practice of the common good.

AN EXEMPLARY TEACHER

Peter Tabichi, a Franciscan friar and science teacher from Kenya, is exemplary in his rights. In 2019, Tabichi was selected among 10,000 teachers from 179 countries to become the best teacher in the world. He was awarded the 2019 Global Teacher Prize. Also referred to as the Nobel Prize of teaching (Shapiro & Stefkovich, 2021), the Global Teacher Prize is a $1 million award that the Varkey Foundation awards annually to a teacher whose contributions to the profession have been deemed outstanding. Tabichi taught math and physics at the Keriko Mixed Day Secondary School, which he joined in 2016. This school feels the impact of famine and drought because of its location in a semi-arid village in the Rift Valley Province of Kenya. The Keriko Mixed Day Secondary School students, where he teaches, have internet access through one computer. For a school with a student-teacher ratio of 58:1, students had to take turns browsing the internet. Prior to joining Keriko School, Tabichi taught at a private school but decided to join this current school despite its limited resources. The majority of his students come from rough backgrounds. They have to walk many miles along dusty roads to get to school. The school community experiences such social issues as teen pregnancy and substance abuse. Yet, Fr. Tabichi unleashed his ability to engage his students because he was determined to give them a chance to learn. His teaching philosophy included turning Keriko School into a place where young people can find direction and encouragement that can help propel them into a brighter future no matter the hardships. Dockrill (2019) reported that Fr. Tabichi donated 80% of his salary to support poor students in the village of Pwani, a remote town in Nakuru where the school is located. Despite the scarcity of teaching materials at this school, Fr. Tabichi launched the Talent Nurturing Club, causing a significant improvement in school attendance. Among many of his other accomplishments, Fr. Tabichi's students reached the Intel International Science and Engineering Fair finals, winning the Royal Society of Chemistry award. In only two years, this exemplary learning leader doubled the number of students attending the University. On winning the 2019 Global Teacher Prize, Tabichi said: "Africa will produce scientists, engineers, entrepreneurs whose names will be one day famous in every corner of the world. And girls will be a huge part of this story" (Dockrill, 2019). He used the $1 million prize money to build a computer lab at Keriko Secondary School. He also sponsored students in need. He created programs to motivate his colleague teachers and initiated an agricultural project whose proceeds would go to the local community. His school principal, Mr. Daniel Mwariri, had this to say about Fr. Tabichi:

> He is one extraordinary teacher. Eighty percent of his salary goes to supporting others, not only from this school but also two other schools. He writes cheques to the school so that the money goes towards clearing fees for needy students. He deserved this more than anyone. (African Impact, 2019)

Like the exceptional teachers in this study, Fr. Tabichi's story stands out as one of altruism and steadfastness in transforming a community. Born in rural Kenya, Fr. Tabichi confided that his family's impact on society inspired him to become a teacher to better the script. His motivation and passion for the education of the little ones caused him to leave his prior job in a private school to dedicate his time and energy to a poor and initially low-performing public school. He overcame the challenges of a lack of appropriate instructional materials, and of a computer or science laboratory, to propel his students to national awards in sciences, which must have required high technologies. Father Tabichi's teaching philosophy also aligns with that of the exceptional learning leaders in this study because it is rooted in and emerges from an altruistic impulse. That this exemplary learning leader donated 80% of his salary to student tuition and equipment says a great deal about his interest in the learning and success of his students. More importantly, Fr. Tabichi used his $1 million award money not toward his own needs but those of the school and his students by building a computer lab and assisting needy students with tuition and school materials.

In this regard, the financial conditions of Fr. Tabichi differ from those of most learning leaders in this study, who identified the insufficiency and/or lack of economic incentive as one of the significant challenges they have faced in their teaching profession. Father Tabichi had the fortune of a religious community that could provide for his necessities while allowing him to use his salary to better his students and their learning. None of the exceptional learning leaders in this study could afford that extended altruistic generosity. However, some of them shared that they took care of some students' financial and social needs. Besides sharing altruistic behaviors with the exceptional teachers, Fr. Tabichi also came across as a caring mentor who dedicated his life to serving his students, engaging them to work for excellence. Remarkably, Fr. Tabichi and the exceptional teachers share a teaching philosophy based on ethics and altruism in a particular manner. However, a caveat exists between Tabichi and the exceptional learning leaders in that Tabichi lives and operates within the norms of his religious order. He will likely avoid some of the challenges that the exceptional teachers must overcome. He can use different strategies than the latter are utilizing in order to remain faithful to their teaching profession. The next chapter presents the coping mechanisms of the exceptional learning leaders.

Chapter 3

Exceptional Teachers' Coping Mechanisms

> "When the door is closed, you must learn to slide across the crack of the sill."
>
> (Yoruba Proverb)

As a follow-up to the findings that emerged from the data collected from the exceptional teachers in South Sahara Africa, this chapter presents the second theme of the participants' coping mechanisms. For memory, in chapter 2, I only presented the first theme, which contained two responses to why the exceptional teachers, those who have conducted themselves in an ethically steadfast manner despite the spoliation of education in their countries, retained their positions for over five years. For this study, I used steadfastness interchangeably with integrity, which can hold various definitions. However, I described teachers who behave with integrity as those who embody the following criteria: a passion to share knowledge; the ability to go the extra mile to teach; unfailing commitment; great humility; excellent punctuality in responding to students' queries and assignments; good communication skills; capability to motivate students; ability to be a professional advisor; ethical leadership; skillful counseling; the ability to align theory with practice; approachability; and selflessness.

The first theme indicated that those teachers held individual motivations that allowed them to resist all kinds of challenges and threats. The second response showed that they operated under some form of altruistic teaching philosophy. After discussing the first theme in the preceding chapter, I will examine the content of theme two: the alternative mechanisms those exceptional teachers utilize for their survival, that of their families, and, ultimately, the survival of their students. Essentially, this chapter has sought to respond to two sub-research questions.

First: How do those teachers cope and make sense of their worth in a society that shows little regard for their role and profession? Second: What other material or non-material means, including artifacts, do they turn to uplift themselves in the darkest moments of their teaching profession? Two survey and interview questions specifically targeted the above sub-questions. One related to the specific financial, social, and personal coping mechanisms, and the other requested that participants describe any artifacts—if any—that might have helped them stay focused on their profession during their lowest moments. After an introduction to the overall coping mechanisms for teachers, I will present the participants' accounts on the two above questions. I will then discuss the results of this research question with the coping mechanisms of teachers in OECD countries and draw some implications. First, an introduction to coping mechanisms or strategies.

A WORD ON COPING MECHANISMS

The APA defines a coping strategy as "an action, a series of actions, or a thought process used in meeting a stressful or unpleasant situation or in modifying one's reaction to such a situation. Coping strategies typically involve a conscious and direct approach to problems . . . " (APA, 2022). As shown in chapter 2, the participants in this study have endured various stressful and unpleasant situations. These participants echo the conclusion by many researchers (Mulkeen, 2010; Katete & Nyangarika, 2020) that those unpleasant factors, also referred to as challenges and threats, directly originated from the social neglect (undervaluing) of teachers' profession. How do teachers in the Global South cope with the neglect and undervalue of their profession? Responses to this question might boil down to two categories of learning leaders as suggested in UNESCO's publication *Corrupt Schools, Corrupt Universities: What Can Be Done* (Hallak & Poisson, 2007): (a) teachers who use petty corruption, know how to navigate the system, and make students pay for the rest of their needs; (b) teachers, including the exceptional learning leaders in this study, who rely on ethical means as they engage in individual income-generating activities. The two categories of instructors must have developed individual, social, and professional strategies or coping mechanisms in the form of actions or thought processes to combat the ill-treatment they receive from their governments and educational institutions.

In common parlance, coping mechanisms refer to the strategies people use to subdue physio-psychological symptoms such as stress, depression, overwork, and the like. This section, however, intends to focus only on the challenges and threats identified in this study, which the participants in this study said they faced. Studies upon studies have concluded that the poor treatment of teachers has contributed to several unintended consequences and unethical behaviors (Transparency International, 2019; Stahl, 2018; Kirya, 2019). In this specific study, factors contributing to the poor treatment of teachers include the lack of value attributed to education, [lack of instructional materials], irregularity or absence of financial incentives including salary, bonus, healthcare, and other monetary benefits, lack of appreciation including lack of respect from parents, students, and educational officials, and lack of opportunities for upward mobility such as promotion to higher positions and responsibilities. Poor treatment of teachers also included multifaceted forms of verbal, physical, and emotional abuse originating from colleagues, parents, or government leaders.

Unfortunately, it was outside the scope of this study to examine the reasons that might lead learning leaders to opt for unethical behaviors, particularly corruption, when facing unpleasant actions or challenges similar to those I just identified. Suffice it to list three major causes of teacher corruption that the United Nations Office on Drugs and Criminality (UNODC, 2022) reported in its document titled "Knowledge Tools for Academics and Professionals: Module 9: Corruption in Education."

1. The high rate of return requirement: "Where school funding or educator remuneration is tied to student performance, there are strong incentives for malfeasance among educators and principals, be it cheating or illicit agreements to attract more students" (p. 12).
2. Teachers' low salary: "In some countries, educators' salaries do not support even a basic livelihood or are perceived as unfairly low relative to the workload—which may lead educators to use their position of power to extract payments and other benefits" (p. 12).
3. Weak ethical standards: In the three countries in this study where corruption is widely prevalent, the propensity to resist corruption has substantially diminished. This factor makes it easier to engage in various kinds of corruption.

To deal with the above factors, other teachers are likely to resort to corruption (Trines, 2017). An idea of corruption in education can provide the reader with a contextual snapshot of education in the countries included in this study. The word "corruption" and similar to it came more than sixty-five times from participants in this study. In survey and interview questions about the most significant threats they faced in their teaching profession, 100% of the participants listed corruption. For example, Linda talked about moral corruption when parents demanded she reconsider the grades she assigned students. She also referred to continuous pecuniary corruption. Kalunga repeated that corruption in its multifaceted forms was the highest level threat their educational institution faced. Innos concluded that it was very easy for good teachers to fall prey to overt and disguised forms of corruption. In the two focus groups I had with students, 95% of participants agreed that teacher corruption was so institutionalized that they did not see any way out.

CORRUPTION AS A COPING MECHANISM

UNESCO defines corruption in education sectors as "the systematic use of public office for private benefit, whose impact is significant on the availability and quality of educational goods and services, and, as a consequence, on access, quality or equity in education" (Hallak & Poisson, 2007). Leading learning stands as a public endeavor, be it in public or private schools, including home teaching, because students receive an education that must position them as future managers and leaders in a society, which by nature is public. Writing for the AntiCorruption Resource Center, Kirya (2019) rightly states that corruption in education is a threat to the well-being of society. It erodes the trust society has placed in it while worsening inequality and sabotages social development while undermining the training of the learner who deserves to become competent and ethical leaders for the labor force of the future. For Kirya, corruption can take the shape of cheating and other academic violations, including bribery, nepotism, teacher absenteeism, and exploitation of learners for sex, money, and unpaid labor. In particular, argues Kirya, poor students suffer the consequences of bribery when families must pay for grades and other services. Even if they wanted to be involved in bribery, they could not afford it because they face financial limitations. Teachers' demand for sex in exchange for grades is likely to cause girl students to drop out of school and others to bear uncontrollable traumas. Table 3.1 reproduces the Anti-Corruption Resource Centre's (Kirya, 2019) examples of corruption that could happen in the education sector, most of which occurred in the three countries in this study.

In a blog belonging to UNESCO's International Institute for Educational Planning, Stahl (2018) argued that petty corruption has affected 74% of public education institutions in Sub-Saharan Africa. The author defines petty corruption as bribery and maladaptive practices, including absenteeism, favoritism, and gift-giving, in other words, "quiet corruption," according to the World Bank (2010). The picture of petty corruption in the D.R. Congo, Ghana, and Uganda (the three countries involved in this study) looks endemically bleak, given the pervasive widespread corruption in their educational institutions.

To give just one example, a study about petty corruption in educational institutions in Uganda (Stahl, 2018) provides the following excerpt and figure 3.1.

Table 3.1 Examples of Corruption in the Education Sector

- Illegal charges are levied on children's school admission forms, which are supposed to be free.
- School places are "auctioned" to the highest bidder.
- Children from certain communities are favored for admission, while others are subjected to extra payments.
- Good grades and exam results are obtained through bribes to teachers and public officials. The prices are often well known, and candidates are expected to pay up front.
- Examination results are only released upon payment.
- Schools nullify the consequences of failing exams by admitting or readmitting students under false names.
- There is embezzlement of funds intended for teaching materials, school buildings, etc.
- Substandard educational material is purchased due to manufacturers' bribes, instructors' copyrights, etc.
- Schools or politically connected companies monopolize the provision of meals and uniforms, resulting in low quality and high prices.
- Teachers on the public payroll offer private tutoring outside school hours to paying pupils. This can reduce teachers' motivation in ordinary classes and reserve compulsory topics for the private sessions, to the detriment of pupils who do not or cannot pay.
- School property is used for private commercial purposes.
- Pupils carry out unpaid labor for the benefit of staff.
- Teacher recruitment and postings are influenced by nepotism, favoritism, bribes, or sexual favors.
- Teachers or officials take advantage of their office to obtain sexual favors in exchange for employment, promotion, good grades, or any other educational good.
- Examination questions are sold in advance.
- Examination results are altered to reflect higher marks, or examiners award marks arbitrarily in exchange for bribes.
- Examination candidates pay others to impersonate them and sit exams for them.
- Salaries are drawn for "ghost teachers"—staff who are no longer (or never were) employed for various reasons, including having passed away. This affects de facto student-teacher ratios and prevents unemployed teachers from taking vacant positions.
- Teachers conduct private business during teaching hours, often to make ends meet. Absenteeism, a form of "quiet corruption," can have severe effects on learning outcomes and de facto student-teacher ratios.*
- Licences and authorizations for teaching are obtained on false grounds.
- Student numbers are inflated (including numbers of special-needs pupils) to obtain better funding.
- Bribes are paid to auditors for not disclosing the misuse of funds.
- There is embezzlement of funds allocated by the government or raised by local nongovernmental organizations (NGOs) and parents' organizations.
- Politicians allocate resources to certain schools to gain support, especially during election periods.
- School management and operation are influenced by informal arrangements driven by political interests.

Source: Kyria (2019). Anti-Corruption Center Resource, pp. 5–7.

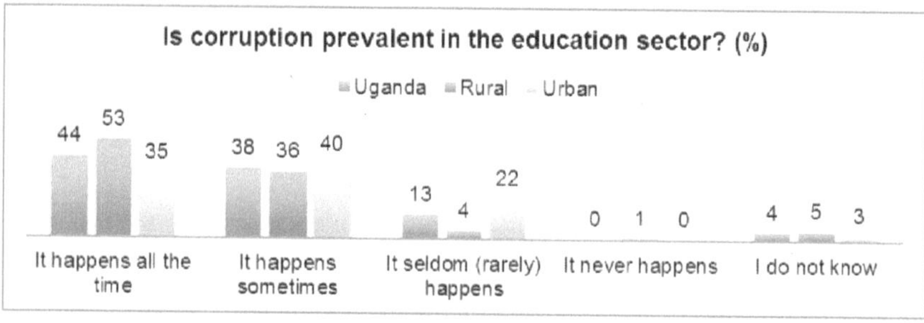

Figure 3.1 Petty Corruption in Uganda's Education. Source: (Stahl, 2018) in UNESCO's International Institute for Educational Planning.

> Ugandan teachers reported that economic hardship, institutional inefficiency, and high living costs drove them to resort to corruption as they had difficulty making ends meet. Furthermore, petty corruption was not necessarily regarded as "something bad" but rather often understood as instrumental strategies to "getting things done," whereby the practices have become an essential feature of mundane day-to-day activities and the normal state of affairs. For example, bribery is a common practice to obtain assistance when sitting national exams to get admission to a school or college. However, the minimum prerequisites are not met to obtain a better position as a headteacher in a more favorable institution ahead of better-qualified candidates (Stahl, 2018).

As we can see, all participants in Stahl's study agreed that petty corruption remains a widespread coping mechanism for teachers in Uganda's urban and rural schools. No participant indicated that corruption never happens. Unfortunately, this figure would also apply to most—if not all of—the educational systems in the other two countries in this study, namely the D.R. Congo and Ghana. The most overt forms of corruption reported in the three countries in this study include sex for grades, bucks for grades, and professor absenteeism.

In the case of Ghana, Transparency International (2019) reported various corruption risks and challenges facing the education system of Ghana. These challenges include the exchange of sex for grades, examination malpractices, fake qualifications, teacher absenteeism, and corrupt recruitment practices. This report has determined that excessive bureaucracy has facilitated the embezzlement of funds and systemic abuses, which have caused a loss of trust and credibility in the educational system. Writing for UNESCO, Akyeampong concluded that extensive corruption exists across the education sector of Ghana and that about a third of people engage in corrupt acts.

"Grade Sexually Transmissible"

Every single college student in the D.R. Congo has heard this French expression "points sexuellement transmissibles" or "grades sexually transmissible" in English. Students who participated in a focus group explained how this aberration begins with a professor forcing a female student into a sexual relationship with him. The instructor informs all his colleagues whose courses the female student—now turned into a girlfriend—is taking to grant her passing grades in their courses. In other words, this practice reveals a more pernicious form of "grade for sex" system (BBC, 2019). This expression, indicating that a quid pro quo practice is very present in the majority of educational institutions, includes secondary schools and colleges in the countries in this study. Instructors demand that female students entertain sexual relationships with them for the former to either enter into the grading system the grades the students earned or grant them better marks. The BBC video "Sex for Grades" investigated four prominent professors (two in Nigeria and two in Ghana) who preyed on their female students.

Ursula recalled that a group of students visited her office in the wake of the broadcast of "Sex for Grades". At first, students expressed their dismay at the discredit brought upon the colonial power, namely Great Britain, which runs the BBC at their university by broadcasting "unfounded allegations" against their professors. Ursula argued with them about the critical importance of the video, which only depicted the tip of the iceberg, that is, the scourge of sexual harassment that has become rampant and systemic on campus. She explained that the BBC's denunciation was somewhat overdue as a means to combat the unethical behaviors of some instructors that have led to widespread sexual harassment of female students and injustice against male students.

> When they understood they had been victims of unfair treatment by their male professors, those students loosened their tongues and recounted their own stories of harassment. One said she resisted harassment and paid for it. She failed several courses and had to repeat some. Each had a story and just hoped the university would sanction the two professors on the BBC video. Unfortunately, they are still working at the university as we speak. (Ursula)

On the other hand, participants in the focus group also agreed that some female students, usually those with serious academic weaknesses, lure their instructors into sexual activities in exchange for a passing grade. Students revealed that the practice of "sex for grades" has been so normalized that instructors would overtly take female students to hotels and hostels where even the staff know what is going on. No one could say otherwise. Several female participants confided that female students avoid receiving appreciation from male instructors for fear of being demanded to enter into a relationship of a sexual nature with the instructor. They would avoid appearing pretty or well-dressed in front of specific (most) male instructors. One focus group participant said, "I pray to God every day I go to campus that I am not noticed by certain predator professors. . . . But it is hard to escape their notice. . . . And once you get noticed, there begin your nightmares." Asked to estimate the percentage of teachers who sexually harass their students, participants' responses ranged from 90% in some departments to 100% in others. Reporting perpetrators to the upper administration can even worsen your case because you will be accused of lying and defaming the instructor. One focus group participant said, "Who do you report to? There is no impartial arbiter because everyone does it." To the question of what they thought about this deprivation, the answer came, "It is widespread. . . . We actually copied it from the US where all bad things come from."

Typically, as a researcher, you would not try to insert your idea or comment amid a focus group session (Danner et al., 2018). However, given the gravity of the topic and the pernicious allegations against academic ethics in the United States, I felt compelled to improvise a teaching moment. I measured my words and my body language to make a statement once and for all. I informed them that every U.S. educational institution includes a clear code of ethics by which teachers, parents, and students ought to abide. Cases of abuse of female students by male instructors might exist, but they are rare.

Wood et al. (2018) conducted on Sexual Harassment at Institutions of Higher Education at eight U.S. college campuses. Across institutions, 16,754 students participated in an online study. Results showed that 19% of students reported experiencing faculty/staff-perpetrated sexual harassment, and 30% reported experiencing peer-perpetrated sexual harassment. These numbers are large, and the consequences of sexual abuse on students are immeasurable. However, African students who participated in the two focus groups reported sexual harassment numbers around 90% to 95%. Statistics on Africa's higher education are even more daunting, according to Dranzoa (2018), who gave the example of Egypt, where 99% percent of women experience sexual harassment, and South Africa, where over 75% of female students experience some form of abuse or sexual violence.

An instructor who behaves like some of those to whom focus group students referred would not only lose their job for good but is also likely to face jail time. The United States Sentencing Commission (2022) revealed that 95.5% of sexual abuse offenders went to prison to serve an average of 211 months between 2017 and 2021. However, should some corruption occur, the concerned institution would be in complicated legal jeopardy. This does not mean that some cases do not slip between the cracks. However, as opposed to educational administrations in the Global South that show either extreme leniency or complicity with the staff perpetrators of sexual misconduct, most institutions in the United States apply swift measures against the delinquent staff. Furthermore, most educational institutions have implemented policies according to which even consensual sexual relationships between students and teachers constitute sexual harassment. The rationale behind such policies is based on the inherent power differential between the two parties, which creates a dynamic that makes mutual consent impossible (Dzeich et al., 1990).

Money for Grades

During a procedural focus group, a student said she did not turn in her final thesis but managed to graduate from the university. She argued that a student might give money to their instructor, who would manage to work on their final thesis or project. I reacted against their notion that a professor would write a thesis, which the student usually defends in front of a committee of professors. However, one of the participants in the focus group gave me her example. She never wrote her program thesis. Asked what she did instead for her to appear to have written and defended her thesis, she stopped short of confessing that she bribed her teacher. Instead, the participant spoke parabolically.

> Imagine that I enter a professor's office, place a substantial amount of money—like $100 on the desk, and say to the professor, "This is for me to pass your class." Would you imagine one single minute that the professor would reject my offer? Rather he will make sure that my thesis is completed, that it is duly filed to the dean's office, and that I graduate without issue.

College instructors would utilize every single means to take money from students and their parents through bribes and sales of course packages called syllabi. Participants in focus groups revealed that professors have become filthy rich. "Imagine our plethoric classes of 500 to 1500 students and a professor selling each course package for a minimum of $10. How much would they get from just one course?" Those professors teach at least two courses per semester, sometimes in as many as five institutions of higher learning. One focus group participant said:

> No wonder, professors own some of the most beautiful cars and houses only politicians can afford. Their children study in the best universities in Europe or the United States. What happens is that at the start of a course a professor comes in and tells you: my syllabus (course package) costs $35. You want to pass my class; you must purchase the syllabus. My assistants will make sure they collect money and turn it over to me. Whether or not they teach the course, you have to pay. If you negotiate with the professor to make a copy from your friend's syllabus, you still have to pay what they call *droit d'auteur* (author's rights), which amounts to half of the total cost of the syllabus. The risk of paying only the author right is the likelihood to fail in the class. Because those who do not purchase the syllabus will undoubtedly fail. On the day of the exam,

the assistants to the professor make sure you show a duly-signed copy of the course package before entering the exam room. Our poor parents scramble to find money to help us purchase sometimes as many as 9 course packages per semester, the value of which varies from \$10 to \$50 depending on the course and the department. It is very . . . very hard to begin the university and finish in these conditions.

In the D.R. Congo, where this corrupt sale of course packages is widespread, students reported that although the government prohibited this practice, it only changed its name from "sales of course package" to "right of authors." Therefore, the system is well alive and intact. In addition to the forced sales of course packages, there exists in the D.R. Congo a well-known and overall normalized and systematized phenomenon called "*Le suivi*" or "branchement" in French, or "follow-up" or "networking" in English, whereby a student who failed an exam or a test follows their instructor to exchange a sum of money for better and passing grades. Teachers and instructors, overtly or through disguised maneuvers, invite students and their parents to this practice by failing as many students as possible in their courses. It remains common practice for a professor to fail every single student in their plethoric classes to stir the practice of "*Le suivi*." The more money a student gives a professor, the better the grades. Some instructors take it so far as to instruct students at the end of a given course on the minimum amount of money they plan to bribe him/her with to expect to pass their class. Parents and other government authorities appear powerless to fix this marram given that some of them not only rely on this practice but also encourage it. Kabasua & Kamango (2021) described all these practices in their investigative article titled "Au Coeur des pratiques de corruption dans les universités de Kinshasa" (At the heart of corruption practices in Kinshasa universities).

This petty corruption is so endemic and systemic that most parents, especially those with some financial means, provide their children with a substantial sum of money (up to \$300) to ensure they bribe professors whose courses they are likely to fail and pass all the courses. One participant in the focus group said, "when you have \$300" for *le suivi*, you are pretty sure to pass all the classes whether you attended them or not. . . ." This system is more widespread than imagined. No wonder a survey taken by Transparency International (2019) on six variables, including education, indicated that 80 percent of participants resorted to bribery in the D.R. Congo. As opposed to those who believed *le suivi* was a wrong and unfair practice, one student participating in the focus group argued that *le suivi* was instead somehow helpful to the student and their family.

Because it allows you the student not to repeat the whole academic year just because of one or two classes that you failed. In my case, I failed two courses

> out of 19. I knew that if I did not do *le branchement* or *le suivi*, I would have to repeat the whole year and retake all the 19 courses. My parents could not afford to lose the money they paid for the previous academic year and pay for another 19 courses. . . . I was compelled to do *le suivi*, gave each instructor something like $10, and I passed the year. . . . That's why I think the system is the lesser of two evils.

The focus group's participants were divided on the merits of *le suivi*. Some considered it a tolerable form of compensation for their instructors, given that the government did not pay them enough. For the majority of them, however, *le suivi* as a coping strategy for professors has become so out of control and so complex that it will be impossible to eradicate. They agree it has gone above and beyond ethics because it has sacrificed their learning.

Like the exceptional teachers in this study, a female student participating in a focus group reported that she stood her ground against *le suivi* and sexual advances from her professors. Her account is one of heroism. She stood as a principled, ethical individual who could contribute to leading the change of the systemically corrupt practices that have eroded the essence of all academic endeavors. This exceptional student recounted the process of her revolt against the system and its nefarious consequences.

> First, I was placed in a working group with five other students, 2 females and 3 males. To complete our assignment and earn a passing grade, two things needed to be done. First, we collected a substantial amount of money for our professor. The money would go through the assistant to the professor. Second, one of the girls in our group must volunteer to bring the money directly to the professor and accept that the professor sleeps with her so that the whole group can pass the professor's class. Please know that all the other working groups must do the same. Since we were only two girls in my group, I refused to be the money-bearer of our group and therefore, rejected to become the scapegoat for the group. My female teammate did not have a choice; she took the infamous leadership . . . and we passed the class. . . . I was disgusted and felt filthy. However, when the final grades came in, I could not believe my eyes. The professor failed me. The three available choices to female students in this context became personal to me. You bribe the professor with money if that's sufficient for him. You bribe the professor with your body if it pleases him and if it is sufficient to him. You pay your grades with both money and your body if all the above failed. And this latter was the choice I was given because of my prior refusals. I decide to do neither.

One can only imagine how disheartening it must be for these powerless female students to claim their right to personal, social, and academic values with no recourse whatsoever. Remarkably, this change-making female student embodied Rosa Parks' admonition, as Wallneau (2021) cited: "You must never be fearful about what you are doing when it is right." She stood her ground to the end:

> I failed the class, had to repeat the whole year, meaning I needed to pay tuition again for 19 classes not including spending money for transportation to campus, food, and the like. My siblings hated me for that. My parents were not pleased with me. For that second year that I repeated, I was ostracized both at home and on campus. I became very secluded at home. I even contemplated suicide. But I praised God who held me in the palm of his hands. I passed that second year without much of *le suivi*, and without being sexually abused by a professor.

Several questions arose that I felt obliged to ask the students who participated in my focus group. For example, to the question of whether bright students—especially females—could succeed and pass classes without compromising their intimacy or bribing instructors, the answer was, "Yes, but it is hard. . . . Some exceptionally bright students are known as such. They can be treated differently." If the majority of students pass classes by corrupt means, how can we be sure that they acquired the required knowledge to perform well in society? The answer came, "It is hard to tell when students just graduate. They have to be tested on the job to ensure they somehow gained knowledge despite the chaos in our education."

However, students participating in the focus group also agreed about a handful of instructors who do their job correctly without getting involved in corruption. One participant gave the example of another student who approached a professor with money after failing their exam. Kindly, the professor responded that he was making more money than the student had imagined and that he could even take the student to a restaurant if his time allowed him to feed the student out of his pocket. The bottom line, the teacher said, "I cannot jeopardize my professional integrity for $10 or any sum of money. I owe it to myself, to my family, and to my departed father." The exceptional learning leaders in this study are heroic teachers who do not practice the phenomenon of *le suivi*, and do not harass their students sexually or financially. Nor do they sell their course packages as a sine qua non prerequisite to success.

Absenteeism

Teacher and professor absenteeism counts among the many other quiet, petty forms of corruption that have eroded education, particularly in the three countries of the D.R. Congo, Ghana, and Uganda. In the D.R. Congo education, three categories of higher education instructors exist. At the bottom level of instructors stand "assistants to professors," usually made up of recent graduates who graduated with such mentions as "cum laude" or "magna cum laude" from their master's degrees and are retained to assist a specific professor in their teaching, grading, and selling courses. These assistants to professors can teach courses on behalf of their "bosses," who are either associate or full professors. Associate professors constitute the larger bulk of those instructors holding any sort of terminal degree such as a PhD. Like full professors, they design and teach their courses and benefit from the service of one or more assistants. Professors hardly show up in classrooms to teach. When they do, students would flood the already overcrowded classes to try to get a glimpse of the professor's knowledge. If they are lucky enough, they would wait additional months before seeing a professor in their classroom. Otherwise, they would routinely continue the remainder of their courses with assistants to professors.

Unlike the "assistant to professors" who can assist only one professor at a time, associate professors and full professors usually hold multiple assignments—sometimes up to five—at different institutions of higher learning. Professors have become rare commodities in classrooms as they engage in multiple forms of absenteeism. The assistants to professors who are usually unqualified to teach courses assigned to them have become more visible to students because they do teach, supervise lab and test activities, administer and correct exams, sell "les syllabus" or "course packages," entertain the phenomenon of "le suivi" on behalf of professors, and fill the pockets of professors with money collected from bribes, "le suivi," sales of syllabi (course packages), and other despicable services. Because of their meager salaries and the overall devaluation of their profession, these professors justify their absenteeism as a mechanism to make ends meet. They believe that working at many institutions at once and engaging in any sort of petty corruption procures them the additional income they need for their social status.

COPING MECHANISMS OF EXCEPTIONAL TEACHERS

The preceding sections presented the strategies many teachers and instructors resort to in order to compensate for the meager salaries the governments of the three countries in this study pay their learning leaders. Suffice it to underscore the ethical and moral despicability of those practices that dehumanize students and contribute to the erosion of the value once attached to education. This study shows that the exceptional teachers owe their professional and ethical reputations to staying away from all the above forms of petty corruption and their corollaries. However, the question remains as to how they survive and take care of their families if they only depend on the uncertain and insufficient salaries from their educational systems. How do they cope without resorting to some of the practices commonly used among and around them? The surveys and interviews I conducted revealed that these heroic and ethical leaders of learning hold permissible lucrative activities outside or alongside their teaching duties. They also draw strength from the supernatural or their inner selves when facing pressure from colleagues or their work conditions.

Farming and Gardening

Many participants in this study revealed that they resort to farming during their weekends and holidays to make ends meet. I have noticed that this activity remains common for rural teachers, most of whom own a piece of land they either purchased or inherited from their parents. For example, John said, "I've got a small project of raising birds, local birds, which can feed on themselves by letting them move around." He raises and sells birds in local markets "to keep moving through the hardships I'm facing financially. Because at one time you find that you are in a position to sell off the birds, then to go away with the financial hardships" (John). Likewise, farming has helped Georg keep out of trouble and support their family:

> I have a garden so that I don't spend the money on feeding my family. During my free time on Saturday, I dig, I go to my garden. I dig, I keep some birds, chicken. So, my free time, I sell that at times and I'm able to supplement the little income I have. I pay, I give, I keep some pigs I sell. . . . So that has kept me going. . . . So those are the things that you do on your free time, on Saturday and after classes in the evening. It does not distract you from your teaching duties because it during my free time. (Georg)

Henry indicated they engage in gardening among other sustenance activities. They use the produce of gardening for domestic consumption. They produce some food to feed their family. They had this to say about their coping mechanisms:

> So like Saturdays, I go to the gardens then produce some, of course for subsistence because the land is not so big for commercial purposes. At least gardening helps to subsidize and to contribute to the feeding of the family. So, though it is a bit tight, but we have to do it. Financially, I even took loan to go back for my studies. Socially, I spend most of the time in school even the evenings, even on Sundays. . . . So on Sundays, I move to different schools. I offer services where priests cannot reach. . . . I go and give their services there, share the services with the faithful. Also, sometimes I go out for sports in the social element. (Henry)

Besides gardening and participating in pastoral and social activities to provide for their family and keep themselves socially sound, Henry also indicated that they took small loans from their schools and elsewhere to curb their financial hardship:

> I use the loan system from the school. The loan is in banks. So, I pick a loan, pay tuition of my children. Then as the salary comes, they keep deducting. The loan has an interest, but it's a low interest compared to the commercial loans. You take a bank slip, then you process it. They pay directly to the account of the school where the child is going. So, for reimbursement, they deduct slowly. (Henry)

Antie has set up some other projects, such as piggery, and poultry, in addition to a nursery school [a daycare]. After probing the participant about when they find the time to juggle among the three major activities given their full-time job at the university, they had this to say: "Full time is not full time. . . . If we have to work full-time, they [the University] have to provide that [financial compensation]. But since we don't get enough, then we cannot say I'm full-time." They confided that they must go get other projects to keep them going. They added:

> The truth is that we have not received the salary since February [and this is end-August], and we are working. No transport. So, you expect me to sit here five hours reading, researching what and what, and how would we survive? How do we move on? And so, we have to look at those other places. So, I have a piggery project. I have a poultry farm and that school [nursery school] where I spend some of my time. Yes, it is my own school where I employ 10 people. No, I am not stretched between two major jobs. And that's the way to go because I can't stay at this one I love to do. I love the institution, but because I cannot . . . then I have to feel the stress. You run here and there. Sometimes you spend sleepless nights, but you have to [juggle to make ends meet]. In the future, they [personal projects] will pay me better than this one [teaching]. (Antie)

Financial and Social Adjustments

University professors discussed several strategies of their own to curb their financial shortcomings, including offering courses at other institutions of higher learning, consulting with private and governmental sectors related to their academic expertise, and the like. For example, Roger stated that they have worked at another academic institution essentially to pay their children's academic fees and finish building the house they have lived in for over 30 years. They underscored the reality that the success of their children in their studies was a consolation and an encouragement to continue to work harder because they had to make that effort to ensure a bright future for their children. Talking about their financial adjustment mechanisms, Simon cited the diversification of their financial sources: "I am a senior researcher in a national research institute and a visiting professor in a university. If we take more than two universities, we will not be efficient. I do consultancy and write bankable projects" (Roger). Likewise, Quella has accepted a consultancy service to local microfinance organizations. She leads conferences and workshops as well as participates in other lucrative entrepreneurship. She confided that she had accepted her life condition and adapted her needs to her financial abilities. Socially, Roger said they have coped by accepting their situation; they remain content with their assets and live within their means. They leave whatever comes beyond their limits to God, the Provider.

I met with Kalunga in their mansion on the outskirts of a large metro city. The size and the glamor of his house immediately caught my attention, given that, overall, professors do not earn enough to afford the structure itself, let alone the fancy cars and trucks that were parked in front of the mansion. Although I had to stick with the order of the interview questions, which he had already answered in the survey I forwarded to him, the burning question was question number 9: "How do you financially cope given the meaningless salaries you receive and the fact that you are not one of those involved in harassing your students for money, as per the community that recommended you for this study?" In his response, he said something to the effect of:

> I cannot trade my reputation and that of the good religious brothers who trained me for a few dollar bills a student would bribe me with. I have been hated by many of my colleagues because many consider that I am showing off . . . or that I am the holiest person on campus. . . . I am sure you have some brave students there who would compare my colleagues to me . . . saying how come you keep telling us you are not well treated; you receive meager salaries and must sell your course packages to survive . . . and get any penny from us. . . . How come? Many of my colleagues, I was saying . . . would not appreciate this kind of comparison. For them, I am an obstacle to their lucrative businesses of abusing students. They would want us all to be on the same corrupt and filthy boat. But I was not raised that way. How do I survive? First, teaching—at least at the institutions of higher learning is a liberal profession, which entails some leeway in terms of how many institutions I want to teach to. Personally, I limit myself to 4 reputable institutions where I offer courses on child psychology, adult student psychology and counseling and the like. . . . I avoid exhausting myself too much with too many papers to read and correct. Let me mention that we do have plethoric classes of sometimes up to 1,500 students. So, how would you do a good job if you stretch yourself too thin? Besides, I do a great deal of consultancy at various governmental and international institutions. I do not understand why my colleagues cannot be creative . . . find some of those institutions that need their

> expertise instead of ruining our already impoverished students. . . . Consultancy pays sometimes 10, to 20 times more than teaching. But I remain in teaching because it is my calling. . . . I have nothing left besides conveying knowledge to younger generations. (Kalunga)

A participant who does not hold any consultancy assignment said that they remain open regarding their financial issues. They make sure to borrow without return interest. Once, they approached the university president and told them, "I am dying." The president, who knew about the constant irregularity in instructors' salaries, did not hesitate to lend them money without interest. Oftentimes, they present their financial issues to village merchants. They would borrow merchandise in kind and pay them little by little when their salary comes in.

Farming and gardening assisted teachers with direct food supply at the primary and secondary school levels, although some produce landed at the market. Other participants in secondary schools, like Pat, said that they bake beignets, biscuits, peanuts, and finger foods, which they sell directly to their students and other colleagues during recessions. It is noteworthy that most schools in the Global South would not provide students with breakfast, lunch, or any meal. Students who can afford some pocket money can buy from nearby local vendors if there exists one nearby. In addition to selling directly to their peers, Pat revealed that she owns a restaurant in the city and uses her daughter as a cashier. She stated:

> I know that the government does not pay us well. I had to organize myself. Selling those small items has helped me to feed my children every day and pay for transformation to school. That's how I have been able to escape bribery from students. It is embarrassing. And when asked for bribery, you lose your personality because you fear the student. You fear to give the student a failing grade for fear they scream, "My father gave you this and this. . . ." That is what I don't like. It's very embarrassing. (Pat)

Beyond looking for extra money to supplement her meager teaching revenue, Ursula indicated that her family gave her the peace of mind she needed to keep going. She is blessed to have the support of her husband. Whenever she gets overwhelmed by the sheer work involved in teaching, setting assignments, marking, grading, researching, and writing, "I can always rely on my husband to take care of the home and the kids. His financial support also balances out the unattractive salary I earn as a teacher" (Ursula). Likewise, Quella confirmed that she finds it soothing to interact with her husband and her children. Additionally, she takes part in prayer groups and actively participates in the apostolate of couples and families.

Coping Artifacts

In *The Stanford Encyclopedia of Philosophy*, Preston (2002) defines "artifact" in a broader fashion that serves the purpose of this section. First, the author acknowledges that experts usually reserve the term "artifact" for physical and durable objects, such as those an archaeologist can unearth. However, Preston contends that many ephemeral or abstract human creations, which ordinarily would not make the list of artifacts, can qualify as such in English, provided that their users made them intentionally for a purpose. "Candidates include musical performances . . . , belief systems . . . , actions and languages . . . , software . . . , normativity . . . , establishments such as restaurants . . . and artifact types" (Preston, 2022). Similarly, when I requested participants in this study to identify and explain any artifact that kept them going during the darkest moments of their learning leadership, they identified both physical and intangible creations, such as meditation and prayers.

Explicitly, participants responded to the survey and interview question, "Share and explain any object, such as a photograph, prayer, symbol, or other object you might have used as a source of consolation and encouragement during your most difficult times." Responses varied from pictures, photographs, and particularly prayers. For example, Maria shared the picture of the "Strength of African Woman." This exceptional learning leader stumbled upon this picture as she reviewed a pile of documents in her office during a rough period at the university where she taught. She was at the confluence of financial, professional, and social pressures. Unfortunately, Maria could not recall the origin of the picture, and my effort to uncover and properly cite its provenance did not return any results. I would not reproduce the picture as it lacks proper identification. The picture represents an ordinary working woman from Africa who is returning from farming. She is an exceptionally hard-working woman who has afforded the bike she is riding. She rides the bike, carrying three children, firewood, and a basin on her head. The basin surely contains some produce from the farm, which she is likely to prepare for her children and her husband upon arriving home. It is easy to imagine that her days begin repeatedly at dawn and end at dusk. When asked why she chose this artifact, Maria responded: "The power of this woman inspires me. She turns her pain into a joy" (Maria). Therefore, each time she was on the brink of faltering, she would look at this picture and say to herself, "If this African mother can carry all these loads with a smile on her face, I can beat all the challenges and threats I am facing for choosing to remain within the ethical norms of my teaching profession."

Participants came with other individual artifacts that helped them cope with the strenuous situations they faced on and off campus. For example, Kalunga confided that they write reflective texts as a way of reframing (Bolman &

Deal, 2022) the scourge their profession brought upon them. Antie meditates on a phrase they received from their late mother, who used to tell her children: "'You sleep over the problem, and the problem will be solved.' Yes, whenever you have a hard problem, saying hardship or what, it passes with time, and then tomorrow you will have a better life. That has kept me going" (Antie). Several participants held pictures of their parents or family in their office. They would look at them and remember the strength a parent or any family member instilled in them. Linda would look at the picture of their late father, a lifelong teacher, who told them that teaching was the most honorable job they could choose because it creates doctors, presidents, and engineers. No other job can boast the honor of birthing all the other professions.

Likewise, Catholic prayer, whether in the shape of orison, meditation, or contemplation over a spiritual object, turned out to be the most common artifact the majority of participants turned to during the harshest of their professional times. Participants Georg and Quella often recite the rosary and go in front of the Blessed Sacrament on Thursday. "And, at times, I go before the Lord in the tabernacle, in our chapel. Basically, that's what helps me to keep going" (Georg).

Henry prays for nine days (novena) to Saint Jude. And when things get tougher, "I go to the grotto of the Blessed Virgin Mary's shrine and pray" (Henry). Chantal even recited their own version of a prayer to St. Jude during an interview session:

> St. Jude you help those who are in need.
> I am here presenting you my needs.
> Please help me reach my prayer to God.
> Help me in this trying moment.
> I'm ready to testify I'm ready to tell your people
> What you have done for me.

Then, continues Chantal, "I say the petitions; then I say the following prayers: our father, hail Mary and other prayers" (Chantal). Another participant uses images and prayers for Divine Mercy in the Catholic Church. They also say Psalm 31: 1–24, which begins with the following three verses:

> In you, O LORD, I take refuge;
> Let me never be put to shame.
> In your righteousness, deliver me and rescue me;
> incline your ear to me and save me.
> Be to me a rock of refuge,
> A strong fortress to save me,
> For you are my rock and my fortress. (The Bible, 2022, Psalm 31:1–3)

BEYOND EXCEPTIONAL LEARNING LEADERS

The above sections presented the findings relative to the second theme of this study. Essentially, the exceptional teachers held specific mechanisms for curving the pressures they received from various sources, including their colleagues, institutional leaders, parents, and students. In the current section, I discuss the coping strategies of teachers in both the OECD and the Global South countries in this study and, whenever possible, compare them with those of the exceptional learning leaders. A review of the coping mechanisms of teachers in the OECD countries yields more differences than similarities with the Global South countries of the D.R. Congo, Ghana, and Uganda. One of the apparent rationales includes the economic disparities between the two blocs of countries, as examined in chapter 2 of this book. Secondly, due to socioeconomic contexts, teachers in the OECD face different problems, although some of them can come close to what teachers in the Global South experience. For example, the nature and scale of petty corruption teachers in Africa face due to the scarcity and/or lack of salaries and financial incentives is conceivably less acute in OECD, if not nonexistent. This financial issue has created challenges and threats for teachers in the Global South countries. They called for specific coping strategies, which should also differ from the OECD countries that do not experience the same educational problems. Whenever the causes of challenges in both blocs seem the same, the same effects appear, as discussed below. "The same causes produce the same effects" (Schmitt, 2014, p. 187).

OECD vs. Global South Countries

When addressing teachers' coping mechanisms in the OECD countries, the challenges that cause readaptation or readjustment of behaviors on the part of the teachers appear to be more in the order of stress, overwork, insufficient training workshops, and lack of better practices and policies (TALIS, 2022). This study and others (Olukya, 2021; Mofokeng, 2020) have suggested that the lack of financial incentives and decent working conditions and infrastructures have led to frustration, stress, and unethical practices, such as the petty corruption I covered in this chapter. In his book chapter on "Teacher Stress and Coping Strategies," Clipa (2017) depicts the coping strategies of teachers, particularly in Romania, who have experienced teaching-related stress and its corollaries like anxiety, depression, and suicide attempts. Although Romania does not count among OECD countries, the findings presented in Clipa's article seem to build a bridge of knowledge regarding teachers' coping mechanisms between the Global North and the Global South. In fact, after reviewing the literature on coping mechanisms of teachers in OECD countries, I posit that OECD teachers, as well as Global South learning leaders, can relate to those issues, although to different degrees dependent on the social contexts in which they operate.

To cope with stress accumulation at their jobs, some teachers in OECD and Sub-Saharan Africa would naturally and freely discuss the problem with their family members, close friends, and trusted colleagues (Aldrup et al., 2017). While in OECD countries, teachers would likely ask for the help of psychologists or counselors because they are available to their institutions, those professionals would be a rare commodity in Sub-Saharan Africa. Teachers in developed countries routinely participate in training workshops to embolden themselves and build self-esteem and resilience (Neves de Jesus et al., 2014; Sandilos et al., 2018; Vita-Agundu et al., 2022). One would also rightly argue that those services are hardly found in most schools in the Sub-Saharan region, given the economic hardships that educational institutions face. To readjust during challenging situations, one would also see teachers elsewhere, including in both blocs of OECD and the Global South, involved in self-examination of their lifestyle (Clipa, 2017). They would consciously or unconsciously avoid situations or people at the origin of their stress. However, people in developed countries are more likely to seek nature, where they can spend their free time or practice physical relaxation exercises in gymnasiums and sports areas (Clipa, 2017). On the other hand, people in Sub-Saharan Africa are more likely to commune more frequently with nature and are unlikely to afford gyms. Some participants in this study mentioned their involvement with outdoor activities such as soccer and volleyball to shake up their accumulated stress. Unlike the exceptional teachers in this study who remained steadfast in their jobs despite multifaceted challenges, some teachers in OECD countries and even the Global South would look for changing jobs (Amitai & Van Houtte, 2022). More likely, in OECD than in Sub-Saharan Africa, teachers it would turn to eating healthy food and taking pills because they can afford Global South teachers would not afford such luxury. UNESCO, OECD, and other organizations have also devised institutional measures to alleviate teachers' sources of professional stress. They have recommended that governments and educational institutions improve teachers' work conditions, increase teachers' salaries, limit to a reasonable level the teacher/student ratio per class and course, implement programs on stress management on the job, and value education and its learning leaders (Clipa, 2017).

It is fair to infer that most teachers in the Global South, particularly the exceptional teachers in this study, also experience challenges similar to those of their peers in the OECD, although they are contextually different. However, in addition, the former has to deal with problems inherent to their social and professional environments, including plethoric classes of 1,500 students in higher education (Gasparello et al., 2022; Green, 2019) and a teacher-to-student ratio of 1 to 60 plus (Shapiro, 2014) in some primary and secondary schools. Moreover, the scarcity of financial incentives further exacerbates the pitiable conditions of learning leaders in the Global South countries in this study. Financial issues became more acutely excruciating for teachers during the outbreak of COVID-19. Writing for the Guardian, Mwesigwa (2022) reported about teachers at private schools in Uganda who received the dreadful message: "No more payments until when schools open." The Ugandan government closed schools for the longest time during the COVID-19 outbreak. While teachers in government-run schools continued to receive their salaries, their counterparts in private schools went without financial assistance all the time the schools stopped operating. Some of the teachers found palliative living means for a while then quit teaching altogether.

Such was the case of Mary Namitala (not a participant in this study), who, according to Mwesigwa (2022), faced the harshest hardship when her private school closed. Her initial financial resolution was to leave their rented house in town and shift to an unfinished house in their village (20 miles north of Kampala, the capital city). However, she fell short of meeting their household demands. Because she had no choice but to find another source of income, she transitioned from teaching to farming, and she even rented another plot of land to grow additional crops. She and other colleagues had to leave with great sadness the profession to which they had dedicated their lives.

As opposed to the context of the Global South, most of the coping mechanisms suggested in OECD educational systems appear to be more institutional than individual. For example, TALIS' survey of about 260,000 teachers and school leaders at 15,000 primary, lower, and upper-secondary schools from forty-eight countries and economies concluded that teachers needed more training in using new technologies. When teachers complained about the need to innovate more and instill a collaborative culture in their schools, governments sought to empower their teachers and school leaders by giving them more autonomy for innovation and peer collaboration.

TALIS: Teachers and School Leaders as Lifelong Learners

Not all learning leaders in OECD countries enjoy close-to-ideal working conditions. In some countries, like the United States and Canada, where individual states and provinces regulate their educational systems, discrepancies in teachers' treatment exist between urban and rural schools and between poor and affluent educational institutions. These discrepancies create their own set of challenges for teachers, which in turn calls for different solutions or coping strategies.

Sugar Daddies

According to Jastich (2019), some teachers with less than decent income in the United States resort to a phenomenon called "Sugar Daddies" as a coping mechanism. Writing for *Yahoo/Lifestyle*, Jastich (2019) published an article titled "Teachers are turning to 'sugar daddy' dating site to supplement their salary" in which he reports on alternative coping mechanisms of some learning leaders in the United States. The author conducted and reported live interviews with some teachers. Those interviews show that the scarcity of teachers' remuneration lies at the origin of the alternative coping mechanism some teachers in the United States have referred to. For example, most of those teachers in the United States who participated in the Yahoo/Lifestyle interview reported using Sugar Daddy dating websites and SeekingArrangement.com to supplement their monthly income and make ends meet. "Sugar daddies are older men who pay younger women or sugar babies for their companionship" (Upadhyay, 2021). Websites like sugardaddy.com and seekingarrangement.com set people up for relationships they call "mutually beneficial." They offer a variety of dating lengths from a single dinner out to a weekend trip or longer. Teachers engaged in these activities (sugar babies) and their sugar daddies determine payment modalities. These dates would add an average of $33,600 to those teachers' annual income, according to *Yahoo/Lifestyle*. Will (2018) estimated that more than one in five public school teachers hold second jobs, of whom 50% work in fields outside of education. Some work as Uber drivers or cocktail servers, according to Education Week (2022). Although teachers in the OECD do not seem to rely on the petty corruption of their counterparts in the Global South, some of their alternative coping mechanisms are ethically questionable.

Jastich (2019) reported a story of a university professor from Arizona, whose first full-time offer out of her PhD program could afford her only a $33,000 salary per year. The inadequacy of this remuneration prompted her to take two additional jobs as a community college staff member and a bartender. From there, she drifted into long-term sugar daddy-like activities where she could earn an "allowance" regularly. Using the Seeking Arrangement website, she met and dated one person for a long time who gave her a substantial weekly amount of money. Another sugar daddy paid her rent, while another contributed to her film project. That website offers an alternative to more than 10,000 teachers who cashed in out of necessity. Other teachers make their money from one-off dates where they charge their minimum desired amount for their time with a given sugar daddy, making between $300 to $10,000 depending on the arrangements. Some teachers became so hooked on dating sites that they quit their teaching positions. On the contrary, others were either shocked by the incredible amount of money they received or frightened by the prospect of being caught by a parent. Jastich quoted one third-grade teacher as saying: "If I saw a parent on there, I would absolutely die," she tells Yahoo Lifestyle. "It would be like the quickest delete that I could ever do." The bottom line is that teachers are becoming sugar babies because of the necessity to supplement their educator salaries rather than taking one extra job. The author advances that teachers involved in the sugar-daddy business explain that their extra earnings have helped them to maintain their modest lifestyle rather than to get rich or quit their teaching profession.

None of the participants in this study alluded to a phenomenon such as sugar daddies as a way of supplementing their meager income. If they had engaged in such practices, I believe the spotters I used for my sampling selection would not have recommended that they participate in this study of learning leaders of integrity. However, the phenomenon might still exist under the U.S. form or any other shape, particularly in the most affluent regions of the countries in this study.

CONCLUSION

In this chapter, I presented the alternative strategies the exceptional learning leaders in this study use to avoid systemic petty corruption in their educational institutions. The study determined that those petty corruptions largely stems from the lack of consideration attached to education in general. The lack of appropriate salaries and delayed payment appeared to be evidence of the undervaluation of education. While most teachers resort to petty corruption as a coping mechanism, the exceptional teachers have proposed ethical coping strategies that keep them away from corruption while allowing them to put food on the table and, more importantly, to keep their professional integrity. Simon rightly encapsulated the spirit of all the exceptional teachers in this study as they stated the following:

> Several principles govern my teaching profession, including (a) the fear of God is the beginning of science, (b) to paraphrase scientists: "science without conscience is the ruin of the soul," (c) being accustomed to living in scarcity and abundance, (d) one does not solve one's problems on the backs of others (students in particular), (e) we are poorly paid but what the Congolese state pays cannot be challenged by a single corrupting student (so we cannot undermine the noble profession as a teacher for \$5, \$10, \$20), (f) our students, our future colleagues, are a long-term investment; the service they will render us in the future is critical.

The following chapter takes it from here to present and analyze the rationale behind the exceptionality of exceptional learning leaders. Specifically, the next chapter seeks to determine whether these learning leaders behave in this fashion out of altruism or because of some hidden self-interest.

Chapter 4

Altruistic or Self-Serving?

Throughout this study, every single exceptional learning leader shared stories of kindness toward their students. Although neither but one—Tata, mentioned the words altruistic and altruism, the analysis of their accounts led to the conclusion that they acted out of kindness. Neither the survey nor the interview questions I administered for this study mentioned the word "altruism." However, when asked why they would commit their lives to teaching in undervalued circumstances, each of the twenty participants used terminologies that connote altruistic behaviors. For example, Participants Antie, Quella, Simon, and Ursula said that their priority was to teach without expecting any return. Chantal said she received generously (education), and she gives back generously. For Maria, giving back to the community without pay constituted her greatest fulfillment. Pat stated that giving herself freely to the service of future generations was her contribution to society. Ninety-five percent of the participants believed that teaching charitably would earn them a heavenly reward in the next life. Thus, the results of this study suggested that exceptional teachers performed their leading of learning out of ethical benevolence, in other words, because of some altruistic impulses. This view begs the timeless leadership ethics question of the existence of altruism. It inquires whether altruism really exists (Batson et al., 2014) or whether a teacher or any other leader for that matter can perform an action for their student or follower without some sort of personal gain (Macaskill, 2016). As a preconception for this book, I posit that there exists no benevolence for benevolence's sake. Any act of altruism involves some form of personal benefit. Says psychiatrist and philosopher Burton (2020):

> There can be no such thing as an "altruistic" act that does not involve some element of self-interest, no such thing, for example, as an altruistic act that does not

> lead to some degree, no matter how small of pride or validation or satisfaction. (Burton, 2020)

Chapter 2 of this book concluded that the fundamental motivation behind participants' integrity, which kept them teaching in their less-than-desirable conditions, also had to do with their teaching philosophies that embody some form of altruism. Besides their teaching philosophies, participants gave many accounts of benevolent acts toward their students. To get to the bottom of why those exceptional teachers behaved benevolently, I endeavor to question their altruistic behavior to understand whether there might be some personal gain under the cover of altruism. This chapter focuses particularly on survey and interview question number 18 which requested participants to select and discuss any self-gratification they found in remaining faithful to their teaching under their current circumstances. The options to select from and discuss included the following: "I feel emotionally satisfied; I pay my due to the community; God will pay me back in the afterlife; I am happy to teach without expecting a return; I hope people will be generous to my children as I am with my students."

In an attempt to closely grasp the essence of participants' altruistic impulses, this chapter analyzes the themes emerging from the above field research in light of Grunig's four models of philanthropic giving and selected ethical leadership theory frameworks that focus in a particular manner on giving for the common good (pure altruism, psychological egoism, weak altruism, and the warm-glow giving theory). Essentially, this chapter seeks to understand the philanthropic foundations behind the behaviors of the learning leaders involved in this study.

EXCEPTIONAL TEACHERS AND FOUR MODELS OF PHILANTHROPIC DONATION

No doubt that the exceptional teachers in this study donated their time and knowledge to their students and the community in a philanthropic manner. Etymologically from ancient Greek, the term "philanthropy" comes from the Greek *(philanthrōpía),* love of humanity, from *phil-* "love, fond of" and *anthrōpos* "humankind." Experts see it as a form of altruism consisting of private initiatives for the common good (McCully, 2009). In this book, I consider philanthropy in its original meaning, which sounds slightly different from just charitable giving to human causes on a large scale, usually in the form of financial assistance. Philanthropy goes beyond charitable donation because it is an effort an individual or an organization makes based on an altruistic desire to improve human welfare (Hayes, 2022). When it comes to imparting knowledge, philanthropy essentially means the benevolent delivery of knowledge including the time, energy, and all the sacrifices a learning leader makes to change the lives of their students. This study further examined this notion of altruistic donation (Routon & Walker, 2017) of exceptional teachers' knowledge through the four models of public communication adapted to philanthropy (Grunig, 1992), which explain fundamental motivations for giving to others. These models of philanthropic contribution as applied to the teachers' altruism beg the following questions: Do the exceptional teachers accomplish their job out of pity for their students (press agentry)? Or for some personal publicity (public information)? Or because they have identified some gain in the process of dispensing knowledge (two-way asymmetric)? Or because all parties gain from their teaching (two-way symmetric)?

Most participants showed a great inclination toward the common good. They expressed this view in a particular manner in their teaching philosophies and personal accounts. Teaching philosophies embodied benevolent language such as "I am student-centered and give myself hundred percent to my students"; "I cannot pretend I am hundred percent altruistic, but I do care deeply about my students, and give sometimes a bit more than hundred percent of my time and energy"; "I treat my students like my own children, that's why I seek to help students to discover their own voice"; "I always make sure that no student is left behind and spend extra energy for the weakest ones"; "I love to see people succeeding; I love to impart the knowledge and see my students succeeding"; "people treated me generously when I was in the wilderness of my life, and I have decided to do the same with every single student of mine"; "despite the low salaries I receive, I give myself wholeheartedly to train psychologists of tomorrow in this country."

To those self-giving languages, participants added stories of their kindness hardly known by people other than their inner circle. For example, Georg, who took care of a child whose poor parents neglected her education, had a similar background: "I'm looking at myself. If somebody had not helped me out, probably I would be something different today." Although they did not earn enough from their teaching, another participant managed to pay tuition for several orphan students who struggled financially. Some learning leaders went so far as to invite some of their needy students to stay with their children so they could afford food and human attention. Stories of elementary and secondary school children, especially in rural areas, who would walk hungry for miles to school abounded. At the higher education level, emotional accounts of students whose parents were either dead or completely deprived of money to pay their children's tuition and/or transportation money were also recurring. One exceptional learning leader in this study noticed that those emotional stories became so frequent that he began questioning their authenticity.

Students knew him as a no-nonsense instructor and overtly opposed to any form of corruption. They began appealing to his emotional side. Some students whom he succeeded in understanding got away with this emotional scheme while leaving the instructor to sort out the authentic stories from the fake ones. The sections below examine the exceptional teachers' exceptionality through my adaptation of Grunig's four models of public communication.

GRUNIG'S FOUR MODELS OF PUBLIC COMMUNICATION ADAPTED TO PHILANTHROPY

As presented in table 4.1, Kelly (1991) used Grunig's (Grunig & Hunt, 1984) theory of public relations models to identify four historical models of advancement communication (or fundraising): press agentry, public information, two-way asymmetric, and two-way symmetric. While these two researchers looked at the receiver's side of either public relations (Grunig, 1984) or fundraising (Kelly, 1991; Bongila, 2002, 2011), I adapted the four models to explore the side of the giver, the philanthropist, or the teacher for that matter. Essentially, the adapted four models of philanthropy concern factors that motivate the donor or the learning leader to make their contribution (money, in-kind gifts, or knowledge) to the receiver (nonprofit organizations, public services, or students). I argue that the four models of learning leadership philanthropy should not be dissociated from their public relations or fundraising origins. The techniques, which organizations or individuals (seekers) used to disseminate information or to attract donors in the past also applied to teachers (donors) who then engaged in the business of donating knowledge. Bongila (2011) conducted research in four Catholic universities in the United States to identify the communication model that had the most effect on donors. One of his findings goes as follows.

> When asked which modes of expression—emotional [press agentry], informational [public information], seeker's interest [two-way asymmetric], and donor's interest [two-way symmetric]—made the donor respond positively to the ask, one advancement incumbent declared: "I'd say the emotional . . . I think probably for most people, I would say the emotional piece is one of the first because you do want to make a difference. I mean, I think there is a helping others component to that. I think for most people, the facts are probably last in terms of giving . . . yes, it goes to emotion." (Bongila, 2011, p. 205)

Press Agentry Model

The beginnings of the press agentry model of fundraising came in the 1800s (Kelly, 1991). Charitable organizations seeking private gifts added the use of

Table 4.1 Characteristics of Four Models of Learning Leadership Philanthropy

Characteristics	*Press Agentry/ Publicity*	*Public Information*	*Two-Way Asymmetric*	*Two-Way Symmetric*
Reasons	Moved by misguided emotions or pity.	Response to dissemination on needs	Response to unbalanced benefits	"Mutual benefits" Teacher/school Student/Com.
Nature of Communication	One-way; truth not essential; dependent on emotions	One-way; truth important; dependent on enlightenment	Two-way unbalanced effects; dependent on strategic positioning	Two-way; balanced effects dependent on congruency
Communication Model	Student → Teacher	Student → Teacher	Student → Teacher Feedback	Institution → Community
Where practiced today	Private faith-based schools	Public schools/colleges	Private education/ public universities	Some universities
Estimated percentage of teachers practicing today	35%	15%	50%	0%

Source: Kelly, K.S. (1991), p. 389.

entertainment and lotteries to their techniques for attracting funds (Bongila, 2011). In the press agentry model of fundraising, charitable organizations sought to affect the philanthropic behaviors of potential donors. These could be impacted by events charitable organizations publicized and staged such as charity balls, fairs, auctions, debating contests, and theatrical productions. Kelly (1991) hypothesized that 15% of all charitable organizations, including two- and four-year colleges, continued to practice this model. Unlike the intentionally well-structured means charitable organizations utilize to attract donors, students do not always intend to stir their teachers' sympathetic inclinations toward them. Rather, I believe the seeming genuineness of students whose unfortunate living and learning conditions move teachers to adopt favorable attitudes toward them. Like donors in the press-agentry model of fundraising, learning leaders were moved by emotions or pity for their seekers. I consider those seekers to be students then in the nineteenth century and nowadays. Kelly (1991) argues that emotional stories meant to move the hearts of donors did not always bear a full degree of truth. By the same token, the account of a participant who pitied his students at the beginning only to realize that other students would return to him with similar stories can give credence to Grunig's (1992) elaboration of press agentry.

However, one would question whether emotional responses to students' poor conditions of life constitute a sufficient rationale to cause teachers to behave ethically. Bongila's (2011) study of the philanthropic communication models at four Catholic universities in the United States suggested that 45% of those institutions used the press agentry model to attract philanthropic donations. I can hypothesize that 35% of teachers or donors of knowledge make their philanthropic contributions out of pity for their students. The communication model is one-way, from the student whose educational conditions call for action from the teachers. Most of these learning leaders feel compelled to act with charity. As seen above in the case of the instructor who realized that students recounted similar stories to attract their attention, the truth does not always matter in press agentry. Playing on the teacher's emotions remains more important than accurately telling a true story. I also posit that teachers in faith-based institutions are likely to remain faithful in their teaching because educational institutions are usually inspired by the social teaching of their religious denominations.

Public Information Model

The public information model emerged as early as 1853 in New York City. Opposed to the previous model was the belief that donors could give more efficiently and with greater morality if the truth and accurate information were disseminated (Kelly, 1991). Cutlip (1965) cited Charles Loring Brace, the founder of the Children's Aid Society, as among the first pioneers to rebel against the then-common cheap exploitation of donors' emotions. The public information model relied heavily on the "Domino Theory," which, according to Grunig and Hunt (1984), maintained that increased communication would lead to increased awareness on the part of the donors.

In turn, the awareness would lead them to positive attitudes and, finally, to positive behavior. Similarly, the exceptional learning leaders have bought into the information about their institution's policies and the need to support both the students and the institution in its trying moments. When asked why they do not behave like other professors who resort to petty corruption to make ends meet, most exceptional learning leaders responded that they abide by the integrity policy of their academic institutions and the recurrent call to duty in support of their students. Like donors who were prepared to make gifts once they internalized the information provided to them by charities (Kelly, 1991), the exceptional teachers in this study might have responded positively to the integrity message of their institution and the information about the scarcity of needs, which called for teaching understanding and steadfastness.

Like the press agentry model, the nature of the public information model was always one way, from the organization (Source) to the public (Donor). In contrast to the press agentry model, truth was important in public information (Kelly, 1991; Bongila, 2011). Bongila's (2011) study concluded that 20% of the four Catholic institutions he studied practiced the public information model of philanthropy. There is no doubt the information the exceptional teachers received from their educational institutions bore the highest level of truthfulness. I can hypothesize that only about 15% of the exceptional teachers in this study relied on the dissemination of policies and needs of their institutions to maintain their professional integrity.

Two-Way Asymmetric Model of Philanthropy

Have teachers identified some gains that might profit their students more than themselves? John Price Jones, a 1902 graduate of Harvard, became well known for his formulation of the two-way asymmetric model of philanthropy (Bongila, 2011). That strategy held that the publicity must reflect the nature of the institution and that the institution must show donors (teachers) the reason for giving (knowledge with integrity). The nature of the public information model utilized by Harvard was one-way, from the organization to the public. For the practitioners of this model, philanthropic communication amounted to telling, not listening. The unbalanced relation between the seeker and the donor gave way to a new communication model, which Grunig and Hunt (1984) identified as two-way asymmetric. By nature, this model described a public communication flowing both to and from the publics, with unbalanced effects in favor of the seeking organization. To shape attractive messages, practitioners of the two-way asymmetric model of public communication/fundraising used research. This model is essentially a two-way unbalanced communication between the institution or the student and the potential donor or the instructor. Kelly (1991) put forth the hypothesis that 30% of all charitable organizations practiced the two-way asymmetric model. Furthermore, she hypothesized that most colleges and universities, either private or public, and most advancement consultants practiced the two-way asymmetric model of raising funds.

Concretely, students would state their present and future interests and "seek" knowledge contributions from the exceptional teachers. Many of these teachers mentioned that they wish to meet their students where they stand academically and socially and team up with them to take them where they want to be in the future. The greatest interests of the institution or the student, as opposed to those of the donor or instructor, are motivating factors. Specifically, most participants in this study indicated their eagerness to make a difference in the lives of their students. Teaching for them amounted to imparting knowledge to their students. A few of them appreciated receiving some form of personal recognition. Most of them would also appreciate fair professional treatment (pay raise and upward mobility) and social benefits (community respect). Some teachers gained respect whenever parents and students themselves approached them with requests similar to "What can my child or what can I do to be just like you?"

Thus, according to the two-way asymmetric communication of knowledge philanthropy, the exceptional teachers give more to the students while gaining a bit in the process. In his study of the philanthropic communication modes of Catholic universities, Bongila (2011) found that 45% of them practiced the two-way asymmetric model. When it comes to the communication of knowledge philanthropy, participants from both private and public institutions indiscriminately showed some propensity toward students' highest interests. I hypothesize that about 50% of the exceptional learning leaders have remained steadfast in their profession because they believe that providing their students with the means to excel in life would yield a greater benefit to their students. This view, however, also holds that the exceptional teachers gain some emolument in the process, although to an unbalanced degree.

The Two-Way Symmetric Model of Philanthropy

Kelly (1991) affirmed that the two-way symmetric model of advancement was a new phenomenon, emerging only in the 1980s. The philanthropic philosophy that Harvard University practiced in the second half of the 1800s under the presidency of Charles Eliot appeared to be the earliest use of the two-way symmetric model. Donors would contribute to a charitable cause should they obtain fulfilling benefits. The goal of the two-way symmetric model of philanthropic giving is a mutual understanding between the seeker and the donor. Unlike the two-way asymmetric model, dialogue, or two-sided communication and mutual understanding, characterize the two-way symmetric model of philanthropy. Grunig (1984) asserted that symmetrical communication is balanced, and it should involve the relationship between the seeker/student and the donor (teacher). Harvard's president Eliot believed that the institution (seeker) should highlight mutual benefits between the institution and potential donors and should emphasize the concept of mutual understanding. The summary in table 4.2 suggested that a donor's satisfaction with their personal interests, as presented by the seeker, would cause them to donate to a cause. Unlike the other models whose communication was portrayed as source and receiver, two-way symmetric communication emphasized the interdependencies of donors and charitable organizations (Bongila, 2011). While Kelly (1991) estimated that about 5% of universities practiced the two-way communication of philanthropy, Bongila (2011) found that 6% of Catholic universities are involved in this model.

That educational institutions in the Global South offer a mutual benefit to both the teacher as the donor of knowledge and the student as the seeker remains very disputable in the contexts of the schools and universities involved in this study. If students (seekers) could think about the benefits teachers receive as a consequence of their work, learners would point to fair salaries and benefits, which unfortunately are elusive in the Global South, as shown in the preceding chapters. The lingering question of this study has revolved around the reasons why exceptional learning leaders keep on teaching despite their unfortunate conditions. Based on the preceding chapters of this book, the two-way symmetric mode of philanthropy, which holds that both stakeholders of the instructors and learners receive mutual benefit, is hardly sustainable. No participant's teaching philosophy alluded to the direct benefit they would draw from their teaching. Instead, the majority of them regretted the lack of fair compensation. In plain terms, mutual benefits would mean that the seeker (student) is satisfied with their learning while the donor (instructor) stays fulfilled with their treatment, including salaries and other benefits that come with it. The discussion of the two-way asymmetric model of philanthropic communication suggested that exceptional teachers might earn some unbalanced benefits from their steadfast work. Although not fulfilled, some participants have no regret about not providing enough for their families (in terms of salary). Yet, that sentiment does not mean they share a mutual benefit of their work with their students. The above discussion infers that no learning leader practices the two-way symmetric mode of philanthropic communication. They certainly have many other reasons to remain faithful to their teaching profession, but imparting knowledge steadfastly to students because they share mutual benefit does not seem to be one of them.

Based on the accounts of the participants in this study, it appears safe to infer that there is always a degree of self-interest in any giving action, whether it is a financial donation or a distribution of knowledge. Only two participants argued that they teach ethically without expecting any return. The remaining learning leaders experienced some benefits. They were emotionally satisfied; they paid back to the community; they hoped their children would be treated fairly; they hoped for an afterlife reward.

Therefore, this more in-depth analysis of the reasons why exceptional teachers might have behaved humanely in the middle of hardships has led to the examination of the four models of knowledge philanthropy. In using the four models, I meant to examine whether the participants pursue any self-interest or whether they act as they do for "no reason." Doing good for no reason would match the statements of most of their philosophies of education. It appears that the press-agentry model of philanthropy—which calls for participants to donate their knowledge out of compassion for their students—aligns to a certain degree with the altruistic statements in their teaching philosophies. The public information model, which is concerned with compliance with the written policy of the institution, does not explain the altruistic impulse of the learning leaders in this study. On the contrary, the two-way asymmetric model of philanthropy shows that the participants always have a certain interest in mind as they teach. The two-way symmetric model of philanthropy—which calls for a win-win benefit for the students and the teachers—stands on the side of "weak altruism" (Kraut, 2020). In the next sections, I examine whether the exceptional teachers owe their exceptionality to pure altruism or some egoistic impulses.

EXCEPTIONAL TEACHERS AND ALTRUISM

Coined by French philosopher Auguste Comte in the 1830s, the term "altruism" has long caused arguments and controversies for academics who have attempted to understand human behavior.

Habito and Inada (2006) pointed out that:

> The original French term "altruism" was suggested by the French legal phrase "le bien d'autrui" (the good of others) and was formed from the Italian equivalent. "altrui," itself a derivative of the Latin "alter" or "other." Altruism is precisely "other-ism": the effort or actual ability to act in the interest of others. (p.1)

Comte himself thought of an altruist as a person whose actions selflessly target other people's good. An altruist holds "love as a principle," "order as a base," and "progress as an objective" (Mangone, 2020). Concretely, an altruistic exceptional learning leader would be full of love for their students as fellow human beings. Like other disciplines, educational leadership and ethical leadership are far from solving the altruism riddle (Lehrer, 2017). Leadership ethics and other disciplines present two views of altruism. On the one hand, altruism bears a categorical resonance, as defined by the Stanford Dictionary of Philosophy (Kraut, 2020) and Ricard, Mandell and Gordon (2015). These sources state that altruism is motivated by a desire to benefit someone other than oneself for that person's sake. In this view, altruistic acts would include only those undertaken to do good to others.

People use the term altruism to oppose behaviors that are "self-interested," "selfish," or "egoistic." These words apply routinely to behaviors that are motivated exclusively by the desire to benefit oneself. On the other hand, experts also come up with a more nuanced understanding of altruism by inferring that one can engage in helping others while benefiting themselves. For example, according to Cherry (2022), "altruism refers to a motive for helping behavior that is primarily intended to relieve another person's distress, with little or no regard for the helper's self-interest" (Cherry, 2022). Even the Stanford Dictionary of Philosophy (2020) acknowledges the nuance, stating that altruistic acts do not need to involve self-sacrifice and that they remain altruistic even when a donor, such as an exceptional learning leader, performs them with self-interest motives.

Leadership ethics practitioners (Flescher & Worthen, 2007; Zoogah & Zoogah, 2020) would agree with other experts who see altruism as benevolence and philanthropy. The guru of leadership ethics, Professor Ciulla (2005), specifies that often people use altruism in contrast with selfishness, that is, a behavior that benefits someone at the expense of others. She argues that both altruism and selfishness imply extreme sorts of drive and behavior. Ciulla rightly disagrees with Edwin Locke (Avolio & Locke, 2002) who argues that altruism is about self-sacrifice. Locke posits that altruistic leaders who wish to be truly altruistic should not expect any rewards or pleasure from the job they chose. Such leaders would give themselves over totally to serving the wants of others. Locke concluded that no one would want to be an altruistic leader. Additionally, no one wants or wishes to have such an altruistic person as their leader. As stated above, Ciulla disagrees with Locke's argument that leaders should act according to their self-interest. However, she also states that it would be problematic to use altruism as a standard of moral behavior for ethical behavior. I agree with Ciulla in her opposition to Locke's view of altruism, which was previously articulated by Ayn Ryan (2020) in her "virtue of selfishness." A caveat remains, however, that

I have merely presented a rationale behind the noticeable steadfastness of the exceptional learning leaders, which boiled down to their philanthropic donation of knowledge. Discussion on whether altruism should become the norm for any ethical leadership amounts to another study of philanthropic benevolence.

In the four models of philanthropic donation (Grunig, 1989; Kelly, 1991) discussed above, I extended this notion of benevolence to the act of knowledge donation exceptional learning leaders practiced. For educational leaders, every single day is marred by teachers' altruistic behaviors because altruism and its motives seem to permeate the teaching profession itself (Olitalia et al., 2013). Oftentimes, altruistic acts might result from acts of benevolence the donor might have received from random community members. In essence, several participants' narratives evidenced their motivation to donate their knowledge in an indefectible manner as a payback to a society that acted altruistically toward them. Georg's account illustrates this point:

> I came not from a well-to-do family. Somehow, I had stopped at senior four because I failed some courses. So, I was in the village serving on the church choir. And then one of my distant relatives came around and was saying, "you young man, what's happening? Why haven't you gone back to school?" I told her my dad is not willing to take me to school and pay tuition. She picked me from where I was and took me to school and paid for it. I was able to go through high school thanks to her support. Then I joined the university. So, when I reflect back, I have a responsibility to help others also who come from where I came from. Because there will be still students who would fail. So, to me, I am there full time. I avail myself to the service of my learners. I always call them. And we chat away forward. I do a lot of counselling to those that seem to be demoralized, those who seem to be having problems in their homes. I am a teacher, I'm a counselor. I guide these learners, and even those who have challenges. . . . Sometimes you get students who are trying to enter into bad habits. So, the moment I learn about it, I bring them very close and make them my friends. We share, and in the process, they succeed, they succeed very well. (Georg)

As it was with Georg, one would also imply that most individuals who are the "targets" of altruistic behaviors are selected for such treatment because of a personal tie between the benefactor and the beneficiary (Kraut, 2020). It did not seem, however, that this participant extended his benevolence in a particular fashion to the learners who related to him through blood or friendship. Rather, most participants' accounts revealed acts of self-sacrifice they sustained when extending their generosity to their students.

Mateer (1993) identified some of the self-sacrificing acts of teachers that go beyond their professional duties. The teaching profession encompasses countless benevolent activities. In particular, the exceptional learning leaders in this study work after-school hours tutoring struggling students; they provide advice or even comfort to students in challenging situations; they are willing to do these things despite a low standard wage; they are concerned with the needs of their students and they volunteer their time and energy to address those needs. Additionally, Konnerth (2017) conducted a doctoral study on "The Cost of Altruism for Teachers." This researcher, who rightly called learning leaders "servant teachers," explored the self-sacrificing altruistic acts of teachers, which eventually lead to burnout. He noted that the provision to render service constitutes a key task of teachers. Although they do not make the list of professional groups like social workers, psychologists, and counselors, teachers align closely with the social and psycho-social care sectors (Konnerth, 2017). The findings of this study suggested that servant teachers who lead learners with altruism show a degree of vulnerability to burnout, entailing some self-sacrifice. The servant teachers in Konnerth's study and the learning leaders in this study share some commonalities concerning altruistic acts of self-sacrifice. Both groups share emotional expenditure for students; they provide a sense of purpose and security to students; they commit to the growth and well-being of students; they volunteer their time in addressing student needs; they often forgo personal well-being and family responsibilities (Konnerth, 2017).

Although the exceptional learning leaders in this study did not dwell on burnout as a self-sacrifice, they indicated some loss of well-being as a consequence of their benevolent teaching. The exceptional "servant" teachers work to settle such issues as health, social, legal, and educational problems, as well as various conflicts that often arise from their educational settings. Besides donating extra knowledge (outside classrooms), the exceptional teachers volunteer extra service to assist in crises both on campus and off-campus, during and after their working times. "In this sense, teachers may go above and beyond even the helping professions that, while their main focus is helping, generally confine their efforts within the scope of their daily jobs" (Konnerth, 2017, p. 57).

As a caveat, not all teacher daily jobs qualify as altruistic acts. The notion of altruism does not apply to every morally motivated treatment of others. Rather, it narrowly encompasses acts that are done out of concern for the good of others—in other words, for their well-being. Specifically, Kraut (2020) explains that altruistic acts are deemed charitable, benevolent, or kind. All these words also convey the notion of acting for the good of others, and not simply toward others. Accordingly, one can also conceive the exceptional learning leaders' act of teaching ethically through the lenses of pure (categorical) altruism and weak (nuanced) altruism as discussed in the next sections.

Pure Altruism

Per its evolution, pure altruism entails the subordination of self-love to the love for others and the satisfaction of their needs as a source of well-being for the individual and society (Mangone, 2020). After a careful review of the literature about altruism, Monroe (1998) provides a six-point taxonomy of what turns out to be a definition of pure altruism.

> (1) Altruism must entail action. It cannot merely be intentions or well-meaning thoughts. (2) The action must be goal-directed, although this may be either conscious or reflexive. (3) The goal of the act must be to further the welfare of another. If another's welfare is unintended or secondary consequence of behavior designed primarily to further my own welfare, the act is not altruistic. (4) Intentions count more than consequences. If I try to do something nice for you, and it ends up badly or with long-term negative consequences for you, this does not diminish the altruism of my initial action. Most analysts now consider motivation and intent critical, even though motives and intent are difficult to establish, observe and measure objectively. (5) The act must carry some possibility of diminution in my own welfare. An act that improves both my own welfare and that of another person would not be altruistic but would fall instead into the category of collective welfare. (6) Altruism sets no conditions; its purpose is to further the welfare of another person or group, without anticipation of reward for the altruist. (pp. 6–7)

Some participants' accounts of dealing with unfortunate students could easily be seen as purely altruistic, that is, detached from any self-interest. Asked what participants gained by being honest in their teaching and by avoiding the corrupting ways that could have made some of them well-off, Tata had this to say: "There is no benefit in what I do. This is a hard question to think about yourself. I do not know if there is a personal benefit. Probably there is not any personal benefit for being in the position that I teach in the university. There is no personal benefit believe it or not" (Tata).

Georg also echoed other teachers' similar message: "I do not expect any return. The moment you do something, expecting a return at times you get disappointed. Because the return may not come" (Georg). One can also infer pure altruism from this statement by Ursula: "I treat my students like they are my children and so in my teaching, I seek to help students discover their voice." In addition to the act of teaching, actions that exceptional teachers undertake, such as hosting poor students in their homes, are also directed toward the wellness of students. It does not seem that the exceptional teachers who engage in altruistic acts with their students, as defined above, behave in a fashion that benefits them. As Monroe (1998) acknowledges it, it does not sound possible to ascertain the intentions of the teachers who endeavor to donate knowledge and wellness to their students. Take the example of Henry, who said they always make sure not to not leave any student behind. And they acted upon this altruistic principle several times. Said Henry:

> When I just joined the institution for teaching, I came across this child who would tell me about the stories at home. Her parents only put the child to school. The teachers only mind about teaching the child. But now the child was running away from school. We interacted along the road. So, I picked up this child, went to her home. At first her parents were very bitter. But later on, as we talked and talked and talked, they said, "Maybe you'll be the one following up the child at the school," a primary school nearby. So, I looked on this child. You'll hear many stories of children like her. Sometimes parents send them to school without breakfast, and the children cannot learn. So, this has pushed me back to school to not only teach the academics, but also exercise mentorship. Every time I meet a child and, the child has maybe moved up to be someone responsible at any level, that keeps me with a lot of passion to continue with the work.

One can only judge Henry and others like him through the good action of bettering the lives of other people, specifically their students. Indeed, there is a presence of some form of self-sacrifice, in which exceptional teachers donate knowledge in unfair social conditions. Furthermore, they spread their African solidarity even thinner when they allow themselves and their families to share their scarce space, food, and intimacy with the students they host. They donate twice or thrice to the common good. Again, judging only by a handful of exceptional teachers' accounts of their actions toward their students, it appears that they worked for the welfare of their students without preconditions or anticipation of any form of personal gain. One might attempt to conclude that these exceptional teachers acted out of pure altruism. At this point, I feel unprepared to make this determination until the examination of the possibility of altruism for altruism's sake.

While I might still be questioning whether altruism for altruism's sake exists, Decision Lab (2022) reports on ethical leadership approaches that believe in the possibility of selfless altruism. A theory called the empathy-altruism hypothesis (Persson & Kajonius, 2016) suggests that often people practice altruism for unselfish reasons. The APA Dictionary of Psychology defines the empathy-altruism hypothesis as "a theory that explains helping behaviors as resulting from feelings of empathy and compassion toward others, which arouse an altruistic motivation directed toward the ultimate goal of improving another person's welfare" (APA, 2022). I agree that there exists a handful of people capable of helping fellow humans out of genuine, empathic concern. This theory argues that should an individual, like an exceptional teacher, hold a sufficient amount of empathy for another person's situation, they will forgo their personal gain and help. Through their accounts of unfailing dedication to their profession, the exceptional teachers sympathized with their students' conditions and decided to act unselfishly. For full disclosure, acting either selfishly or unselfishly did not seem to cross the teachers' minds. They just acted in favor of their fellow human beings. However, the theory of psychological egoism denies the very existence of pure altruism.

Psychological Egoism

As an antithesis to the above view, according to which some exceptional learning leaders might have acted with pure altruism, the theory of *psychological egoism* (Wayment & Bauer, 2008) would maintain that they continued to do their job because "we humans always do what is in our own self-interest." Therefore, any good action they took toward their students (or any action of love for that matter) was done primarily benefit themselves. In addition, the theory of ethical egoism (Gotthelf, 2006), which is often associated with psychological egoism, would imply that the exceptional teachers always profit from their teaching because "we ought to do what is in our own interest." This view also aligns closely with Ayn Rand's *The Virtue of Selfishness* (Gotthelf, 2016), which argues against the possibility of any kind of altruism that would claim itself to be pure or deprived of any conscious or unconscious personal gain. Although I have maintained this view as a working premise, I should quickly disclose that I led the data of this study guide the theories and not the other way around. Coincidentally, the findings of this study have suggested that altruism, not necessarily pure altruism, has been the driving force that propelled the participants toward the good action of teaching and caring for their students. Yet, *psychological egoism* goes so far as to question even the existence of pure altruism.

It pays to recall that philosophers and experts in ethical leadership (Ciulla, 2014; Marion & Gonzalez, 2013) as well as educational leadership (Johnson, 2015; Shapiro & Stefkovich, 2021) have long argued about the very existence of altruism. Those on the side of pure altruism would argue that the exceptional learning leaders in this study acted selflessly to benefit their students out of kind sympathy and an inherent quality of goodness. Scholars on the other side would maintain that there is always an ulterior motive behind the acts of altruism the exceptional teachers enact. Those ulterior motives could include the desire to appear good in the eyes of the community (Wilson, 2015), or the hope in an afterlife reward. Proponents of psychological egoism would summarize their denial of pure altruism by echoing biologist Michael Ghiselin's saying, "Scratch an altruist and watch a hypocrite bleed" (De Frans de Waal, 2009, p. 10).

According to the Stanford Dictionary of Philosophy (2022), psychological egoism holds that all human action is ultimately motivated by self-interest.

This theory concedes to the commonsensical idea that humans often seek other people's benefit besides their own. In other words, there always exists a personal benefit when humans seek the benefit of other people.

Accordingly, humans do not care about others for others' sake, which entails the nonexistence of altruism. The Stanford Dictionary of Philosophy (2022) acknowledges that this formulation of psychological egoism is least open to objection. This source suggests that:

> We always do find some self-interested motivation that accompanies altruistically motivated behaviors. It is difficult to refute that proposal. We should not pretend that we know all of the considerations and causes that underlie our behavior. Some of our motives are hidden, and there is too much going on in our minds for us to be aware of the whole of our psychology. So, for all we know, we might never be pure altruists. (Stanford Dictionary of Philosophy, np.)

Weak Altruism

The above explanation of "altruism" leaves room for self-interest while one is in the process of helping unselfishly. It prompts us to further probe the motives behind exceptional teachers' propensity to help while seemingly sacrificing their own interests. As suggested above, this same source points out what it calls "weak altruism." Consider a participant in this study who stated: "There is a personal benefit I get from teaching at the University. Maybe the people who get results from corruption, are benefits to them. Mine are the time and the space the university has given me by nature of the job description. . . . Bottom line, I would fit into my being emotionally satisfied" (Ursula). Because of the personal benefit attached to the work of this participant, one would see their act as weak altruism. Assuming the participant declared that they shall never do anything unless doing so would be best for them, they would refuse to sacrifice their well-being even to the slightest degree. Yet, this participant "could have altruistic motives for some of what he does" (Stanford Dictionary of Philosophy, np.).

This source establishes an interesting distinction between a pure or strong altruistic act, a weak altruistic act, and an altruistic individual. In the strong sense, an act is deemed altruistic when it is performed entirely from benevolent motives and is completely without self-interested reasons. In some cases, but not always, the benefactors performing a purely altruistic act can sustain some loss of well-being. In the weak sense, as in the case of the above participant, an altruistic act can be motivated by some interest to the benefactor or someone else besides the beneficiary of the act. However, the benefactor of the weak altruistic act might not be recognized as an altruistic individual. Accordingly, all the exceptional learning leaders in this study have completed altruistic acts owing to their faithful teaching in unfair contexts. However, the majority of them would not be deemed altruistic individuals due to their weak altruistic acts, which include personal gains, be they intentional or unintentional. At this point, it feels safe to infer that all four models of philanthropy (Grunig, 1984; Kelly, 1992; Bongila, 2011) covered above concern weak altruism because they seem to pay attention in a particular fashion to the interest of the donor or the teacher, for that matter. Participants' accounts confirm this point.

The survey and interview question 18 asked participants whether they found [pursued or obtained any self-gratification] as they remained faithful to their teaching under their current circumstances. "I feel emotionally satisfied; I pay my due to the community," said Kalunga. While this response indicates self-gratification on the part of this participant and others, it prompted me to further probe Henry about his self-interests, if any.

> What do I gain for teaching the way I do? . . . I feel emotionally satisfied. . . . It's overall God; God is every really the one we think pays back everything. . . . Then, I'm happy to teach without expecting a return. The other self-interest I gain from teaching with ethical integrity is of course for my children. Our dad used to tell us that I'm known to surviving on your grandfather's property. So, I'm surviving because I've worked hard to put up with what I have. Okay. I picked that where I'm teaching my children. . . . I bring them up to live on their own, to sustain themselves, get the best upbringing. I teach two because of the emotional bit of it, the passion in it, and two it's my job. I would continue to teach even without self-gratification. Why? Because I'm very hopeful. If I may not get it now, but I'm rendering a service. Okay. I'm doing a service. I'm not looking at it as a self-satisfaction, but I'm seeing it as the only way I can contribute to my society. (Henry)

> You know that according to what they call *psychological egoism*, you cannot perform an act that doesn't benefit you. That's what I was asking you. But there's a theory also *ethical egoism* that says that you ought to do only what is in your interest. So, there's nothing that you can do that doesn't benefit you. Even the fact that you are having children is self-interested because it benefits you to share your love with your offspring. So that's why my question comes back to you. After this explanation, would you have continued to teach, even though there were no benefits to you there?

> I think no, I would not be teaching. (Henry)

Not many exceptional learning leaders involved in this study concluded they would quit teaching if they did not find any self-gratification. However, Joseph's teaching motives qualify as acts of weak altruism because the participant received a certain degree of personal reward. My next conversation with Bill reached a different conclusion although still in the realm of weak altruism.

> I am committed to my teaching because I believe that people will be generous to my children because I have been to their theirs. (Bill)
>
> Okay this is not always obvious because you might be generous and other people may not care much about your own children. But you are hoping that that's what will happen, right?
>
> It is my hope because if they see my good services then they can transfer the same to my offspring. (Bill)
>
> In short, what would you say to my question, "What are you gaining by teaching?" You know you could have chosen another profession. What do you gain besides the fact that people would take care of your children? That's in the future, and you don't know if it's going to happen. But what do you gain by teaching?
>
> So being a government civil servant at least at the end when I retire, there is that retirement package. (Bill)
>
> So, you keep teaching because there will be a retirement package?
>
> At least it can help me in retirement age. (Bill)
>
> Okay so without that you wouldn't be teaching.
>
> Not necessarily but the demands, and the community expectations of serving have kept me serving. I want to serve my people. (Bill)
>
> Would you have the same retirement package if you were in the private school system?
>
> The private schools also benefit from the National Social Security Fund which is continuously deducted from one's salary per month in that particular case. So that's what the [private school teachers] get at the end of the profession. (Bill)
>
> So, without that incentive would you have continued to teach?
>
> Yes. (Bill)
>
> Why?

I would continue because this now means income currently. (Bill)

No. I understand, but if the government didn't offer you anything after your retirement would you have continued to teach?

Still, I would continue. (Bill)

Why?

Because it is the vocation, I selected myself and it is where my base is. So, it's where I am based. (Bill)

Like Bill, several others expressed their determination to continue to work even though the little benefits they received from their educational institutions were to vaporize. Despite the reality that a handful of exceptional learning leaders pursue self-benefits, all of them endeavored to do good for others. Their self-interest, coupled with altruistic acts, places them in the realm of weak altruism. For this reason, it would be misleading to say that Henry, and others like him, fall under the category of altruistic persons.

Mixed-Motives Altruism

Leadership ethics experts and other scholars such as Hu and Liu (2003) also identify more nuanced weak altruism as mixed-motive altruism for the simple reason that the benefactor holds various motives when acting benevolently. For example, a teacher's altruistic acts might include both actions undertaken to do good to their students and those undertaken to prevent harm to their learners. Those altruistic acts may or may not involve self-sacrifice. The online Encyclopedia (Encyclopedia.com, 2022) explains that many human actions involve mixed motives. Often, people, including the exceptional teachers in this book, would act in a way that benefits the common good. However, they would only act so partly because they would expect benefits in return. The benefit could be immediate or at some future time. Ethical leadership experts also describe this behavior as *reciprocal altruism* because what motivates the benefactor is not just their own self-interest. On the other hand, pure altruism, which is the sole concern for the interests or well-being of the recipient, might not always motivate the agent either.

For example, Roger's account contains mixed motives. He taught for a while in the D.R. Congo, then had to leave his teaching position for safety reasons, only to return when it became opportune. He explained that his departure to a foreign country was motivated by the lack of security in the D.R. Congo and the opportunity to work and study for his five children in safe conditions. His salary decreased after only two years in a ministerial structure where he worked as an advisor. He returned to a state university in the D.R. Congo where he was invited to participate in the launch of psychology studies. Despite a rather low salary and the increasing expenses for his children's studies, he became passionate about imparting his knowledge to the first graduates in the Psychology Department he created. He began coordinating a master's program in Family and Community Therapy. This paraphrase of Roger's account includes several motives within their decision to continue to donate their knowledge with integrity to students of her country. First, one could see pure altruism as she indicates that her main goal was to heal the countless young men and women who fell victim to the senseless invasion war in the region of the country where she taught. She selflessly underscored the need to contribute to the training of psychologists and therapists who would serve their local populations. Second, to the act of altruism, there is also some form of self-sacrifice to the participant's family because she agreed to return to a country and take a low salary, which was hardly enough to support her children's education. Third, this participant had to act to provide safety for her own family and work to ensure her retirement, making the latter act somehow self-interested. Fourth, this participant took action to do good for her local population while working to prevent harm to both to her family and the victimized population of the region where she works. This specific example illustrates what Kraut (2022) calls altruism with "mixed motives." Roger, like many others, is careful always to do what is best for himself while pursuing such personal interests as retirement security.

The Warm-Glow Giving Theory

Even emotional self-gratification, which does not yield a palpable reward to the teachers for doing good to their students, would not make the exceptional learning leaders altruistic individuals. The warm glow-giving theory (Andreoni, 1990; Evren & Minardi, 2017) attempts to explain it. For example, Antie stated:

> When I do something I want to feel like doing so satisfies me. Because I am making a difference in the lives of students, I emotionally get satisfied. That is how I gauge it. . . . Assuming one of my students becomes like a university president somewhere, it brings me satisfaction. Just like this lady who is now president of the Guild [the student body]. I say yeah that is our [my] student who has handled that [responsibility]. So, you feel that you did, you had added something to her or his life, and that person has become somebody. But then it fulfils you emotionally. You become happy because that is only something that we want as teachers. You want your students to have success. . . . As to whether I would have been teaching or continued to teach if teaching did not provide me an emotional satisfaction? I would say: Teaching because of money you can

> teach. But when you are frustrated!! Like maybe if all my students were failing; that would be a challenge if I saw that I was not making anything good in it. I would say well bye-bye to this profession. Maybe I am misplaced. My call is not here. Then I have to change and go to the other side. (Antie)

The above narrative displayed another case of weak altruism as the benefactor pursues both the interests of their students and their own in terms of emotional satisfaction. Regarding emotional satisfaction, the warm-glow giving theory (Andreoni, 1990; Mark Ottoni-Wilhelm, 2017) claims that the joy an individual feels because of helping others constitutes their best reward. Like Antie and many others, people experience a level of joy and satisfaction from contributing to the betterment of others. Andreoni calls that satisfaction the "warm glow" or the selfish pleasure that comes from doing good whether or not the act of generosity produces a positive impact. To be fair to Antie, their warm-glow seems *a posteriori* (after witnessing the impact of their act of generosity) rather than *a priori* (before the impact) as explained in the warm-glow theory. This theory indicates that the benefactor rejoices upon performing the act of generosity. They do not care whether the consequences of their act result in positive or negative outcomes. On the contrary, most participants in this study exult when their gift of knowledge yields positive results while they might consider quitting the teaching profession should the consequences of their teaching fail to better the status of their students.

The warm-glow framework goes so far as to claim that people may be "impurely altruistic" because they might simultaneously hold both altruistic and selfish motivations for giving (Andreoni, 1990). In the case of the exceptional learning leaders in this study, it would be hard to detect the impurity of their altruism from their own accounts. While they are intentional in their vocation of serving their students, their selfish motives seem unintentional. Mixed motives altruism and weak altruism might better explain the nature of the exceptional teachers' donation of knowledge. The two approaches are rightly present in the formulation of the warm glow theory. This statement by Andreoni feeds into this understanding.

> When people make donations to public goods such as charities, there might be many factors influencing their decision other than altruism. . . . People are sometimes motivated by the desire to win prestige, respect, friendship, and other social and psychological objectives. . . . Apparent charitable behaviors can also be motivated by the desire to avoid scorn of others or to receive social acclaim. . . . Clearly social pressure, guilt or sympathy or simply a desire for a warm glow may play important roles in the decisions of agents. (Andreoni, p. 463)

Indeed, the desire to maintain the esteem of herself and to remain loyal to herself seems to motivate Quella in her teaching integrity. She added that she stayed honest in her teaching because she is very jealous of her personality and her dignity and will not stand for a day when people say that she is soaked. "God, my husband, my children, and everything that believes in me gives me the strength to always move forward well" (Quella). She believes that by teaching with integrity, history will witness it so that her grandchildren can say that they had a grandmother of integrity and be proud of it. More importantly, Quella concluded with this powerful statement:

> My mother told me, "When you take food from the pan, never empty it because someone can come in the middle of the night, and you need to serve him." It will mean that I must live; but beyond that, I must use, communicate and transmit virtues to others. So, my pan of virtues must not be empty. Values must not be exhausted, and we must not get tired of being able to live honestly because future generations will have to draw from my pot. (Quella)

That Quella evokes maintaining her dignity as one of the reasons that prompt her to teach with integrity might easily sound like serving the purpose of the warm-glow theory. Many participants have expressed similar feelings. Unlike the proponents of warm-glow theory who might see Quella's preservation of personal dignity and moral values as merely selfish and non-altruistic, it can be safe to side with either the mixed-motive approach (Hu & Liu, 2003) or the weak approach to altruism (Morris, 2005). For one, the exceptional teachers ought to maintain their dignity, though this could be a selfish reward to themselves. Second, and more importantly, they hope to selflessly impart not only knowledge but also their steadfastness for future generations to follow. This mixture of motives that may appear selfish with those that are objectively within the realm of altruism makes the participants' acts altruistic although on the weaker side.

Tata stands out as the only learning leader who used the word "altruism" when she stated in an interview, "I can't say I am altruistic. I can't say I love them [my students] so much. It is my ethical approach to teaching. I heard it in the past that I was dedicated to my job. If I have to do it, I like to do things properly. I have never overthought it; I've never thought there is altruism to it. . . . I cannot pretend that I am 100% altruistic. . . . I do not think so."

Per the definitions discussed above, one would agree with Tata that she is not altruistic because her motives for teaching with integrity amid unfair hardship still bear some self-interests. She made this point when she stated, "Because I do think about things like salary and compensation . . . but I do think about my well-being." The same reason holds for all the participants in this study, making their acts of benevolence altruistic while it would not be prudent to give them the altruistic epithet. None of the learning leaders in this study have been identified as such. They all have posed altruistic acts, though.

Yet, their approach to imparting knowledge indicates they hold mixed and/or weak altruistic motives. Getting to understand the rationale behind the behavior of the exceptional teachers immediately begs the question of how those individuals acquired the ethical invisible mover called altruism. Without getting into unfinished questioning, it would suit to also ponder why the exceptional teachers gave themselves up, so to speak to donate knowledge and why the majority of the teachers in the Global South countries in this study do not care about professional integrity.

FROM CULTURE TO ALTRUISM ICEBERG

Culture Influence

The exceptional learning leaders' noticeable sense of practiced altruism had to come from somewhere. Allen (2018) authored a white paper prepared for the John Templeton Foundation by the Greater Good Science Center at UC Berkeley titled "The Science of Generosity." The project addressed three relevant questions: 1) "where does this generosity come from? 2) What are the benefits that result from helping others? 3) And how can generosity be further cultivated within individuals and in society as a whole?" (p. 18). The first question directly addresses the potential origins of the altruistic behaviors the exceptional teachers have shown throughout their careers. This chapter presents key findings of studies from many fields, including neuroscience, economics, psychology, sociology, and ecology. For example, according to Kramer (2005), the evolutionary roots of generosity suggest that humans are both selfish and generous. In other words, altruism is not just the product of culture; rather, it has deep roots in the natural evolution of the human species (Kramer, 2005). Theories that hold biological roots of altruism suggest that because of evolution, humans are born with biological "hardware" made up of altruistic behaviors. A study by Zaki and Mitchell (2011) suggested that extending generosity to another person activated the orbitofrontal cortex, responsible for intrinsic reward when a person extends generosity to another human. However, a question still lingers as to why only a few learning leaders exceptionally thrive in their altruism if all teachers bear generous impulses in their DNA. Yet a study by Knafo and Plomin (2006) on identical twins concluded that they had a genetic predisposition toward altruism, while other studies indicated that women have a higher inclination toward generosity than men (Son & Wilson, 2010). Undoubtedly, it was beyond the scope of this study to determine whether the teachers who imparted their knowledge ethically and altruistically did so because their genes were prewired with generosity impulses.

Important for this current investigation is the study by Henrich and Henrich (2006), which recognized culture as an evolutionary force and theorized that many behaviors of a generous nature could be the result of a gene-culture evolution. Yet several scholars of educational leadership, including Ciulla (2014), would recommend looking into culture to uncover the roots of altruistic behaviors.

In his book *Beyond the Dichotomy between Altruism and Egoism*, Mangone (2020) writes:

> The attitude and actions of individuals towards each other are therefore influenced on the one hand by culture, and on the other, by the indissoluble link with context and everyday life. Thus, we move away from the search for the cause of a phenomenon (principle of causality) to focus instead on those overall interactions (relationality) that Sorokin (1948) had defined as indivisible sociocultural trinity (society, culture, and personality). (p. 159)

Likewise, I have avoided looking into the cause of each act of altruism undertaken by exceptional teachers, for example, what caused Bill to take a struggling student into his home. Rather, altruism as a general ethical way of behaving, which those learning leaders have displayed, has to do with the society that nurtured them, the culture in which they grew up and lived, and the character they fashioned. Since altruism cannot happen in a vacuum, Mangone (2020) and Sorokin (1962) focus its occurrence on human relationships. Concretely, the exceptional teachers in this study must have developed their altruistic impulses in relational contexts whose ways were prepared by their own culture. To further explain the role of those human relationships within a culture, Sorokin (1962) divides them into (1) ideological culture, (2) behavioral culture, and (3) material culture. The ideological culture includes meanings, values, and norms an individual holds because of their interactions with other people. The behavioral culture encompasses every meaningful action-reaction an individual engages in. In turn, those actions-reactions reveal pure meanings of the norms and values a society conveys. On the other hand, the material culture only represents the physical manifestation of the content of both the ideological and behavioral cultures of individual actions or reactions.

Although Sorkin's framework can explain in part social and relational rudiments of altruism, I will depart from his notion of ideological culture because of its rapprochement with politics (Reese & Rosenfeld, 2016), which can include conviction, loyalty, and empathy that are captive to political views. In an ideological culture, "Each ideology projects its own particular mythology, sacred history, icons, prophets, heroes, saints, martyrs, villains, and demons. . . . People close their ears to opposite arguments. . . . " (Gat, 2022, p. 307).

On the contrary, I maintain that foundational culture—as opposed to ideological culture—can partially provide the rationale for the practice of altruism that the exceptional teachers in this study engaged in. Thus, the foundational culture of altruism would include teachers' attitudes, beliefs, religious and social expectations and values, and the like, as portrayed in figure 4.1. In particular, Question 7 of the interview/survey of this study asked the exceptional teachers what motivated them to remain in their teaching positions all those years. Most responses evoked the foundations of their cultures. Innos and others believed that it was their duty to train future generations as they themselves were trained. For the majority of them, the social teachings of their respective religions instilled in them moral values, including particularly that of giving selflessly, even to strangers. The behavioral culture of the exceptional learning leaders indicated that every altruistic behavior the exceptional teachers displayed originated, one way or another, from the ethical foundations of their cultures. These behaviors include, but are not limited to, such actions as teaching benevolently, assisting students outside of classrooms, and treating students like their own children. As Sorkin (1962) would argue, the self-manifestation of the exceptional learning leaders' altruistic acts constitutes what he calls physical culture.

All the above considered, trying to conceptualize where exceptional learning leaders' altruistic disposition comes from simply amounts to two aspects of altruism: one is visible, the other is not. Figure 4.1 represents the top and

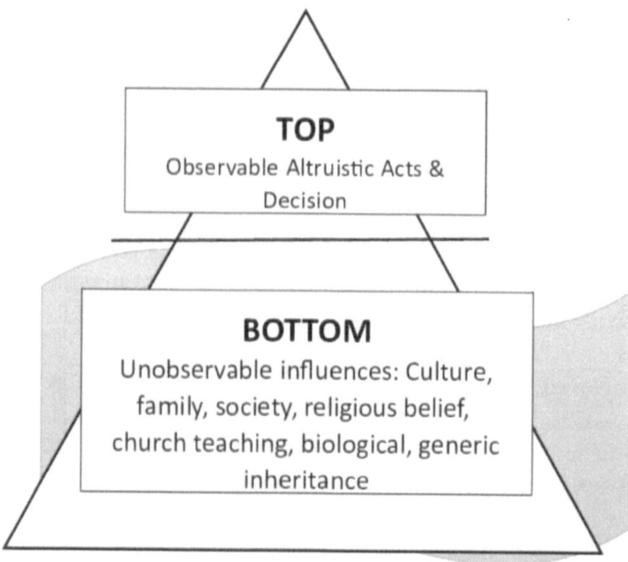

Figure 4.1 Altruism Iceberg.

bottom sides of an altruism iceberg. Like an iceberg, only a fraction of the reality manifests itself to the outsider while the more potent invisible reality remains unlikely to be known to the actor.

Altruism Iceberg

Up to this point, this study of the exceptional teachers in the Global South has revealed that there is more to their altruistic behaviors, and particularly the sources of their moral generosity. The rationale for this sophistication stands for the simple reason that it remains elusive to try to exhaust the bases of why they are essentially altruistic. Perhaps understanding the observable and non-observable facades of altruism might provide some response to the foundations of the exceptional teachers' generosity. In the 1970s, anthropologist Edward T. Hall (1976) developed the Cultural Iceberg Model to represent most prevailing codes in societies. Inspiration for this model came from polar seas' icebergs, which include visible parts on the surface of the water and invisible parts underwater. Experts estimate that up to 90% of an iceberg remains below the water. In the same way, argues Hall (1976), culture and behaviors encompass both visible and invisible components. On the one hand, the observable part of culture refers to the way people live and interact with each other, their traditions, food, and attire. On the other hand, the non-observable part includes people's preferences, values, beliefs, and value systems. "Just as much of ninety percent of an iceberg remains hidden underwater," says Hall, much of the culture and behavior remains hidden though influential.

It is now safe to infer that, just like culture and behaviors, altruism as practiced by the participants in this study involves two facets relevant to our quest for understanding the sources of teachers' generous donation of knowledge and other services to their students. Table 4.2 presents both sides of the altruism iceberg. First, the top of the iceberg altruism is made up of the altruistic acts and actions that are observable. More explicitly, exceptional learning leaders, their communities, and society—for this matter—could only witness the altruistic side of these leaders that was observable to them. This visible

Table 4.2 Altruism Iceberg

Altruistic acts	Family influence
Benevolent behaviors	Society influence
Observable activities	Religious beliefs
Explicit actions	Church social teaching
Extracurricular counseling	Unknown sources
Conscious self-sacrificing decisions	Biological and evolutionary sources
	Instinct for generosity, evolutionary culture, generic inheritance

side of their altruistic iceberg encompasses such items as acts of kindness, benevolent behaviors, explicit actions, extracurricular counseling, conscious self-sacrificing decisions, and the like. Second, the bottom of the altruism iceberg includes unobservable elements that, however, influence the visible altruistic acts posed by the exceptional teachers. The exceptional learning leaders have argued that they received their altruistic impulses from their families, societies, churches, social teachings of their religions, and unknown sources. To these, one should also add the immaterial sources discussed above (Allen, 2018) including biological and evolutionary sources, instinct for generosity, evolutionary culture, and genetic inheritance. One could argue that 95% of teachers who have been exposed to the very same sociocultural and religious-ethical conditions never developed the kind of selfless drive that those in this study excelled in. Table 4.2 also pictures the invisible/unobservable sources of teachers' altruism, which the exceptional teachers—like any other human in their situation—are unable to adequately conceptualize and properly deduct from the teachers' accounts, which I have represented in the below iceberg.

CHAPTER SUMMARY

This chapter interrogated the rationale behind the obvious altruistic behaviors of the exceptional teachers toward their students. As summarized in figure 4.2, I used two theoretical rationales: Grunig's (1991) four models of public communication as applied to philanthropic giving (Kelly, 1991; Bongila, 2011) and a leadership ethics framework of altruism. Throughout this chapter, I premised that the exceptional teachers are involved in the business of philanthropic distribution of knowledge. The four models of philanthropy handily explain the results of this study, which consisted of examining the real reasons that have motivated the exceptional teachers to keep on working despite the undervaluation of their profession and their work. The four models of philanthropic giving (Grunig, 1992) (press-agentry, public information, two-way asymmetric, two-way symmetric) discussed the exceptional teachers' drives to good action. The first model, *the press agentry model,* explained that a sizable number of the exceptional teachers in this study donate knowledge because they are moved by emotion or by pity for their students. Second, *the public information model* of philanthropy holds that about 15% of the teachers in this study extended their "charitable" hands in response to the information put forward by their educational institutions. Third, *the two-way asymmetric model* explained that the majority of participants in this study (50%) make charitable contributions of knowledge in which they reap personal gains, although to a lower degree than the recipient

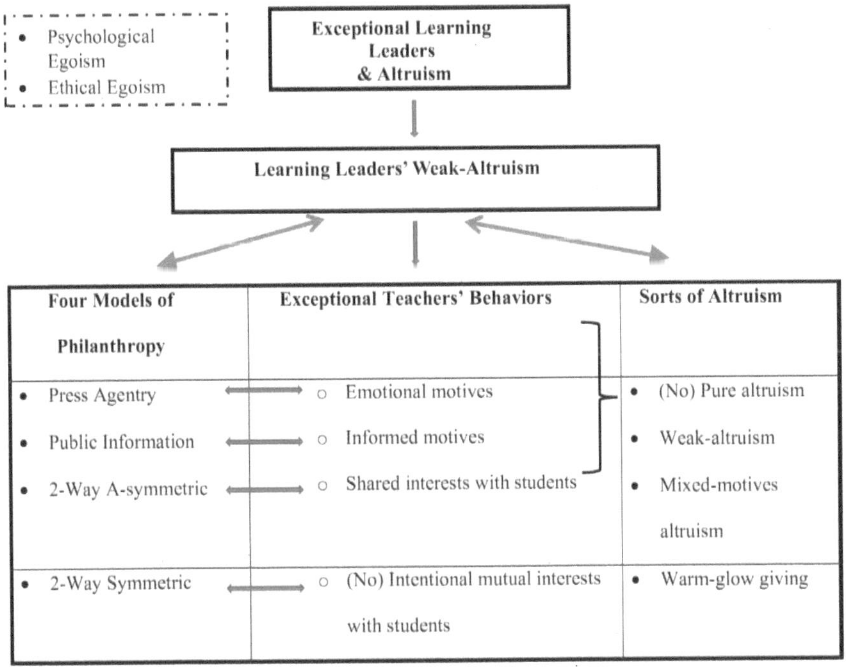

Figure 4.2 Exceptional Learning Leaders' Altruistic Behaviors.

students. Fourth, the *two-way symmetric model,* consisting of a mutual benefit between the donor (teacher) and the seeker (student), could not explain whether participants in this study intentionally sought their own self-interest as they equally did the well-being of their students. However, no matter the participants' reasons for imparting knowledge, this model indicates learning leaders always benefit, although to varying degrees. The leadership ethics framework of altruism, as applied to the contexts of the exceptional teachers, explained that these individuals have likely imparted knowledge out of some forms of altruistic motives. Some participants might have acted out of pure altruism, that is, without any personal gain intention. A further examination of the data through psychological egoism denied that the exceptional teachers might have acted exclusively in students' interests. Weak altruism, mixed-motive altruism, and the warm-glow giving theory suggested that participants engaged in altruistic acts. However, they might not bear the epithet of altruism because their motives for sharing knowledge held some degree of personal reward. Finally, this chapter led us to the examination of the very sources of altruism, as to where the exceptional teachers might have gotten it from. Discussions of this latter point were funneled into an altruism iceberg (figure 4.1), which indicated the visible and invisible sides of this rather complex phenomenon.

Chapter 5

Leadership Ethics of Voiceless Teachers

"You can teach other people how to learn other languages,
But you can't teach them how to govern themselves."

(African Proverb)

This chapter serves as a synthesis of the above presentation of the contexts of charitable self-giving by the exceptional teachers in chapter 3 (thesis) and the theoretical analysis of their altruistic conduct in chapter 4 (antithesis). It argues that notwithstanding their probable self-interested motives inherent to our human nature, the exceptional teachers have dedicated their lives to serving charitably and honestly numerous children and future leaders, and their contributions to the learning of countless students should be deemed priceless and timeless. Their respective teaching institutions, their communities and countries, as well as all educational leaders, should applaud these teachers' dedication. Indeed, whatever visible and invisible factors that motivate these "selfless" teachers to continue to work tirelessly—including what Dale Carnegie (Carnegie, 1998) identified as the craving for honor—is worth praising and sharing with other people in the leadership of educating the youth. A popular saying goes that "one of the deepest desires of human beings is the desire to be appreciated." This chapter posits that although their overall society and political leadership might have devalued the teaching profession, a handful of their population feels and acts otherwise. To redecorate the blazon of an underappreciated profession, this tiny group of role models should grow and be allowed to speak up.

One could argue that these "heroes" of teaching are enabling a system of corruption that requires defiance or some other measure to initiate change to the system. They could raise questions such as "Who benefits from praising steadfastness in a corrupt system? What change, improvement, or shift is brought about through this praising?" While I concede that steadfastness for steadfastness' sake does not yield change in corrupt educational systems, I see the exceptional teachers' integrity as an antithesis to the corruption of their educational institutions. Should one deplore the corruption of educational institutions, one should therefore admire the integrity of those teachers, who constitute a resistance—although passive—to the less-than-desirable education systems.

The underpinning question of this chapter can be read as follows: What are the ethical leadership implications of the selected teachers' steadfastness for educational leaders in the Global South and beyond? Chapter 4 identified "altruism" as one of the main reasons that motivate the exceptional teachers to work with integrity. However, altruism is only a tiny sector within the field of leadership ethics. Besides altruism, there might have been many other unidentified rationales behind the teachers' behaviors, most of which can sit well in the domain of ethics while others could amount to the social and spiritual upbringing of the exceptional instructors. For organization's sake, this chapter intends to use a leadership ethics framework presented by Bongila (2013) in his book *Grounding Leadership Ethics in African Diaspora and Election Rights* to draw some implications from the words and behaviors of the learning leaders who participated in this study. To begin with, it pays to define "leadership ethics" as this discipline can bear varying definitions dependent on contexts and experts who use it.

ABOUT LEADERSHIP ETHICS

Professor Joanne Ciulla can rightly be seen as the pioneer scholar of leadership ethics (Northouse, 2019). Her publications have borne great authority in this discipline since the 1990s. For example, in her *Introduction to the Ethics of Leadership*, Ciulla (2003) wrote:

> The central issues in ethics are also the central issues in leadership. They include the problem of authenticity, self-interest, and self-discipline, moral obligations of justice, duty and the greatest good. In leadership, we see morality magnified. The actions of leaders usually have a greater impact on a greater number of people than the actions of other individuals. We look to leaders as role models. (p. xi)

Ciulla's view identifies leadership ethics as leadership infused with ethics, distinguishing it from one that does not involve morality or ethics. Although Ciulla's perspectives arose mainly from her studies of Western and Asian philosophies (Ciulla, 2005), her global understanding of ethical leadership ought to include African cultures. This study of the exceptional ethical leaders in education in the Global South infers Ciulla's views of two kinds of leaders. First, counted as leaders are those individuals deemed ethical due to their work ethic, authenticity, selfless interest, and moral obligations toward the common good. It is fair to believe that this first category of leaders exists even beyond the exceptional teachers whose communities recommended them for this study. Secondly, global history, including that of Africa, has known countless leaders who do not abide by the norms of ethics and cannot, therefore, fit into the category of ethical leaders. These include educators, teachers, and instructors who rely on corruption, bribes, sexual harassment, and illicit sales of course packages to compensate for the lack of fair treatment their educational institutions and governments have inflicted on them.

Fortunately for educational leadership, there is this "immaculate" group of learning leaders who happen to distinguish themselves by their altruism. For Kanungo and Mendonca (1996), leadership ethics was nothing but altruism.

Although this study came to the preliminary conclusion that the mover that drove the exceptional leaders looks altruistic, I quickly concede that altruism cannot encompass the whole field of ethical leadership. Nor can any of the major standards of ethics including duty ethics, utility/utilitarianism or consequentialism (Mill, 1987), ethics of duty (Kant, 1997), ethics of care (Gilligan, 1982), ethics of professionalism (Shapiro & Stefkovich, 2021), and virtue ethics (Ruggiero, 2024). Virtue ethics has been seen as encompassing altruism or charity, also known as benevolent love. Ciulla (2005) adequately addresses this issue when she writes to the effect that some leadership scholars, including Kanungo and Mendonca (1996), wrongly "use altruism as the moral gold standard for ethical leadership" (p. 6). In fact, in their book *Ethical Dimensions of Leadership*, the two authors maintain that the leaders of organizations are more effective when their motivation is a concern for others. Additionally, they keep on being effective when their guiding principle is the benefit to others, even if the result of their decisions and actions would have a cost to themselves.

I remember teaching two leadership ethics classes for the MA and doctoral students at the University of St. Thomas. One was called "The Intellectual and Ethical Foundations of Leadership" and the other "The Ethical Dimensions of Leadership." To define leadership ethics, I methodically guided students through a heuristic process that involved a discussion of (a) [in] adequate] definitions of ethics; (b) the particularity of ethical leaders versus other leaders; and (c) an application activity highlighting the differences between ethical leaders and other leaders.

[In]adequate Meanings of Ethics

Writing for the Markkula Center for Applied Ethics at Santa Clara University, Andre and Velasquez (2014) quoted sociologist Raymond Baumhart as asking businesspeople, "What does ethics mean to you?" I use the same introductory question to engage students in a debate of whether each of the following definitions would be adequate to understand the whole field of ethics.

> Ethics has to do with what my feelings tell me is right or wrong.
> Ethics has to do with my religious beliefs.
> Being ethical is doing what the law requires.
> Ethics consists of the standards of behaviors our society accepts.
> I don't know what the word means.

Understandably, some graduate students agreed with either of the above meanings of [mis]conceptions of ethics. Meanwhile, through some form of Socratic process, I would urge other students to either raise their support or argue against any student who holds one of the above views. In general, these bright graduate students would easily hint at arguments explaining the fallacy of each of the above assertions.

Explicitly, ethics is not a matter of following one's feelings because they can cause us to err (Ruggiero, 2024). For example, students who participated in focus groups for the purpose of this study reported that most of their instructors would routinely feel it was a good idea to recommend their family members to their colleagues for better grades. This occurred particularly when their child, niece, or nephew performed poorly in a course taught by their colleagues. Students themselves indicated that this sort of feeling was ethically wrong because it disadvantaged other students who did not have anyone to plead their cause.

Ethics should not be identified with religion for the simple reason that even non-religious people can be ethical. "Religion can set high ethical standards and can provide intense motivations for ethical behavior. Ethics, however, cannot be confined to religion nor is it the same as religion" (Andre & Velasquez, 2014). However, religion provides a great impetus for people to act ethically. I posit that 99% of professors, teachers, and instructors in the three countries in this study are religious people. When asked the percentage of their instructors who might be directly involved with unethical actions or petty corruption, students responded about 95% of them. Given that most of these teachers practiced one form of religion, it stands as evidence that religion did not make them ethical, nor is it equivalent to ethics.

A law-abiding person is not necessarily ethical, given that the law—like feelings—can deviate from ethical standards. For instance, in some of the countries in this study, the law allows university professors to hold teaching positions at other institutions of higher learning. Out of curiosity, I asked a law professor about the maximum number of universities where an instructor can realistically teach at once. There was none: professors could teach at as many universities as they were capable of. It is worth noting that professor absenteeism acutely plagues the great majority of institutions of higher education in the Global South. Professors who teach at five universities are abiding by the law, but their actions do not meet any standards of ethics.

Ethics is not equivalent to "the standards of behavior our society accepts" since communities or societies can also err (Ruggiero, 2024). In chapter 3 of this book, I discussed the phenomenon of "suivi" or follow-up. It is customary in some countries involved in this study for parents to hand over cash to their college children at the end of class sessions for "suivi." Parents know that whether their child has succeeded in some given courses, instructors can still fail them to collect money from students. Therefore, students must follow up with instructors with a monetary bribe and/or sexual relations for the instructor to either restore students' real grades (in case they succeeded) or offer them a passing grade (if they failed in the class). Although this horrendous practice has been normalized—in some communities/societies, in no way can it become ethical.

After I had led students to refute all the above assertions as not comprehending ethics, I usually ask that each student privately craft their definition of ethics. They would then read their definitions aloud for the whole class to appreciate, critique, and edit. Then I would run for them the following for their appreciation and adoption. What is ethics? First, there is normative ethics, which prescribes how one ought to live ethically in any given society. "Ethics refers to well based standards of right and wrong that prescribe what humans ought to do, usually in terms of rights, obligations, benefits to society, fairness, or specific virtues" (Jenkins, 2003, p. 4). As an illustration, ethics refers to those standards that impose reasonable obligations to refrain from harassing students, stealing from them, exchanging sex for grades, committing assault, slander, and fraud. Normative ethics includes ethical standards that enjoin virtues of honesty, compassion, and loyalty. Additionally, ethical standards—such as utilitarianism, deontology, and virtue ethics—include values relating to rights. Among those rights, one would count the following: the right to life, the right to freedom from injury, the right to privacy, and the right to education. Secondly, there is metaethics, which refers to the study and development of one's ethical standards. This aspect of ethics is meant to control such elements as feelings, laws, and social norms, which can deviate from what is ethical. Therefore, metaethics calls for the continuous effort of studying our own moral beliefs and our moral conduct and striving to ensure that we, and the institutions we help to shape, live up to standards that are reasonable and solidly based (Andre & Velazquez, 2014). In addition to the above essence of ethics, Ingram and Parks (2002) provide what I can call the function of ethics, which is to clarify the nature of right and wrong, good, and bad. "Besides clarifying the meaning and justification of ethical ideas, ethics tells us how we ought to behave" (Ingram & Parks, 2002).

Particularity of Ethical Leaders

In this section, I still refer to the two ethics classes I taught at the University of St. Thomas, MN for both the MA and Ed.D students. To get to a definition of ethical leadership, I guide students by presenting to them these two seemingly opposite notions of a leader. First, I ask them to read this statement regarding who might be a leader: "Such despots as Hitler should be ranked among tyrants, not among leaders because 'a leader and a tyrant are opposites'" (McKenna, 2010). Then students would struggle to respond to the following questions: "Is ethics a *sine qua non* for leadership? In other words, how can you fathom a leader without ethics or morality?" Discuss your response.

Second, after discussing the idea of a leader from McKenna's book, I request that students turn their attention to the next statement and reconcile it with the previous view: "Stalin, Hitler, Mussolini, and Mao Zedong were regarded as good political leaders at some point in time by a certain element of the population. History has proven, however, that each was guilty of an immoral use of the tremendous power his leadership afforded him" (McKenna, 2010).

I believe the above dialectical activity prepares students to think of three essential features of an ethical leader, which they can incorporate into a definition of ethical leadership. As far as the course goes, I only suggest two essentials of an ethical leader (means and ends) to allow students to continue to build a workable definition of ethical leadership. Finally, I lead students to an application of a definition of ethical leadership based on the overall means and ends a leader has used. I broadly defined an ethical leader as one who pays attention to both the means and the ends in their decisions and actions. As indicated in table 5.1 (Ethical Leadership Matrix), I drew a matrix with the "means" on the horizontal axis and the "ends" on the vertical axis, generating four quadrants representing four types of leaders as far as their ethics were concerned.

The first quadrant of table 5.1 represents *Ethical Leaders* who conduct people with honorable or effective means toward good/ethical ends or goals. The second quadrant belongs to the *Well-Intended* or people with dishonorable/ineffective means and good ends/goals in mind. Quadrant 3 belongs to the *Tyrants*, leaders with honorable or effective means but bad ends or goals. Finally, the fourth quadrant is that of the *Adventurous*, individuals with dishonorable means

Table 5.1 Ethical Leadership Matrix

	"Honorable"/ Effective Means	"Dishonorable"/ Ineffective Means
Good Ends/ Goals	Ethical Leader	Well Intended
Bad Ends/ Goals	Tyrant	Adventurous

and bad ends or goals. In a warm-up activity, I engaged students in a discussion of the definitions of the terms I had suggested. Eventually, we adjusted word connotations as needed to stir critical discussions in their small groups. The purpose of the application activity was to compare ethical leaders with other competent leaders. The student group assignment consisted of identifying four leaders who could fit each of the four quadrants and explaining their choice to the rest of the class. In response to this activity, students easily classified such leaders as Mother Theresa of Calcutta, Gandhi, Fr. Maximilian Kolbe, Martin Luther King, and Nelson Mandela among the ethical leaders. Without hesitation, I would place all the exceptional learning leaders who participated in this study among the ethical leaders. Their ethical goal was to turn their students into educated citizens who act wisely for the common good. Their main honorable means was to care for their students with great altruism.

In sum, I like this short, simple, and encompassing definition of leadership ethics that Moore (2022) provides on the website of Greatworklife: "Ethical leadership is the art of leading people and making good decisions based on a defined set of values, such as fairness, accountability, trust, honesty, equality, and respect. These values form the core foundation of ethical leadership" (Moore, 2022). To this definition, it is only fitting for the leadership ethics scholar to add the central elements of means and ends. Therefore, one can conceive ethical leadership as an approach to guiding people toward good ends, including the common good, by using honorable means based on ethical standards of utility, duty, care, justice, professionalism, and virtue. In his book *Leadership: Theory and Practice* (2010), Northouse describes the principles of leadership ethics, including respect for each other's views, service to others, honesty, justice and fairness, and community building, to which Bongila (2013) added ethical decision-making. Armed with the above understanding of leadership ethics, particularly its focus on the centrality of honorable means and ends, it suits to examine the implications of and recommendations from the exemplary life and work of the exceptional learning leaders in this study.

LEADERSHIP ETHICS OF THE EXCEPTIONAL TEACHERS

This study has suggested that despite the multifaceted devaluation of education in several countries of the Global South, which has caused massive nefarious consequences on the part of the learning leaders, there exist some bright spots. These are teachers, professors, and instructors who have fought the pernicious corruption of education to stay afloat as role models. For most of the time, they have been voiceless, but their actions speak loudly about them. Figure 5.1 represents a synopsis of what emerged as the leadership ethics of the exceptional learning leaders in this study. As discussed in the above sections, those teachers targeted an honorable/good end, namely the education of future generations as a common good. Their specific means to reach that end included their steadfastness, their resistance to contextual hardships and petty corruption, and particularly their altruism. Additionally, they extended their *kimumtu* to a larger community than their own extended families. In the following sections, I examine how the exceptional teachers embodied the five major tenets of leadership ethics, namely respect for others, service to others, justice/fairness as well as building community. Along the way, I will first draw some implications from the behaviors and actions of the exemplary teachers. Second, I will quote and paraphrase their voices on the

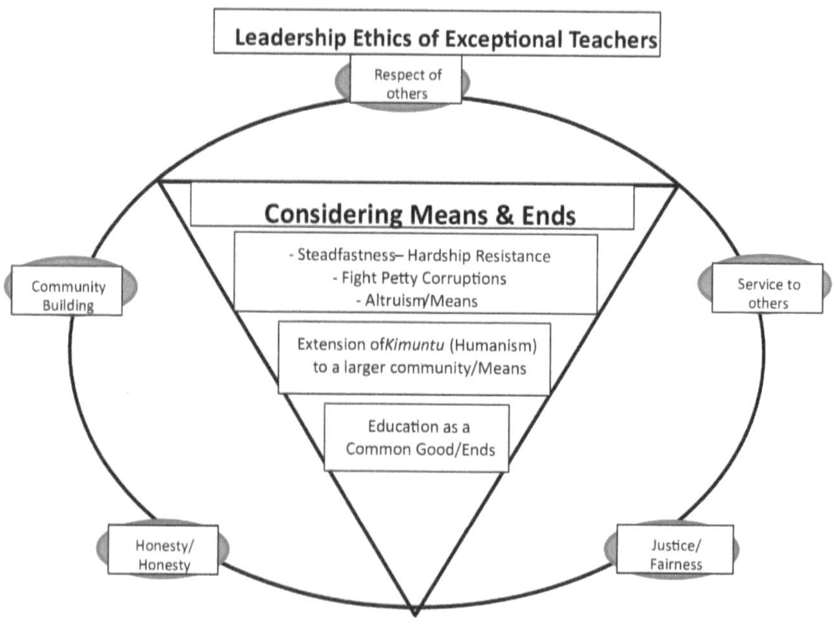

Figure 5.1 Leadership Ethics of Exceptional Teachers.

recommendations they yearn for to redecorate the tarnished blazon of education in the Global South and, why not in the world. The implications and recommendations are based on the principles of ethical leadership (Bongila, 2013), which the exceptional learning leaders have incarnated throughout their years of donating knowledge.

Respect for Others

Learning leaders who dedicate their lives to teaching their students show them respect because they deserve to be treated as humans. In his elaboration of duty ethics, philosopher Emmanuel Kant (1724–1804) declared that it is our duty as humans to treat other human beings with respect. He further clarified that treating others with respect means treating them as ends in themselves as opposed to means to ends. Although the term respect can bear several meanings, leadership ethics scholars such as Moore (2022) identify it with showing "regard for the wishes, feelings and right of others." Others might have different feelings and wishes, which the would-be ethical leader should strive to respect, appreciating the fact that people may look and behave differently for a reason. A great mark of respect stands for the ability to learn to respect the differences in us all. No one would completely comprehend human differences, but it pays to consider their existence. Over time, respect for others may call for admiration because there is always something to admire in any given human being. The admiration one gives to others is likely to be given back to them. How and to whom did the exceptional learning leaders in this study show any form of respect?

By remaining faithful to their teaching profession for the sake of students despite the hardships they faced, the exceptional teachers in this study considered that their students have value inherent to their common humanity. The fact that students are humans has value in itself, which, in Kant's words is treating them as an end in themselves because they are worth it. These teachers care about the good of the students for their sake. They did not instrumentalize or objectify their students for their personal gains or satisfaction. Some of the exceptional teachers took some students under their wings, and their families said a great deal about the respect they had for human beings. The exceptional teachers respected the wish of their students to acquire learning in a safe and caring environment. They respected the rights of students to a just and fair education by showing up prepared for their class lessons, showing up in class on time, uplifting their students, correcting their assignments, giving them the grades they earned, reporting their grades promptly, communicating with parents as needed, and encouraging them to work harder. Some exceptional teachers reported paying attention to their students' differences, particularly those mentally or socially struggling. They would dedicate more time to making sure they were on the same page as the rest of their classmates. Take the example of a learning leader who counseled and encouraged his students who confided they contemplated priesthood; the teacher admired the student's determination although they knew his weaknesses. They encouraged the students to focus on their strengths rather than on their struggles. Eventually, their students reached the goal of their lives because a teacher treated them with respect.

Above all, the exceptional teachers showed respect for themselves. Recall the environment in which these heroic leaders operated: most [not all] instructors and teachers do not show up in class for no reason; they financially, morally, and sexually abuse their students, trash students' grades or do not even grade papers, expect bribes for grades. These exceptional teachers resent those dehumanizing practices because they have great respect for their integrity, for the profession, and particularly for their students. It is a situation where not conforming to the toxic environment of corruption means ostracization and emotional and even physical threats. Antie stated that she was once so insulted and physically threatened by a colleague that she quit eating meals with the group for fear of being poisoned. Bill said that some of his colleagues repeatedly told him to look after himself and that "I look for cheap popularity from the learners." Linda had her office burglarized in the aftermath of an altercation with her department chair who demanded that she give a passing grade to a student who rarely attended her class. Maria said, "I live in constant fear that anything can happen to me," recalling "the only incorruptible colleague" who passed "under suspicious conditions. . . . He was also hated by almost all his colleagues."

The exceptional teachers extirpated themselves from ruining their reputation, as one said, "I am very protective of my reputation. I will never trade it for any amount of money or any bribery for that matter." I do believe the community that recommended such teachers for this study knew them as people who also respected them because they were flag-bearers of educational integrity. These teachers have recommendations for various constituencies that deal with students.

Teachers Deserve Respect

Respect for the teaching profession and the main agents of education, the teachers, is paramount. Although the exceptional teachers did not raise any complaint, they just hope that their governments and educational institutions will treat them as an end and not as a means. It is common knowledge that the teaching profession is the least paid in many countries of the world, particularly in the Global South. This situation has greatly contributed to the erosion of educational value and integrity. Worse, many students I spoke with in focus groups enjoined their governments and educational institutions to pay their teachers a market salary. In chapter 4 of this book, I discussed the issue of respect (or lack thereof) given to the teaching profession. I quote Dolton (2013), saying that governments that respect their teachers should look seriously into their status and remediate such situations by paying them the right salaries. Countries that respect their teachers the most, like China, Malaysia, and Korea—not the United States—treat their teachers as medical doctors (Global Status Index, 2018). Although treating instructors with respect would not solve all the rampant and systemic corruption in educational settings, it would cut it by a large margin.

Money alone will not redecorate the tarnished business of teaching as far as its respect is concerned. I can only underscore the importance of festively celebrating October 5, World Teachers' Day (Koreabridge, 2011), which I discuss in the Introduction of this book.

Small communities often make a difference when it comes to the implementation of such changes. When governments or school districts do not take the lead, I can see those small school districts and villages start celebrating teachers of the year, as I described in my anecdotal story in the Introduction. As to why we should put such an emphasis on honoring and respecting teachers, one exceptional teacher had this to say: "Teaching is the mother of all the other professions. There would not be any engineers, any doctors, any lawyers, any professors without teachers. No one neglects their mother."

Students Deserve Respect

The exceptional learning leaders in this study appeared to champion student respect in multiple ways. One thing is to talk vaguely about students' respect; the other is to draft, implement, promote, and enforce policies about respecting students as humans (as ends in themselves) as opposed to means for personal enrichment and satisfaction on the part of vicious instructors. I am still shocked at the reaction of a focus group student who stated that the level of corruption in their schools and colleges, which they shared with me, was a copy from the United States because "that's where all the bad things come from." My reaction was stern as I immediately told them, "You do the kind of things you tolerate here; you face jail time, and your profession is forever done." Students in the United States are respected and protected by clear policies that have been implemented and enforced. For example, before taking students to a study abroad program in any given country, the assistant director of the program and I must attend a compulsory session on sexual harassment policies.

To respect and protect students, policies prohibiting financial, physical, verbal, emotional, and sexual abuse of students should be implemented and enforced, particularly in the schools and universities that participated in this study. The systemic practice of "suivi" or following up with instructors in the aftermath of exams and tests for a better grade is a disgrace and a lack of respect for students who might have worked very hard to succeed in a given course. Also distasteful is the official sale of course packages to students for which each professor sets the price at their own will. Poor students unable to purchase course packages are already doomed to fail. It's noteworthy that some governments proclaimed the abolition of that practice, but to no avail because there was no enforcement. Enforcement of such prohibition can include official blame, suspension, and/or exclusion from the teaching profession of any instructor caught in the activity of selling course packages to students. At best, academic institutions can take the reins to collect, print, and sell those packages in the university bookstore. Some proceeds can be returned to the instructor—if the institution allows for individual professors' copyright materials. If not, all course packages should become the property of the university, which—as mentioned above—should pay instructors fair and market salaries out of respect for their learning leadership.

The exceptional teachers in this study also deplored the rampant and systemic sexual abuse of students. One participant in this study decried the inertia of their academic institution to sanction professors who were featured as sex abusers of students in the aftermath of the publication of the *Sex for Grades* video by BBC. Respect for students who are at the center of the teaching business should be sacred. Again, it should begin with clear policies prohibiting any form of sexual harassment from the instructors, the staff, and the students themselves. Given the power play in this situation, academic institutions should prohibit or refrain from any form of sexual relationship between professors and students during students' academic years. Yet, the sensitivity of this matter also requires that the recalcitrant benefit from due process, and if found liable, be reported to the legal system for a follow-up process, whose endgame should be the protection and respect of all students. Our bright spots, like parents of young female students, know the pernicious emotional and psychological trauma students would go through for the longest time because of sexual exploitation for grades purposes. To gain respect also requires that one respects oneself. Although this assertion was not alluded to by the exceptional teachers in this study, all focus group students agreed to the fact that some female students—who are academically weak—provoke male professors and lure them into sexual relationships to get better grades. They recounted the story of one male professor who told a provocateur female student that he saw her as his daughter and was more interested in her brain than anything else. Such rare incidents of a few gregarious female students should not deter those who day in and day out strive to learn and succeed honestly. Academic institutions should also come up with policies sanctioning such gregarious behavior. However, students should abide by this timely recommendation from Fyodor Dostoevsky: "If you want to be respected by others, the great thing is to respect yourself. Only by that, only by self-respect will you compel others to respect you." Yet, the sacrifice of the one female student who participated in a focus group should be ever more praiseworthy and adopted for change to happen.

In chapter 3, I told the story of one student participant in a focus group for this study. Out of respect for herself, she refused to bribe her professors for grades; she refused to contribute to collecting group money to operate the "suivi" (follow-up) with the professor; she did not sacrifice her intimacy for grades; she accepted repeating a whole year, to undergo the ostracism from her own family; she finally passed the class with great respect for herself and from her peers. I believe some other students who are now voiceless are seeking the opportunity to stand against the lack of respect for their intelligence and their bodies. One can only imagine the day when most students will stand against academic abuses and say, "enough is enough." Figure 5.2 summarizes recommendations on how to show respect.

Service to Others

As noted throughout this book, exceptional teachers have championed altruism and its corollary service or stewardship (Bongila, 2013). Quella well underscored the purpose of teaching as a service. This is how she responded to the question, "why have you chosen to be a teacher?"

> I want to start with how this desire to become a teacher came about. Since my childhood I have always wanted to be of service to others since we grew up surrounded by precisely Protestant missionaries. This education allowed me to

Summary Recommendations for Showing Respect

- Pay the right salaries to teachers
- Celebrate World's teachers' Day – October 5
- Honor teachers as you would mothers
- Forbit financial, verbal, sexual exploitation of students
- Abolish the practice of "suivi"– following up teachers for grade adjustment
- Abolish sales of course packages by professors
- Discipline perpetrators of money and/or sex for grades
- Students to stand up against any form of exploitation

Figure 5.2 Summary Recommendations for Showing Respect.

> see the world differently in relation to my friends which created a climate of divergence. Already at school we always had divergent points of view in relation to life, in relation to some, in relation to education and these are elements that challenged me. Me, even if with my brothers and sisters in the family we had the same vision, I, personally, often asked the question to Dad: "But why did they not think or orient their thinking like us?" to this question we understood that education was for a lot because we received a solid education so I had this concern there I said to myself: "If friends don't have what we have, what should we do?" So, we have to share knowledge with them and that's how I've always been involved in groups, associations, sharing a little, showing our point of view or our vision to help solve certain societal problems. (Linda)

In *Grounding Ethical Leadership in African Diaspora and Election Rights*, Bongila wrote: Many scholars of leadership ethics, including Gilligan (1982) and Greenleaf (1977), have maintained that the primary engine of ethical leadership is service to others. For Senge (1990), the stewardship of leadership consists of clarifying and nurturing the vision set forth for the people, a vision that is greater than the individual ambitions of the leader. Greenleaf (1977) added the important aspect of waiting on the have-nots to the heart of servant leadership (p. 137).

Northouse added a relevant component to the understanding of the notion of service when he wrote that "leaders who serve are altruistic," placing the welfare of their followers foremost in their plans. In educational settings, one can observe altruistic conducts in several activities, such as when an instructor mentors, empowers behaviors, and engages in team building and citizenship behaviors (Kanungo & Mendonca, 1996). The exceptional teachers' teaching philosophies always included an element of service, which translated into the overall theme of altruism. Every single exceptional teacher who participated in this study indicated they are in this business to serve one way or another. As an overall recommendation to other teachers, Bill had this to say: "The interest should be providing the services more than the gains for the outcomes of your effort. So, it is for the good Lord to pay us for our services and for delivering the good message from him to his people."

However, the notion of service to people could be very diluted in many African traditions as it might apply in priority to one's restricted family members and friends. Bongila (2013) maintained the same claim when he presented a paper on "Understanding the Disparity between African and Asian Conception of the Common Good: Leadership Implication for Social Development" at the African Studies Association. This scholar argued that one of the African morality tenets about the common good (including education) is the greatest happiness and the good of the tribe as the end and aim of each member of the tribe (Gyekye, 2010). The standard of well-being, which includes economic happiness through education, is therefore utilitarian in African tradition. However, the governing academic and educational officials, and by extension instructors and teachers, do not seem to hold the duty of ensuring economic sustenance or good education to all people. Rather, such basic needs as food and education are provided by "He who supplies the needs of His creatures," understanding the higher being or God (Mbiti, 1999).

In most African traditions, service to others becomes, therefore, the duty to give preferential assistance to the members of one's family/tribe/ethnicity understood as the largest human community beyond the immediate extended family. Note that in Africa, ethnic identity refers to a group of people with common ancestry, language, symbol, and territory (Tarimo, 2008). The combined memories of the past and common expectations of one group constitute its identity. Therefore, the African conception of service and stewardship as applied to basic needs differs from that of Confucianism. On the one hand, Confucian teaching compels Asian leaders to care for the welfare of their people, understood ethnicity and country. On the other hand, traditional African leaders only prioritize the common identity of their immediate family, clans, and ethnicities. The traditional African leader does not feel the same urgency or duty to serve the larger community, including their diverse schools, colleges, and universities.

The above cultural underpinning should not justify or excuse the behaviors of most teachers who serve themselves rather than serving their students and the community good. Many factors other than a decaying traditional philosophy, egoism, and ethical gaucheness might account for the lack of teachers' stewardship in the Global South countries involved in this study.

Therefore, the exceptional learning leaders in this study should be commended for bypassing the nefarious aspects of the African tradition as depicted above. Taken at face value, that tradition would prevent them from serving all students, most of whom are unrelated to them by blood or friendship. It is critically important for the entire academic and educational leadership to be cognizant of the less-than-favorable conception of service and stewardship in traditional Africa, so they can serve their extended family, including the whole nation, particularly in this time of globalization. With that in mind, the well-informed teacher and professor will behave differently. Some recommendations follow.

Using the *African Baobab* tree model of decision-making, national, educational, and academic leaders should get together and reexamine the roots of African traditional philosophy about education service, which prevent policy-making and implementation of service and volunteerism. Of critical importance, these leaders would foster the extension of the utilitarian view of extended family to the duty of serving others for the common good. By nature, education is the best means to nurture engagement to the common good of a nation and of future generations.

Rather than requesting the favor of another colleague for their family members or close friend who failed in class, they will consider other parents' children who might be in the same situation but do not have the means and will to push their children forward even when they fail.

Those informed learning leaders (teachers, instructors, or professors) will refrain from contributing to lowering the standard of their children's education by requesting that they learn harder to perform well in the workplace instead of resorting to bribery and quid pro quo.

To ensure that their children receive a quality education in a harassment-free environment, teachers with means secure their admission to schools, colleges, and universities in Europe, Canada, and the United States. Instructors with financial means find it their duty to protect their children from sexual harassment, bribes, and the like, which are prohibited by school policies and are meticulously enforced. These learning leaders entrust the care of their children to the service of other instructors abroad. They could also serve their countrymen and women in the ways their counterparts do for their children. In the formulation of his categorical imperative, Kant espoused the golden rule to "do unto others as you would have them do unto you" (Mat. 7:12, Lk. 6:31).

Not only will ethical learning leaders extend the notion of the African extended family to their countries, but they will also practice the African virtue of *kimuntu,* or humanness, which includes service and generosity toward others. Writing about *Kimuntu*, Bongila (2013) argued that this foundational principle articulates the conviction that each African becomes a whole human being only in the fellowship of life with other people. Ideally, the *kimuntu* principle does not refer exclusively to members of one's own family, clan, and ethnicity, although these groups constitute the basis for larger relationships. Rather, it goes behind the close family ties to embrace the view that humans act more effectively when they hold fast to solidarity with their kind. It, thus, includes participatory compassion and charitable contributions that encompass universal perspectives to uplift the community and the country as a whole.

Not to mislead the reader; noticeably, the principle of *kimuntu*, as described clashed with the African tradition I discussed in the above section in that it goes further than the latter in its service to other human fellows. While *kimuntu* represents the ideal societal virtue, its practicality in African traditions is rather restricted. Therefore, exceptional learning leaders and I would recommend going back and implementing *kimuntu* in our dealings with students.

Concretely, when an instructor remembers to show *kimuntu* to their students, they stop their eagerness to collect money or other dishonorable services from students in exchange for grades. Instructors would remember to atone for the coins of the poor students' parents that made up their ostentatious houses, their expensive cars, and their unprofessional and unethical pleasures. They would strive to keep some of their children in local schools and colleges to ensure that they receive the same learning services as other students of the same education or academic levels. I summarize recommendations for rendering service to others in figure 5.3.

Justice and Fairness

The majority of the exceptional learning leaders in this study believed that it was fair to immerse themselves in the education of the students they pledged to educate fully. Some of them even believed they would cheat students should they not deliver on that pledge, which entails teaching them based on the money they (or their parents) paid and the dictates of their professional ethics. Others, who had their children in the best schools in the country or even abroad, also felt it was justice and fairness to treat others' children as their counterparts elsewhere were treating their own children.

Moore (2002) argued that as humans, we expect to be treated fairly and strive to treat others fairly. The opposite of fairness would consist of treating

Summary Recommendations for Service to Others

- Extend African utilitarian views of extended family beyond ethnicity
- Refrain from academic nepotism and favoritism
- Teachers should serve their country fellows based upon duty ethics: "Do unto others as you would have them do unto you" (Lk. 6:31).
- Educational leaders to extend *Kimuntu* – humanness – to include each student regardless of backgrounds
- Teachers/administrators should avoid quid pro quo in exchange for academic/pedagogic services.

Figure 5.3 Summary Recommendations for Service to Others.

people with favoritism or differently in the same situation. For a leader, being fair to followers can amount to taking disciplinary measures against those who misbehave while avoiding unequal discipline for the same issue across diverse followers.

Bongila (2013) wrote:

> An ethical leader practicing justice also places fairness at the center of the leader's decision making. The notions of justice and fairness work alongside each other, implying that no one should receive special treatment in normal conditions, except when an individual's particular situations demand it. . . . The core deontological and moral standard, held by most ethicists such as Kant, Rawls (1971), Shapiro and Stefkovich (2021), and others calls for reciprocity that is translated into the Golden Rule: "do onto others as you would have them do unto you." . . . The principles of distributive justice outlined by Beauchamp and Bowie (1988) . . . can serve as guidelines for ethical leaders in assessing fairly the benefits and burdens of external franchises. (Bongila, p. 138)

Those principles of distributive justice should apply, in different situations, to each person. They consist of "an equal share or opportunity," "according to individual need," "that person's rights," "individual effort," "society contribution," and "merit or performance" (Northouse, 2022, p. 437).

The exceptional teachers in this study have also lamented the unfair treatment they received from their colleagues, parents, educational officials, and sometimes students just because of their rectitude. Verbal abuses such as "Do you think you will be the one to change this system?" are frequent. Expectations are that every learning leader should be ethical because of the nature of their impeccable interactions with students. However, it appears frequent for teachers to display unfair and unjust behaviors. Therefore, I recommend that leaders of educational systems put in place policies, including a clear teachers' code of conduct, and organize workshops and retreats on leadership ethics in education. A review of the policies on collegiality, teamwork, and ethics of justice, to mention a few, will help to build a bridge of understanding among colleagues and erase the unfair treatment of those who excel as ethical leaders.

As discussed in the case of respect, justice and fairness should start with offering teachers and professors fair market salaries. In countries like Uganda, the officials must revisit their policy that gives unfair advantages to science teachers over liberal arts and social science counterparts. Huge gaps and unbalanced benefits between the two groups of colleagues create resentment and unhappiness among teachers that unfairly affect the learning of students.

Justice demands educational institutions enact a policy that restricts university professors from being full-time at mulitple institutions at once unless they receive explicit written authorization to help one other institution on a part-time basis. Because professors cannot bilocate or be present at several universities at once, they pick and choose institutions according to their time, their state of mind, and their health. This practice fuels professor absenteeism, lack of preparedness, and serious pedagogical delivery issues.

This study recorded several accounts of teachers and instructors who held students' grades hostage to receive unfair emoluments in terms of bribery and sexual favors. Students in a focus group even recounted the story of professors in crowded classes of over 500 students. Unable or unwilling to go over students' final papers, they designed an answer sheet and gave it to a relative or even a street merchant to do the correction and hand the teacher the final grades. What usually happens is that the grader would secretly inform students that he had their papers and solicit several of them, ten to twenty depending on their greed, to contact him/her with a certain amount of money in exchange for a passing grade. The higher the amount of money, the better the grade. The grader might not have time to correct all the papers. They would make sure those from whom they received the cash passed the exam and then "too bad" for the rest. Being strangers to the subject matter, those graders would not know all the nuances of the discipline to assign the right grades. Most students were penalized, especially the brilliant learners who worked honestly, expecting to pass the class. Many students would pass who did not deserve it, while others would fail the class and possibly repeat the whole year because of careless professors.

Justice demands that students speak up and raise their voices against these unfair and unjust practices, particularly those of "grades for sale." Their silence will only be complicit in the endemic erosion of the whole education system and undermine their future.

Justice demands that the officials—most of whom are aware of this horrendous practice of trading and selling grades—take quick action to eradicate it. Since individual students would be scared to speak about this system, which will punish them, the authorities could conduct focus groups with students from various institutions, as I did for this study. They will gather workable data that should prompt swift measures, leading to warnings, putting on leave, or the dismissal of the perpetrators, depending on the gravity of their liability.

It is paramount that the D.R. Congo eliminate the practice of "grade retention" in higher education. Neither Ghana nor Uganda hold such policies at the university level. Mainly used for primary and secondary education in many countries including the United States (Education Endowment Foundation, 2022), the process of grade retention or grade repetition forces students to repeat a grade after failing the previous year. As an alternative, some countries have opted for a policy of social promotion, which emphasizes the importance of students staying within their same age group. Debates about using one system or the other are looming depending on necessities.

However, this practice seems very uncalled for at the higher education level—at least—in the universities involved in this study.

I salute some experimental curriculum reforms in some countries that will—among other elements—get rid of the widespread policy of "grade retention" at the college or university levels. It stands as ethically fair to students, parents, and the community at large to abolish that archaic tradition. The practice of grade retention requires college students to repeat a whole academic year because they failed a few courses. A student could fail two to four major courses out of a nineteen-course coursework and be forced to repeat the whole year and retake the nineteen courses, including the other fifteen to seventeen subjects they had passed. Many ill-intended instructors take advantage of this policy to entice students to bribe them one way or another for fear of repeating a whole year, with all the financial, social, and psychological implications that come with it.

Table 5.2 represents this corrupt and unfair grade retention in higher education in the D.R. Congo. All begins when a student fails or is failed (by the professor) in two or more core classes. This failure prompts the student to prepare for a follow-up (suivi) with the professor to improve their grade. To protect their reputation, the professor does not appear to be expecting bribes or sex from students. Did not Machiavelli have it that the Prince should appear to be virtuous? But they have tacitly or overtly directed students to their mediums, usually their assistants or family members in charge of collecting money and other low services. The poor student should be looking for means to please the professor of one course before moving to a second, and the following professors depending upon the number of courses they failed.

The worst implication consists of forcing the whole social fabric into academic corruption: students are scared to repeat the year; parents become unnerved to spend twice for tuition, room and board, and transportation; siblings blame the increased household scarcity on their brother/sister who dares to accept repeating a year; the repeating sibling is looked upon as a failure or incapable of maneuvering their way to academic success. All the above implications, and others, constitute a complex recipe for systemic academic corruption. The price for exceptional teachers who do not participate in this systemic corruption is scorn and hatred from the administration and their colleagues. They all see them as uncompromising and uncooperative, a showy bunch of hypocrites.

As a note of caution, it is fair to acknowledge that a few institutions, particularly those run by religious organizations, intentionally and often successfully resist and fight the rampant cycle of corruption detailed in table 5.2. For example, there have been some rare accounts of professors who have been sanctioned because of their unprofessional behaviors. Also, a law professor advised that the grade retention policy is likely not to be retained in the experimental revision of the national curriculum in the D.R. Congo. However,

Table 5.2 Corrupt and Unfair Grade Retention in DRC's Higher Ed.

Systemic Corruptor	College Grade Retention	Beneficiaries
How does this corrupt system work?	Student fails or is failed in 2+ classes; Student prepares for "suivi" or follow-up, requests money from parents; Professor hides behind mediums (assistants, parents, friends to request bribery or sex); Student finds mediums and pays the bribe (cash and/or sex); Student secures passage of the class; The student repeats the cycle with other courses they failed; If the above fails, the student repeats the academic year and retakes all passed and failed courses	Unethical Professors
What perpetuates this unjust system?	Unhinged Instructors; Administration silence; Students' fear of repeating a school year; Parents' pressure not to repeat; Siblings and colleagues' pressure; Students' fear of being looked down upon; Students' fear of being singled out	Unethical Leadership
System losers	Scorned exceptional teachers; traumatized students; ruined parents; cheated country; sacrificed next generations	
Beneficiaries		Corrupt & Unethical Instructors

before then, it is imperative to grow the pool of exceptional teachers, exceptional universities, and exceptional students for the change to happen.

Show Honesty and Integrity

The main criteria for the selection of the participants in this study was their integrity in the teaching profession, which their school and academic communities confirmed through their recommendations. Asked what they thought about being recognized by their communities as people of great integrity, some of them said they were surprised that people even noticed their performance. For others, it was only a fight against the anti-values of corruption, harassment, absenteeism, bribery, and the overall spoliation of educational institutions. They believed that ethical leaders ought to oppose these with strong integrity, honesty, and trustworthiness (See Figure 5.4. Recommendations for Honesty and Integrity).

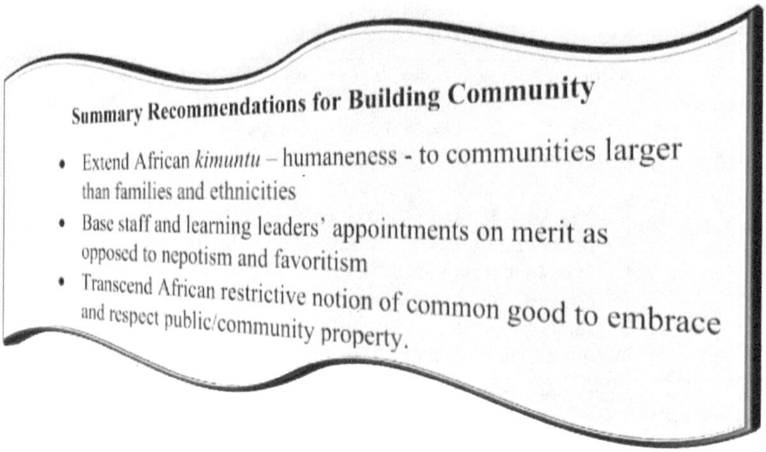

Figure 5.4 Summary Recommendation for Honesty and Integrity.

Various participants' accounts evidence these values. Take the example of Antie, who reported that some of her students said they came to class not because of academic obligation, but because of who was teaching the class. Her integrity attracted students to her class. She pursued:

> Maintaining my integrity is key. That's me personally. Because there are so many people who can lose their integrity when it comes to hardships. But the way we are trained cannot allow us. . . . You feel you are cheating; you feel you must fulfill your duty so that you get a better society. Suppose you cheat for a student. The following day how would the student judge you? Ask yourself those questions and you feel you need to maintain professionalism. (Antie)

African traditions recognize the necessity of teaching the value of integrity to children early in their young age so that they will not lose their moral compass. No wonder African proverbs frequently remind children that "a liar is a thief" and "a person who always lies about being attacked by a leopard will be killed by a leopard" [because no one will believe them the day the leopard really attacks them]. To be a good person or a good leader means to embody truthfulness and honesty, and therefore become a person of integrity. "To be a good leader, one must be honest" (Northouse, p. 437). Moore (2002) adds that honesty feeds directly into trust, and the ability of the leader to discuss openly and honestly important issues around them is key to the integrity of relationships. Jaksa and Prichard (1988) analyzed the importance of honesty by considering its opposite: dishonesty. For them, dishonesty is a form of lying, a way of misrepresenting reality. A dishonest leader projects their image as being undependable and unreliable. The consequence of a leader's dishonesty is the loss of faith in them by their followers. Being honest goes further than just telling the truth. In their book, *The Ethical Imperative,* Dalla Costa (1998) made the point that not deceiving is one thing, being honest is another and more. Concretely, for the leader, being honest means the following: (a) promise only what you can deliver; (b) represent facts accurately; (c) be upright, meaning avoid hiding "behind spin-doctored evasions"; (d) embrace obligations; (e) open up to accountability; (f) ensure that business pressures from the most powerful do not excuse you as a leader from the responsibility to respect the dignity and humanity of one another. Furthermore, according to Dalla Costa (1998), the organization should uphold the duty of recognizing and acknowledging the necessity of honesty. Additionally, it should reward honest behaviors within the institution.

Dalla Costa's above taxonomy should help to examine the question of how the exceptional leaders in this study showed integrity, honesty, and trustworthiness. I believe the promise they made to themselves and to the institutions they served was included in their teaching philosophy, which was deemed altruistic as a research of data analysis. Because some form of altruism involves self-sacrifice (Mangone, 2020), it is fair to infer that the exceptional teachers went beyond their call of duty to fulfill their promise. The facts participants presented in this study zeroed in on the challenges they faced as a consequence of their integrity. Those challenges were common knowledge in their educational environments, and the individual threats they faced were realistically the result of both their steadfastness and the logical implications of those challenges. These teachers stood against unethical behaviors and actions that tarnished the sanctity of the education profession. They did not follow Machiavelli's advice to the Prince that he should pretend to be virtuous whenever necessary. Their communities recognize them as authentic, upright, and ethical leaders. They embraced and went above their obligations to work professionally and morally for the learning of their students. They met the moral imperatives of classroom leadership (Fullan, 2003). Their reputable standing was a statement of their accountability as students appreciated their class and flocked to them in times of crisis. For example, when students learned about BBC's (2019) "Sex for Grades" featuring prominent professors at Ghana University who sexually harassed female students, groups of students quickly consulted with trusted instructors. They chose instructors based upon their proven accountability in this area, which over time has translated into openness and trustworthiness.

Because corruption in education can be systemic in several institutions, one can only imagine the tremendous pressure the exceptional teachers were under when an injunction would come from the upper hierarchy to act in an unethical fashion. Fortunately, they resisted those pressures, oftentimes at the risk of losing their jobs. One can only wish that all the educational and academic institutions where the exceptional teachers and others operate upheld integrity to the highest esteem and implemented mechanisms for rewarding it. A few recommendations can emerge from the behaviors of the exceptional learning leaders as far as their integrity and honesty are concerned.

First, it would be a wonderful activity for educational institutions to identify these usually voiceless ethical leaders and give them a voice. One way of doing this would be to invite them to mentor, coach, or assist other instructors who might be struggling in one way or another. Three potential benefits can emerge from promoting the voices of these exceptional teachers. First, as Dale Carnegie (1998) would maintain, there is nothing that a human would crave than honor. Recognize the integrity of these teachers, and their numbers will blossom through an osmosis process (Bandura, 1977). Second, you would apply the major advice of Tom Rath in *Strength-finders* (2007), which is to tap into a human's strengths rather than failures. The exceptionality of the participants in this study lay in their integrity to the job. An institution would strengthen that area for the teachers and their colleagues if it decide to give a voice to the exceptional teachers. Change should happen if you work from the bottom up (Bolman & Deal, 2021).

Some participants in this study reported that their institutions were forced to promote them to higher positions when they were faced with chaotic uncertainties. Participants' integrity became so evident and so handy that the administration had no other choice but to promote them. I applaud these institutions for recognizing order amid chaos (Rowe, 2023) and hope for the continuation of such positive change.

However, for those changes to take root, they should be paired with enforced integrity policies. Institutions could make sure that each year, teachers and instructors review and recommit to those policies, keeping the records in case of infringement. Some students who participated in focus groups reported a handful of schools that have implemented such zero-tolerance policies concerning student grade manipulation and grade trafficking. Ultimately, to avoid professors' feelings of impunity and to instill objective accountability, students must assess professors' teaching and behavior.

Every single university in the OECD countries, including the United States, and some institutions in the Global South countries of Uganda and Ghana, have adopted some form of accountability measure. In the United States, people are familiar with the Individual Development and Educational Assessment Survey (IDEA) that students are requested to complete at the end of each class to rate their learning on relevant course objectives, and the overall quantitative and qualitative performance of the teacher in the class.

This rating determines whether the course and/or the instructors are excellent, great, good, average, or mediocre. Instructors who perform poorly should receive mentorship. In the case of recidivism, poorly performing instructors should be either put on probation or dismissed. A student course evaluation of their professor will solve several issues that have plagued educational institutions and contributed to petty corruption. For example, instructors will not be able to hold several simultaneous teaching positions at various universities. They will realize that absenteeism, unprepared teaching, disrespect of students, and petty corruption will affect their performance. Poor performance is likely to be reflected in the students' survey of their course(s), which in turn will affect their annual rating as an instructor and bring about consequences that might include dismissal from the teaching profession.

The implementation and effectiveness of the proposed student survey of courses will ultimately depend on the seriousness of the administration in using it as one of the objective tools for teacher performance assessment. Should the administration somehow benefit from the systemic corruption described above and operate on a favoritism or nepotism basis, this call for accountability will remain muted, and the exceptional teachers unsupported in their resolve for integrity and steadfastness. On the other hand, and this is my hope, should the administration believe that professor accountability is a major way out of the pedagogical and academic ills of the moment, they should learn from Machiavelli:

> There is no more delicate matter to take in hand, nor more dangerous to conduct, nor more doubtful in its success, than to set up as a leader in the introduction of changes. For he who innovates will have for his enemies all those who are well off under the existing order of things, and only the lukewarm support in those who might be better off under the new. (Machiavelli, [1514] 1961, p.27)

Rather than discouraging the Prince (understanding education or academic administrators), Machiavelli invites them to be as bold as the exceptional teachers, go head-on against the anti-values, and reframe (Bolman & Deal, 2022) the crumbling educational systems. Those reprehensible and unethical behaviors include—but should not be limited to—teacher absenteeism, sale of course packages, sexual harassment, late arrivals, early departures, and "no call, no show." Honesty demands that students receive the required quality of learning they expect, which is a function of the professor's timely presence in class and dedicated teaching. As described earlier in this book, clear and enforced policies coupled with no-nonsense administrations can break the cycle of corruption, neglect, and abuse in the educational systems of Global South countries, particularly those involved in this study.

Students should reclaim their right to hold their instructors accountable for quality learning to happen. They should request and obtain the policies that present to them the steps to follow to report any form of abuse. Machiavelli's above statement applies even more dangerously to students who wish to report—say an instructor—who abused them. Students who participated in the focus group recounted that making such a report would backfire detrimentally for the student. They will undergo tremendous pressure from their classmates, other instructors, and—sometimes—from the administration, parents, and siblings. To avoid this boomerang effect, the majority of students have—unfortunately—resorted to passive resilience. However, students should remember the hero leaders of the past, including Rosa Parks (1913–2005), Martin Luther King Jr. (1929–68), Nelson Mandela (1918–2013), Steve Biko (1946–77), Mary McLeod Bethune (1875–1955), to mention a few, without whom there would only be socio-political status quos. I believe these heroes exist among current students because I trust that some of the women students will complete their education without bribing their instructors. They are heroes who deserve our praises. I also trust that some students have resented the systemic academic abuses to the point of becoming advocates of changes in education, just like Greta Thunberg has been fighting for better treatment of our ecosystem, and Malala Yousafzai for the education of girls in Pakistan and throughout the world. Figure 5.5 summarizes the recommendations for Building Community.

Summary Recommendations for Honesty and Integrity

- Spot and recognize voiceless exceptional learning leaders
- Establish and enforce integrity policies
- Implement student evaluation of professors at the end of each course
- Administration to be bold in making changes toward education as a common good
- Students to reclaim the right to hold instructors accountable

Figure 5.5 Summary Recommendations for Building Community.

Building Community

The exceptional leaders are resolute in their belief in a better future and in working toward it so that the materialization of a better community cannot be delayed. One explicated, "The future generation needs a role model. I would like to believe that it is we who must contribute to building a just society. It starts with a small step that everyone can take and when there are several small steps the world will change, and life will be better for all. Values must be defended at all costs in our community" (Quella). Building a community meets the goal of leadership, which is "a process whereby an individual influences another individual to achieve a common goal" (Northouse, 2022). This scholar adds that "achieving the common goal" gives an ethical dimension to leadership. When the leader takes into account both their purpose and that of their followers toward a direction that is beneficial to both of them, that individual encapsulates the essence of ethical leadership. The author also argues that building community and other principles of ethical leadership can vary from one culture to another. I rather like the nuance proposed by Resick, Hanges, Dickson, and Mitchelson (2006), who suggested that "ethical leadership dimensions of character/integrity, altruism, collective motivation, and encouragement were endorsed across all cultures but the importance of each dimension varied by culture" (Northouse, p. 439). Central to leadership ethics is the notion of a leader as a servant and custodian of the common good, understood as whatever contributes to the standard of well-being in the local or global community.

In the context of Africa, Kwame Gyeke (2010) makes the point about reciprocal obligations by using such Akan proverbs and maxims as "the wellbeing of a man depends on his fellow man." This particular wisdom-bound adage advances the fact that a community member can count on other members for goodwill, sympathy, compassion, and material support (Bongila, 2013). Gyeke argues that mutual aid constitutes a moral obligation for African cultures in general. For example, if a community member needs help on their farm, they are likely to receive that support from other members, who should expect the same behavior from him or her. The fundamental moral value in African ethics circles around altruism or *kimuntu*. *Kimuntu* is critical in that world because people can easily get overwhelmed by the contingencies of daily life. Additionally, states Gyeke, traditional wisdom requires one to share one's roof and food with a stranger.

Yet, Bongila (2013) had a note of caution about African traditional altruism—*kimuntu* as presented. First, in reality, the reciprocity wisdom does not go far enough to include people outside of one's extended family, clan, village, or ethnicity. Second, African tradition does not explicitly oblige leaders—in politics or education—to enter a reciprocal relationship with their followers, including students, to share material, psychological, and social values. This notion could emanate from the divine status given to leaders in African traditions. By extension, nowadays, professors with the highest university degrees are regarded as individuals set apart from the common people who might not have to share their *kimuntu* with their followers, the students. Third, many popular sayings about the common good depict the sad reality that any public good belongs to no one, understanding that no one takes care of the common good. Tarimo (2008) argues that "the African understanding of the common good is still limited to the framework of the ethnic community. That is why city dwellers are sensitive to the needs and interests centered on their village of origin and ethnic group" (p.12). People see the ancestors of their ethnicity as the guarantors of their traditional moral standards, including their needs and interests. It follows that the destruction or vandalism of a structure or work believed sacred to the ethnicity amounts to an infringement of the dictates of the ancestors. People are likely to respect their ethnic "communal goods" more than they would public treasures beyond ethnic boundaries. In a presentation at the African Studies Association in 2011, I posited that Asian leadership rooted in Confucianism (Bretzke, 1996) and its emphasis on stewardship has contributed to the socio-development of Asian countries. However, African philosophy may encompass elements that diminish leaders' responsibility toward public assets, including government, churches, and schools. Take the example of these typical sayings in some African cultures: "the good of the Church," "the good of the State," stressing that whatever belongs to the church, or the state is public property and therefore subject to carelessness. Similarly, a typical Congolese proverb could say, "You'd better strive to eat the food prepared by your own mother," [assuming one's mother's cuisine is not delicious] to mean that one is required to protect family patrimony at all costs. The rest of the public patrimony pales in comparison with the family or ethnic needs.

In reality, the treatment of the larger community's common goods, those usable beyond one's ethnicity, is often met with a hands-off attitude. No one takes ownership of those goods, and no one bothers much about them. When I take U.S. students to study abroad in Global South countries, we visit private and public schools, private and public hospitals, and private and public enterprises. Students are quick to notice the startling differences between the private and the public, with the latter often being in less-than-desirable conditions. Why? Because no one cares that much about what amounts to public property.

Fortunately, the exceptional teachers have transcended that restricted conception and practice of the common good to include those students who might not be related to them by blood or law. They have also taken ownership of the common good, which they strive to improve. More importantly, they endeavor to build a local community. Quella stated:

> I strive to show young people that excellence is possible, that you can work, win and succeed without relying on corruption but because you are better. If, on the contrary, you win because you have corrupted or relied on someone, tomorrow in working life, reality will catch up with you. That is the reason for my determination to make a change in our community. (Quella)

In chapter 2, I recounted the story of Friar Peter Tabichi, a teacher in a Kenyan village who won the prestigious Global Teacher Prize, and the "Nobel Prize in Teaching," in 2019. It is worth underscoring the reality that Tabichi was selected out of 10,000 teachers from 179 countries. The particularity of his story lies in two factors. First, as a simple rural teacher, the humble Tabichi managed to capture the attention of the entire world by being named the best learning leader in the world. Second, like the exceptional teachers in this study, his story is one of altruism (generosity/*kimuntu*) and a fierce steadfastness that transformed a community and inspired the world (African Impact News, 2019). Tabichi transcended the African tradition and practice of a restricted common good that involves only extended family members and friends to embrace a whole variety of students. He transforms the lives of the wider community because his generosity extends beyond the classroom to embrace education as a common good. UNESCO holds that maintaining education as a common good remains fundamental to ensuring equity and social justice while underpinning the human right to education (Locatelli, 2018). Tabichi has joined the bandwagon of exceptional learning leaders who empower the community through education and other social activities. A few recommendations are warranted.

Expanding *Kimuntu*'s Extended Family

As a follow-up to prior recommendations, it is paramount for the educational and academic leaders in the Global South to participate in what Bongila (2013) identifies as the *African Baobab tree* or public sphere (Habermas, 1991). Sequential reflection and decision-making forums from the lowest units such as schools, departments, and school districts to the highest ones like the country can yield critical pathways toward positive change in communities. Such change will begin with a reframing of African traditional features, including but not limited to the myopic notion of the "extended family" that prevents leaders and followers from looking past their kinship. They would make real the notion of "Ubuntu or kimuntu" with its idealized motto of "I exist because you exist" once the administration gives the tone by breaking the boundaries of kinship. As a consequence, teachers will teach students without consideration of their social, ethnic, or religious origins and status. Instructors would offer the same treatment to all students, those of their kinship as well as others whose origins are unknown or dubious to them.

Administrators will appoint teachers and headteachers based on their professional and moral merits, regardless of ethnic or tribal backgrounds. This particular recommendation to extend *kimuntu* to the largest community is neither utopian nor dystopian (Mohr, 2018) because exceptional leaders and learning leader Tabichi have exemplified it. The attitude of these learning leaders has met the core characteristic of transformational leadership, as Northouse (2022) explains, paraphrasing Burns (1978) as saying that such leaders move the group in a direction that is beneficial not only to the leader but particularly to the followers. In this globalizing world, teams need diversified teammates to function efficiently, each bringing a different type of skill.

Like Confucianism (Bretzke, 1996), African philosophy should be reshaped to make it shameful and horrific for family members, relatives, and ethnic groups to accept undue favors from corrupt leaders who do not move forward the causes of the whole community. It is critical to build on other African values that foster broader visions, including proverbs such as this: "If you travel alone, you will go fast; but if you travel in a group, you go far." However, for such a group to perform effectively, the merits of each community member ought to take precedence over kindred affinities.

Transcending the African Notion of Common Good

To combat the accepted insensitivity toward the abuse of common properties, particularly those committed by educational and academic leaders, will require a whole change of mentality. The exceptional teachers in this study and the best teacher in the world, Tabichi, offer concrete examples of African learning leaders who have transcended the traditional African restrictive notion of the common good. Quella exemplifies her contribution to education as a common good as she states:

> I have just finished my course at the University of The Common Good (pseudonym). There I correct the students' tests while I have not yet received the envelope of my services, but it is not the essential, the essential is first communicating knowledge, transmitting what I know to others, and giving the best of myself to continue a chain but if I put money in the foreground, it will be a problem on how to salvage our wrecking education. I must do it out of love for future generations. (Quella)

Tabichi's award saw him win the coveted title and a prize of $1 million. He did not use this money for his immediate extended family or his ethnicity. Instead, he used it to build a computer laboratory at Keriko Secondary School, sponsor students in need, create programs to motivate fellow teachers, and establish an agricultural project to benefit the local community. I believe he poured this money into education because he saw it as the ultimate common good. The hope is that other teachers and community members will follow the pathway of these role models to empower small communities and work toward education as a common good for all. Locatelli (2018) agrees that empowering communities to make important decisions about the institutions in which they live is probably the most effective way to make educational opportunities and governance more sustainable and equitable (p. 12). At the same time, the author acknowledges the challenge of identifying context-sensitive solutions that contribute to a paradigm shift.

I believe the community in which Friar Tabichi invested much of his $1 million prize to build a computer lab will protect this precious gift as their own. I guess that the community, the school district as well, and the school established various small committees, each with the responsibility to care particularly for a specific area of the laboratory, from keeping it clean and fire-proofed to protect the valuables against potential vandalism and theft. A community like a school district could endeavor to award a competitive teacher of the year award and then give the name of the laureate to a classroom. The teacher of the year would symbolically own the class. The laureate would teach the majority of their courses from that classroom, provided that they take sparkling care of the class and urge students to do the same. Owning a classroom students who follow their example would give them a sense of entitlement and lead students to see in that classroom a real good for the community. Academic leaders willing to make a difference can be creative in their own right to empower students. This empowerment can consist of assigning the care of small units of the college (library, computer lab, recreational areas, and others) to the care of small committees or teams of students. Although this service will look like volunteerism, each committee will have to report to managers or leaders with more power than that committee. Students are likely to take care of the goods entrusted to their care when they feel a sense of entitlement and ownership.

Operating a paradigm shift in Global South's schools and colleges to better care for the common good constitutes a dynamic process that requires continuous examination considering changing times. Tensions will arise even from the small care committees of teachers or students I have proposed. Yet, tensions provide opportunities for all to work synergistically to care for any public and/or common good. In the words of Locatelli (2018), "empowering communities to make important decisions about the institutions in which they live is probably the most effective way to make educational opportunities and governance more sustainable and equitable" (Locatelli, 2018, p. 12).

CONCLUSION

In this chapter, the silent steadfastness of the exceptional teachers has spoken to all through the implications of their behaviors and messages. Those messages have yielded some recommendations for various educational and academic institutions in the Global South and, by osmosis for those in the Global North as well. The exceptional learning leaders in this study ought their exceptionality to generosity, better identified as altruism. They are, above all, ethical leaders because they embody the five major tenets of leadership ethics, including respect for fellow humans, serving them, treating them with justice and fairness, and building community.

Although Friar Tabischi did not participate in this study, his behavior toward his students in rural Kenya, and particularly the use of his $1 million award for the best teacher in the world, makes him an exemplary and ethical learning leader similar to the exceptional teachers in this study. When considering the professional contexts of these ethical leaders and their heroism in the teaching profession they so enjoy, every ethical leader should pause. These teachers' behaviors constitute an incentive for those in the Global South countries and particularly in the OECD countries like the United States to stay in the profession. They are calling for a change in the treatment most instructors in the Global South inflict on students, who also deserve respect due to our common "*kimuntu*" or humanity. Educational and academic administrators should meet under the African Baobab trees and fight against the multifaceted abuses that devalue education, which is rightly considered a common good. These teachers are certainly operating in conditions worse off than those in which their OECD counterparts work. If the former can remain steadfast and function with integrity, their messages and acts should be an incentive for many to stay in the profession. In turn, not only do these ethical leaders deserve our consideration and respect, but they ought also to be treated with justice and fairness. In addition, their example of honesty and community building should be moved past the simple African practice of the "extended family" and "the common good" to include the larger community of our nations and our globe.

Conclusion

The foundational disciplines of this *magnum opus* revolve around the still-evolving ethical leadership, global leadership, and educational leadership, given their influence on my teaching and professional engagement. In particular, I situated the topic of this study within the ongoing discussion on teacher attrition and retention in the global contexts of the Global North and the Global South. For the former, I limited my comparative analysis to the OECD countries, while the latter included the three countries in this study, namely the D.R. Congo, Ghana, and Uganda. In these three countries, I examined the exceptionality of teachers in the Global South who have remained in their teaching positions despite facing socioeconomic hardship. The study was built on the premise that most participants would advance some form of ethical altruism (Ricard, Mandell, & Gordon, 2015) as the main reason for their unfailing pursuit of the teaching profession. I founded this preconception on my background in ethical and global leadership. Still, I used constant reflexivity approaches as demanded by qualitative inquiry (Merriam & Tisdell, 2016) to bracket myself to let the data—and not my preconceived idea—lead the investigation. The investigation shed light on the exceptionality of those exceptional teachers.

As the book concludes, my mind became fixated on the hypothetical question of what if we did not have any exceptional teachers because all teachers, instructors, and professors behaved like those in this study. The hypothetical would have defeated the purpose of this book as I would not have had the opportunity to dig out elements of systemic corruption in Global South education. Nor would I have described at length the unethical behaviors the exceptional leaders have avoided to keep their integrity and that of the profession they cherish. This book has put into perspective the plow of the voiceless heroes and their tenacity in the face of social and systemic adversity. Yet, the reality is the participants in this study constitute a tiny bright spot. In line with Foucault (1995) and other critical theory experts (Adorno, 1973), I brought to the surface some unfortunate conditions that created the exceptionality of the learning leaders who participated in this study. Using a critical pedagogy lens, I hoped to let the readers and those with political and educational power take it from there and initiate the necessary change. However, the ethical leader in me called for recommending some honorable means that should lead to implementing practical change and the emergence of more exceptional teachers. They constitute a bright spot in the Global South's chaotic whirlpool of educational leadership. Besides the practical recommendations suggested in chapter 5, the change this study is proposing consists of a call to action to increase the pool of the current exceptional leaders. I agree with Caroll Galligan (1982) that ethics of care should be central to those who want to join the pool of exceptional teachers who demonstrate both care and altruism.

INITIATE CHANGE

As concerns change, Psychologist Jonathan Haidt (2021) used an analogy of the elephant and its rider to explain two independent systems at work at all times in our brain. First, there exists the emotional side, which constitutes the part of the instinctive individual that feels pain and pleasure. Second, there is the rational side of the brain, also referred to as the reflective or conscious system. This side of an individual is in charge of deliberation, analysis, and looking into the future. Haidt (2021) calls the emotional side the elephant and the rational side the rider. For change to take place, both the emotional and rational sides of an individual should collaborate to get on the path together. The rider takes the lead in responsibility and direction and appears to be in charge. However, in the event of a disagreement between both, the elephant usually wins.

Chip and Dan Heath (2010) build on this analogy to talk about directing the rider. In their *New York Times* No. 1 bestseller book titled *Switch: How to Change Things When Change Is Hard,* the authors indicate that the Rider is the rational brain responsible for planning and direction. However, the Rider can become paralyzed by overthinking things and motivating the Elephant, the emotional brain, which prefers quick gratification over the long term but can also get things done. To make sustainable change, one should first direct the Rider while avoiding the paralysis of figuring out how to measure intangible things like knowledge-sharing success. Then, get the elephant and the rider to happily go on the path together. The authors identify three areas that can foster individual change. First, there should be a long enough cooperation between one's emotional side, "The Elephant," and their rational side, "The Rider," for the desired change to occur. Second, there needs to be the existence of an appropriate surrounding environment, also known as the "Path." Third, behavior can change if the individual directs the Rider, motivates the Elephant, and shapes the Path. The authors posit that someone must start acting differently for anything to change.

The change framework Chip and Dan Heath (2010) utilized in their book can rightly apply to the case of the exceptional learning leaders in this study. The Rider portrays the educational leadership or the administration who are also thinkers of systemic change within education and academic institutions. As indicated in chapter 5, the gathering of the administration under the African Baobab tree should become the locus of the rational brain, which sets the guidelines and policies for the renewal of educational systems in the Global South. Most of their guidelines will consist of various ways to bring on board the huge number of other players, including teachers and professors who have become comfortable with the status quo. In proposing that the administration play the role of the Rider, I remain cognizant that not all members of a given administration would behave in a rationally leading role. However, given the authority power (Bolman & Deal, 2021) granted to them, one would concede them the role of riding the rest of an educational institution that appears to linger in apathy.

The Elephant represents a good portion of the teachers, instructors, and/or professors who feel comfortable with their country's chaotic state of education. This emotional brain of the institution encompasses the majority of those teachers and instructors who prefer quick personal gratification and are likely to succumb to petty corruption, including bribery, money, and sex for grades. This does not mean that unless one is an exceptional teacher, one would embrace unethical behaviors. Do not get me wrong. On the one hand, I concede that many teachers at present would not make the pool of those I have called exceptional teachers in this study, mainly because of the high standards I set for this specific cohort. However, on the other hand, I believe in the existence of a considerable number of teachers who behave ethically but would still fall among the elephant or emotional brain category. The rationale lies in that those learning leaders feel comfortable with the status quo in the educational systems in their respective countries. For example, they would not go the extra mile to advocate for the teachers' salary increase or fight to end the horrific practice of trading grades with unethical practices.

The Path can represent both the social and economic conditions that are ripe for change as well as the path already paved by the exceptional teachers through their ethical behaviors. For the educational administration under the baobab tree (Bongila, 2013), this means that wanting the rest of the teachers (Elephant) to exhibit certain behaviors would require removing the points of friction that keep them from choosing the right behaviors that have characterized the exceptional teachers. In essence, the exceptional learning leaders represent the path toward the ethical change an institution should desire. In many instances, the educational leadership (administration) appears to be in charge—as it should—at least in the contexts of the Global South countries involved in this study. However, experience has it that most of the faculty (Elephant) always win in conflicts between both. A case in point is that of the D.R. Congo, where the administration decided to abolish the practice of selling course packages to students because it maintained a systemic injustice against students who did not have sufficient means, gave an undue favor to professors, and maintained systemic corruption. This decision died upon arrival: the faculty (Elephant) perpetuated the same practice by changing its wording. Instead of "course package sales" (which the administration prohibited), they have called it "paying for the right of the author," who happens to be the course package designer and, therefore, the professor. The Elephant has won again. Chip and Dan Heath (2011) would argue that change fails because the academic administrator in charge (the Rider) cannot keep the faculty (the Elephant) on the road long enough to reach the destination. Additionally, say Chip and Dan Heath:

> When people try to change things, they're usually tinkering with behaviors that have become automatic, and changing those behaviors requires careful supervision by the Rider. The bigger the change you're suggesting, the more it will sap people's self-control. And when people exhaust their self-control, what they're exhausting are the mental muscles needed to think creatively, to focus, to inhibit their impulses, and to persist in the face of frustration or failure. In other words, they're exhausting precisely the mental muscles needed to make a big change. (Chip & Dan Heath, 2011)

One would contemplate various changes based on the exceptionality of the participants in this study, and the cultures in which they operate. Further consideration of the recommendations proposed in chapter 5 can yield changes at the individual, organizational, and cultural levels. Each category might contain behaviors that are deemed automatic, while some would be significant enough to consider tackling immediately. Regardless of the size of the issue, change processes can be scheduled on a long-term, mid-term, and short-term basis depending on the importance and urgency of the matter. I agree with Chip and Dan Heath (2011) that the administration (the Rider) should tactfully approach challenging behaviors and proceed from smaller to bigger ones. These authors also underscore the fact that decisions are the Rider's turf, which requires careful supervision and self-control.

Table 6.1 represents a sample of the key changes that need to happen to redecorate the blazon of educational leadership in the Global South within the scope of this study. I listed issues in terms of my perceived order of importance

Table 6.1 Sample of Changes Needed

Issues in Order of Importance	*Individual Change Timeframe*	*Organizational Change Timeframe*	*Cultural Change Timeframe*
Spotting & recognition of voiceless exceptional learning leaders		Short Term	Short Term
Right salary for teachers		Short Term	Short Term
Policy enforcement on financial, verbal, sexual abuses of students	Short Term	Short Term	Short Term
Abolition of student grade retention		Mid-Term	Mid-Term
Implementation of student evaluation of professors		Mid-Term	
Pompous celebration Teachers' Day		Mid-Term	Mid-Term
Teachers/administrators to extend *Kimuntu*—humanness to include each student regardless of backgrounds	Long-Term	Long Term	Long Term
Conduct student-focus group on academic challenges		Short Term	
Policy on one-professor, one-institution		Long Term	

and indicated whether change should be made at the individual, organizational, or cultural levels. I also added an estimated time frame to process each issue. For example, it is critically important that organizations and communities spot and recognize the voiceless, exceptional teachers who are the driving force behind a reframing (Bolman & Deal, 2022) of educational and academic systems. Next, in order of importance, are the right salaries for teachers, which should be dealt with in the short term. Enforcing policies on the financial, verbal, and sexual abuses of students—wherever they exist—and creating new ones where they are absent appears to be one of the most important issues to address in a very short term at all levels (individual, organizational, and cultural). Although important, a policy on one-professor one-institution might be dealt with in the long run by institutions of higher learning as it sounds complex and big. Rightfully, Chip and Dan Heath (2011) advised that big problems rarely get solved with commensurately big solutions. Rather, institutions of higher learning can solve this particular issue of one-instructor one-university by a sequence of small solutions over periods. Issues such as this requires a careful analysis, which ethical leadership offers.

When it comes to solving such complex issues or dilemmas, which should allow the Rider to provide clear directions to the Elephant, leadership ethics comes in handy. In particular, a methodology for solving ethical dilemmas used by Kramer and Enomoto (2007) and Bongila (2013), consisting of

Description, Interpretation, Rehearsal, and Rediscerment (DIRR), constitutes an ultimate tool for sound leadership directions based on ethical decision-making (see figure 6.1).

As is often the case in qualitative methodologies, Description refers to the first step of the ethical analysis. It includes exhaustive details of the situation, the environment, the location, and the stakeholders involved in the dilemma. The researcher gathers information to answer questions similar to: What is at stake? Who is involved? When, and where it happened? After Description comes Interpretation, the second step of ethical analysis. It is conceived as an exploratory attempt to theorize the dilemma through ethical language. It also serves to identify tensions among ethical standards and inquiries: what of the universal values versus desires, or what of the personal life/interest versus public life/interest is at issue? For example, one side considers that a policy of teaching at one single university should be upheld at all times, while another group maintains that university teaching is a liberal profession. They argue that the number of universities where an instructor can offer their courses should be left to each professor's discretion. There appears to be tension between the two groups of stakeholders. Enomoto and Kramer (2007) argue

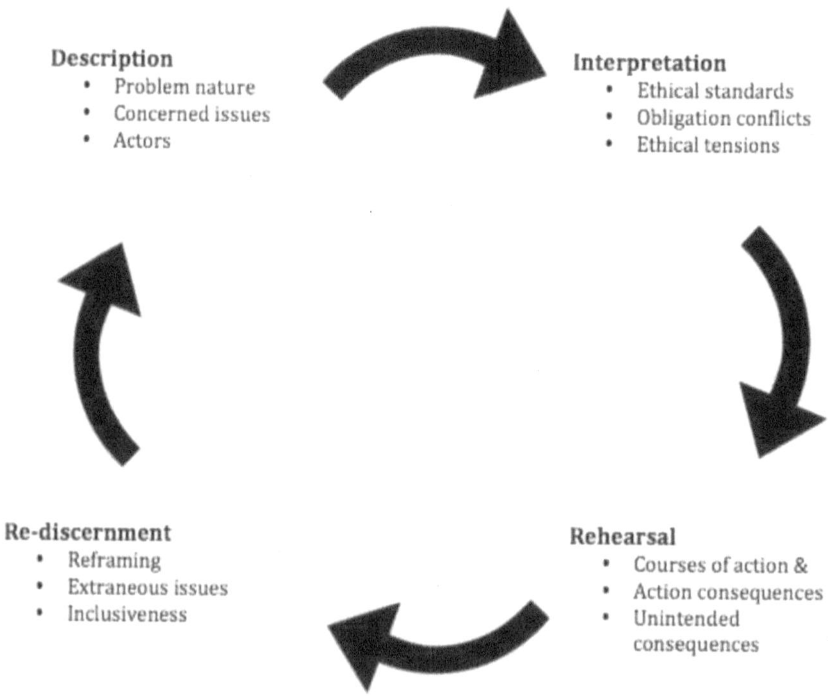

Figure 6.1 DIRR Steps of Ethical Decision Making. Source: Enomoto & Kramer, 2007.

that Interpretation calls for the examination of ethical standards, including what is virtuous for individual members versus what is virtuous for the group or whether it is a question of duty versus utility.

The third step in the DIRR is Rehearsal. It consists of laying out all possible courses of action, namely all decisions that can be taken as a result of the dilemma analysis. Enomoto and Kramer (2007) maintain that the above analysis of the tensions between ethical standards prepares the leaders to predict what might occur given the wants and desires, as well as the duties and responsibilities of those in the decision-making process. In addition, leaders would be able to carefully scrutinize the positive and negative consequences, including long-term and short-term outcomes, of each possible course of action. Rediscernment is the fourth and last step of this ethical process. It requires that the leader reframes the dilemma in more vivid and creative language, such as a simile, a metaphor, and other visual techniques. Bongila (2013) asserts that this step presents a synoptic view of ethical tensions, consequences, and possible decisions. It also encompasses all viewpoints after giving them due consideration in resolving the dilemma in question. Rediscernment, or the revision of the picture of the dilemma, might prompt the leader to consider extraneous elements that can heighten the chances of compromise and consensus. Compromise points to the middle-ground viewpoint. It entails the loss or win of something by the parties involved, whereas consensus calls for better understanding the situation before taking action.

Although the DIRR method of solving the dilemma is not flawless, it would guarantee that the Rider who leads the discussion under the baobab tree provides the elephant (the rest of the faculty or teachers) with informed directions. Another important caution stems from the fact that not all the issues identified in table 6.1 comprise dilemmas, which can be defined as "a situation that requires a choice between options that are or seem equally unfavorable or mutually exclusive or problem that seems to defy a satisfactory solution." Furthermore, "a moral dilemma exists whenever the conflicting obligations, ideals, and consequences are so very nearly equal in their importance that we feel we cannot choose among them, even though we must" (Bongila, p. 6). Therefore, I posit that many potential changes I listed above would become moral dilemmas when digging into the details of their interpretation or implementation. For example, spotting and recognizing exceptional teachers should be a matter of common sense. A dilemma would appear when it comes to whether an individual teacher meets the moral and professional criteria to be recognized as such. Another example concerns creating or enforcing clear policies protecting students against any financial, moral, and sexual abuses. Presenting it as a "whether or not" dilemma would not be professionally or ethically acceptable. Rather, a dilemma can come from each violation case'sparticularities. For example, whether or not a particular teacher's behavior can amount to sexual harassment. While the policy should be unambiguous, cases that arise might present gray areas that call for the DIRR resolution.

Although using the DIRR does not make one become an exceptional teacher as defined within the scope of this study, the method encourages making decisions that take into consideration both the ends and the means and, therefore, eliminates the chances of erring. One of my graduate students who took my class on the Intellectual and Ethical Foundations of Leadership, in which I teach the DIRR method of decision-making, wrote the following in the course survey:

> If the day ever comes when I am the principal of an elementary school it will be my responsibility to lead in an ethical manner. . . . No matter what foundational approach I take when making decisions I will first need to view the dilemma using the DIRR model. This protocol will be extremely helpful because it is an established process used by leaders to gain better understanding of an issue and provides clarity for how to proceed. First, it will be important to describe the issue at hand and take time to think about all the key facts/players and what brought about the dilemma in the first place. It will be important to then Interpret what has been happening along the way based on conversations, observations, and data. Next, it will be crucial to take time to Rehearse, or in other words, think about all of the possible outcomes that could result from various scenarios. And finally, before any type of resolution or decision can be made, I must Re-discern or re-frame the original dilemma. Doing so will allow me to reflect on the entire process because certain aspects of the dilemma could have changed along the way or perhaps certain viewpoints or perspectives were missed and not taken into consideration. (Beekman, UST. Ed.S student) (Bongila, 2013, p. 5)

I doubt any of the exceptional teachers apply this peculiar method of decision-making in ethics. Nonetheless, I posit that their altruistic and caring approaches to leading the learning of students make them ethical leaders in their own right. The next section covers some takeaways from the exemplary leadership of those exceptional learning leaders in the Global South.

COURAGE UNDER DURESS

The example of Dindo comes to mind as he wondered whether his colleagues were right and he was wrong in his respect for academic norms, particularly about students' exams and grades. Dindo received countless voice messages and calls from his "trusted" colleagues at the end of each exam session. Some would request he meet with them about their niece, son, or family member who failed his course to readjust the grade and let them pass the class. Others would encourage relatives who failed Dindo's class to visit him with recommendation notes, some of which contained bribery money from students, parents, and other stakeholders. Worse, those unofficial recommendations even came from high-ranking administrators of his institution. The pressure was so intense that he wished to find an ally who would hold his moral values and teach integrity. There was none because the last professor he counted on for comfort and consolation had died under unknown circumstances. His late colleague's steadfastness and integrity only brought her scorn and hatred from most of the academic community. During a face-to-face interview with me, Dindo took his head in his hands and murmured pitifully, "I always wonder whether I am wrong, and they are right." My dismay was at its highest level as I told him that he was right and brave and that any chance of change could only come from the handful of ethical leaders like him who endeavor to become the path (Chip & Dan Heath, 2011) for others.

That the exceptional teachers demonstrated exceptional courage in the face of educational adversity constitutes an understatement. These educational heroes operate with moral courage, that is, with a willful intention to act and execute actions "after mindful deliberation involving an objective substantial risk to the actor, primarily motivated to bring about a noble good or worthy end despite perhaps the presence of the emotion of fear" (Rate, Clarke, Lindsay, & Stenberg, 2007, p. 95). As demonstrated in chapter 3, the exceptional teachers face a set of particular challenges beyond what the general population is accustomed to. No wonder, Ganu (2018) wrote that "Africa likely brings to mind mixed thoughts—corruption, ethnic violence, poverty, AIDS, malaria. . . . Many have attributed the challenges in Africa to a lack of ethical leadership; however, underneath ethical leadership is the moral courage to face those challenges" (Ganu, 2018). Harvard Business School (2022) came up with five characteristics of a courageous leader that suit the characteristics of exceptional leaders, namely authenticity, resilience, emotional intelligence, self-discipline, and commitment to purpose. Communities that recommended the exceptional teachers for this study did so because they recognized in them people who were true to themselves and demonstrated trust and performance. They showed resilience thanks to their capacity to endure great challenges and get stronger in the midst of them. It is safe to infer that the exceptional teachers relied on their emotional intelligence as they cultivated, enhanced, deepened, and learned to trust their self-awareness. They self-disciplined by acting with their calmest selves under a considerable amount of pressure. Finally, they showed commitment to the learning of their students and focused on working for the common good.

COMPARED WITH OECD CONTEXTS

Most learning leaders in the Global North are oblivious to the extraordinary pressure the exceptional teachers in this study go through day in and day out. The former benefit from the protection of their educational institutions through various enforced policies and laws, while the latter rely only on their conscience to keep themselves afloat. On the one hand, their conscience frees them from the heavy remorse one would feel for breaking ethical norms. On the other hand, it cannot always protect them against any form of peer pressure that can threaten their health and the cohesion of their families. Dindo's above example of his colleague who might have lost her life for pursuing what was deemed ethically laudable was very telling. Not to mislead the reader, professional codes of ethics and academic policies on grading, peer harassment—you name it, do exist—at least in the books of the educational and academic institutions of the Global South. Unfortunately, they are hardly upheld and often bypassed by those Riders who are supposed to enforce them. Note that those who trespass those policies often operate covertly for fear of compromising their already tarnished reputation if their turpitude becomes known to the larger community. However, they often find themselves shielded by the system that has become increasingly corrupt.

As previously stated, this study does not wish to paint all institutions in either the Global South or the Global North with the same brush because it only covered a few entities. Nor does it maintain that petty corruption does not exist in educational systems in the Global North because it does. There exist also questionable ethical practices in the United States, like sugar daddies, which female teachers use as an alternative coping mechanism to put food on the table. To my knowledge, no one has yet observed such a practice, at least in the three countries involved in this study. The difference, though, stems from the fact that academic systems in the OECD, to mention only this Global North organization, tend to enforce their policies and fear the laws. The literature I reviewed for this study has suggested that teachers' conditions worldwide show some similarities, with a few exceptions in countries that value education and treat their teachers well. Many voices have joined those of teachers to request better working conditions, particularly a marketable salary comparable to other professions with the same workload or same education level. Teachers' conditions vary from one country to another, from one state to another, and even from one school district to another within the same state or the same country. However, the gap in teachers' living conditions remains considerably large between the Global North and the Global South. When compared to their counterparts in the OECD countries, it is safe to infer that the working environment of the exceptional teachers in the D.R. Congo, Ghana, and Uganda is less than desirable. Their working conditions are calling for extraordinary changes, starting from their insignificant and sometimes delayed and absent salary. They are left to resort to alternative coping mechanisms that are ethically sound and admirable. In addition, this study has suggested that not only do the exceptional teachers in the Global South show profound care for their students, but they also go further to practice altruism because they love their profession and, above all, the students they have been called to serve and lead. I can only imagine that some learning leaders in the Global North, particularly those in the OECD and the United States, can be struck by the moving stories of these Global South teachers, who have chosen to stay firm in their decision to train future generations. A Global North teacher might think, "if they can remain in the job with their meager conditions . . . I could stay teaching because I am in a better condition, though not ideal." Those exceptional teachers truly represent bright spots whose ethical compass should invite people to rather inquire "how we can do more of it?" (Chip & Dan Heath, 2011).

EXCEPTIONAL LEARNING LEADERS' LEGACY AND EXHORTATIONS

The last two questions of the survey and interview I administered to the participants in this study targeted their legacy as well as their message to the larger community. Explicitly, the two questions read as follows: What do you want to be known for by future generations in your community and beyond? What message do you have for teachers in your area and worldwide who might be struggling to remain steadfast in their teaching because they face conditions similar to yours?

As Concerns Their Legacy

I noticed that it hurt their humility trying to talk about themselves. Understandably, the culture in which they grew up finds it boastful or bragging to put ostensibly personal merits on display. However, some reported that they wished to be known as a person of humility, which, for a participant, meant "being so down to earth, open to people, and socializing and associating with the members of my community around me." Most participants wanted future generations to remember them as people who helped others transform lives, especially people who have been in poor living conditions. Others desired to be recognized for helping people to reach some status. "That's what I want to be known for by the children that I've taught. If I can get a few people to recognize that in one way or another that I have made a contribution in their life, that will give me happiness" (Eliza).

Some of them explained the rationale behind their legacy wish:

> The reason as to why am saying that is I came from very far. I come from a very poor family background and I did not even expect to reach where I am. It might not be the best position, but at least I'm somewhere because people helped me and transformed my life. So, I feel I should be remembered for transforming people's lives. (Antie)

More importantly, these exceptional learning leaders hope future generations will remember them for having rendered loyal services with honesty and competence. "I want to be known as a visionary who saw beyond the present needs of my students in the classroom," said another participant. Still another said, "let people remember me as a teacher of integrity and dedication, rigorous in training, and transparent in evaluations." Finally, they wish future generations to know them for passing the torch of education, honesty, and integrity onto them. "May future generations continue the immense work of training real skilled people for our populations," concluded Quella.

Exhortations

The last question of my survey and interview concerned a message the exceptional learning leaders could have for other teachers throughout the world. I recall one participant who said they would not have any message for those colleagues in the world who do not have any regard for the teaching position, and who insult the core ethics of this noble profession by engaging in petty corruption. Having said that, the participant joined the other learning leaders' bandwagon to encourage teachers worldwide to love their profession, to see it as a vocation, and to give it precedence over money. Since this book has also aimed to provide a voice to those voiceless teachers, I summarized their message below after making sure I avoided obvious repetitions. Instead, I kept the substance and tone of their exhortations as they came out of the participants' mouths.

> Teaching is a vocation, and it should not only be on a monetary basis. Whoever does it as a job should follow the example of the great teacher Jesus who taught in his time and delivered the message as expected. So, it should not be attached only to monetary value as it is important for survival. So, the interest should be providing the services more than the gains for the outcomes of your effort. So, it is the good Lord to pay us for our services and for delivering a good message from him to his people.

I just encourage teachers who are on the verge of abandoning teaching to love their profession. Once you love this profession, you love your learners, you try as much as possible to treat them in a way that you would feel the best way. So, I encourage them to love their profession and also abide by that teaching professional code of conduct. I encourage teachers to remember why they went into teaching in the first place and know that the work we do is what keeps the world sane.

The message I have for teachers is if you don't love the job, you cannot deliver well either. If you're money-minded, you may not teach well. When you are in a private institution, salaries might be delayed, and if you are money-minded in that delay, you may do a disservice in the class. So, it's all about like you should love the job and you should accept to work in any condition, that's when you can deliver well.

I tell colleague teachers that teaching as a profession is a call from God as you are modeling many lives of people into better citizens. God will reward you, so I argue with them not to give up. Let's stay and do the work heartfully and tirelessly. Despite other challenges we face we know we have word repercussions at the end.

My Message for other learning leaders is: Abide by the essentials of our profession. You have to love this profession. I like to teach, to transmit what I have as knowledge to others, to love the people to whom we transmit, to have the desire to improve the future, to contribute to this education, and to transmit the values worthy of an integrating person.

Dear Colleagues, I exhort you to become increasingly aware that teaching is a really beautiful profession that gradually transforms children into competent men and women. And continue to practice this profession by participating in the work of empowering young people to rebuild our country. This is despite the limited material conditions and especially the lasting social insecurity.

The teaching profession is one of the few disciple-training professions, with the number of good disciples trained being the indicator of a good trainer. A student is a long-term investment. The benefits (honor and services to be enjoyed) of being a trainer far outweigh the small shameful benefits of anti-values. Let us be honest in the practice of our profession, and God will reward us justly.

> Scarcity of basic means. That's why they [other people] run away from the teaching. And even here [in the Global South], they do run away—many of them, but it's because we don't diversify the ways we look at our sources of income. We should look at how we do this as a vocation, and then look at how can we survive, and how can we sustain ourselves financially outside the teaching.
>
> We have not sold this profession to younger generations as a great and noble profession. And that is what we should do. And even let the children love the profession. We should sell the profession because most children we teach, you ask who wants to be a teacher. No. None of them wants to be a teacher. Why? Because we've not become their role models.
>
> Here is my message to those teachers who wish to quit: Teaching is a call and teachers ought to appreciate this call. For example, if we all quit, if there are no teachers, then who will take on the generations to come? It is a poor-paying profession. It is disregarded. Teachers are being abused here and there. But I think we have to go back to the roots and say supposed I was not helped, supposed I was not told abcd, how would I be? As we are looking at social status, we want to be rich, we can invest in some other investments as we protect the teaching profession. It is the mother profession of all these other professions. If the teachers are not there, who will teach the doctors? Who will teach the lawyers who teach? It is the basis of our society. . . . Whatever is going wrong in our countries, in our societies majorly it is the role of the teacher to amend that. So, we should love the profession with all that surrounds it, but you do not simply quit, but look at solutions to those problems. That is the message I have for the teachers: let's be those teachers who love our work and maybe fight to make it a better profession like other professions.

When Friar Peter Tabichi received the 2019 Global Teacher Prize, he made this proclamation about a bright future for African students and the education they have received as a means to reaching the common good:

> Every day in Africa we turn a new page and a new chapter. This prize does not recognize me but recognizes this great continent's young people. I am only here because of what my students have achieved. This prize gives them a chance. It tells the world that they can do anything.

Mr. Sunny Varkey, the founder of the Global Teacher Prize, seconded Tabichi's message by adding that his story was likely to inspire people who are thinking about joining the teaching profession. He proceeded by stating that the prize would shine a spotlight on the incredible work teachers, particularly those who lead learning with ethics and altruism, do in Kenya and elsewhere in the world.

Future Research Prospects

The attitude with which I started this book has shifted during the writing process, though my enthusiasm for putting on display the hidden perceptions of those who tacitly influence education in the best possible way has remained intact. Yet, I thought this book would be my *magnum opus* because it would exhaust most of my academic professional engagement, including four research areas: grounding ethical leadership, comparative educational leadership, organizational leadership, and the pedagogy of global positioning leadership. As I reach the end of this book, I realize that I have made great use of the first two areas, while the other two have remained almost untapped. I have hardly alluded to my organizational theory specialty or global positioning leadership.

Had I approached this research with the mindset of an organizational theory scholar, I would have conducted a case study (Yin, 2017) and delved into framing and reframing selected educational and academic institutions in the Global South. Bolman and Deal's (2021) four organizational frames (structural, human resource, political, and symbolic) would have provided the underlying theoretical framework to approach a study of that nature. When discussing Bolman and Deal's human resource frame, I would have dedicated a whole chapter to analyzing the particularities of the school or academic body, which could have led me to identify the exceptional leaders as potential outliers. Since my study did not address this topic, chances are that anyone interested would take it from here to develop a compelling future study.

I could have also used global positioning leadership (Bongila, 2017) as a framework for my coining. It is defined as a capacity that makes leaders aware of the socioeconomic contexts of both the Global North and the Global South position themselves globally. A study using this framework could have helped to examine the exceptional teachers in broader contexts of education, healthcare, economy, and governance. I would have engaged my graduate students who participate in my yearly study abroad in a Global South country as co-participants in a grounded theory study (Charmaz, 2014). Any other scholar can conduct such a study to dig out the real challenges of leadership that those exceptional learning leaders face day in and day out while looking for ways out.

The above potential studies would use qualitative inquiry methods with their richness in collecting the views and perceptions of the direct actors of the phenomenon. Other scholars who find issues with the reliability or transferability of qualitative studies could conduct case studies on what makes some teachers more exceptional than others. Scholars undertaking such a study might dovetail quantitative and qualitative approaches and sample teachers from more Global South countries and various educational and academic institutions.

The exceptional teachers have been identified as such for unethical behaviors they do not ascribe to and for the ethical conduct they excel in. Most of the unethical conduct participants stay away from has had consequences on them and constituted professional and ethical challenges. For example, by refusing to falsify student grades in exchange for money, sex, and peer recommendations, these teachers have met the scorn and hatred of a portion of their school and academic community. A quantitative or qualitative study can investigate the impact those challenges—including but not limited to student abuses and petty corruption—have had on the mental and social psyche of the exceptional teachers and/or their students. A study of the nature of ethical leadership could provide guidelines based on the ethics of utility, duty, virtue, and profession (Shapiro & Stefkovich, 2021).

This current study has suggested that exceptional teachers owe their exceptionality to their altruistic acts both in classrooms and off-campus. To a probing question of what ingredient of any nature compelled these teachers' altruistic behaviors, this investigation suggested there was an iceberg of altruism with an observable and an invisible side. Since this study only dealt with the visible portion of the altruistic behaviors the participants in this study displayed, another inquiry could gauge the invisible aspects of altruism that make them outstanding. Quantitative research could examine a large number of variables while a qualitative grounded theory could yield a theoretical understanding of the phenomenon of exceptional teachers' altruism.

Furthermore, participants in this study exhibited altruistic behaviors and engaged in benevolent actions despite experiencing social and professional duress. However, the study did not conclude that they were altruistic people because they reaped some form of personal benefit from their seemingly selfless actions and decisions. Participants' accounts revealed that both the teachers and the beneficiaries of their altruistic acts—their students—harness the power of altruism to aid in making the world a better place (The Decision Lab, 2022). Their altruistic actions included—but were not limited to—teaching students, volunteering, donating time and money, and working for organizations that focus on the common good. However, some studies have suggested that people who engage in altruistic behaviors can reap such benefits as better health, life satisfaction, and a high level of well-being (Mark Ottoni-Wilhelm, 2017). In line with the warm glow-giving theory (Mark Ottoni-Wilhelm, 2017), one can rightly ascertain that altruism made both the exceptional teachers (the givers) and the student (the receiver) feel good (The Decision Lab, 2022).

Furthermore, the warm glow-giving theory (Mark Ottoni-Wilhelm, 2017), according to which integrating altruism into daily lives yields some benefit to mental health and well-being, would explain that the joy and satisfaction the exceptional teachers felt from helping their students was their best reward.

Still, one could hypothesize that this theory also explains why the exceptional leading learners engaged in altruistic actions. A study of a quantitative nature could investigate the correlation between several actions that qualify as altruistic and their effect on the mental and somatic health of a larger population of teachers who are deemed exceptional. Additionally, a qualitative case study could examine participants' feelings after engaging in acts of benevolence.

Finally, the warm glow-giving theory holds that altruism is not necessarily "selfless or selfish." Yet, the self-accounts of the participants show their altruistic actions and decisions were more motivated by selflessness than selfish impulses. To the ethical dilemma of whether or not the participants' altruistic actions benefitted them more than they did their students, Aristotle's Golden Mean (Aristotle, trans. 2007) allows us to infer that both the giver and the receiver win, although to different degrees as discussed in the Two-way asymmetric model of philanthropy in chapter 4. The warm glow theory would argue that participants' help to their students resulted from genuine care for their well-being and the warm glow the teachers felt thereafter.

Appendix A

2018 Global Teacher Status Index

COUNTRY	INDEX RANKING	ACTUAL TEACHER SALARY ($USD, PPP, ADJUSTED)	PISA RANKING (1=HIGHEST PISA SCORE, 35=LOWEST PISA SCORE)
China	100.0	12,210	7
Malaysia	93.3	18,120	NOT AVAILABLE
Taiwan	70.2	40,821	3.5
Russia	65.0	5,923	15
Indonesia	62.1	14,408	27
Korea	61.2	33,141	6
Turkey	59.1	30,303	25
India	58.0	21,608	NOT AVAILABLE
New Zealand	56.0	33,099	11
Singapore	51.7	50,249	1
Canada	49.9	43,715	3.5
Greece	48.3	21,481	23
United Kingdom	46.6	31,845	12
Switzerland	43.7	77,491	10
Panama	42.0	16,000	NOT AVAILABLE
United States	39.7	44,229	18
Finland	38.0	40,491	5
Japan	37.4	31,461	2
Egypt	34.8	6,592	NOT AVAILABLE
France	33.7	33,675	14
Germany	33.4	65,396	8.5
Chile	33.1	20,890	24
Portugal	32.9	35,519	13
Netherlands	32.2	43,743	8.5
Peru	31.1	12,478	29
Colombia	30.3	18,806	26
Spain	29.1	47,864	16
Uganda	25.1	4,205	NOT AVAILABLE
Hungary	24.4	16,241	20
Czech Republic	23.9	18,859	17
Argentina	23.6	10,371	22
Ghana	18.9	7,249	NOT AVAILABLE
Italy	13.6	33,630	19
Israel	6.6	22,175	21
Brazil	1.0	12,993	28

This PISA ranking by country is based on the average actual PISA scores in Mathematics, Science and Reading reproduced in Appendix C section 6 for only the 29 countries in our data that are also included in the PISA survey

Figure A.1 2018 Global Teacher Status Index. Source: Varkey Foundation (2018).

Appendix B

Gallup Poll (2014)

In your opinion, which of the following is MOST valuable for someone in [this country] to have in order to succeed in life?

	Education	Family/friend connections	Strong work ethic	Intelligence
Botswana	73%	10%	4%	13%
Ghana	72%	12%	9%	7%
Zambia	64%	19%	9%	8%
Liberia	63%	15%	11%	2%
Tanzania	63%	5%	12%	20%
Malawi	61%	4%	18%	17%
Sierra Leone	59%	21%	10%	6%
Kenya	58%	17%	11%	13%
South Africa	51%	25%	11%	12%
Zimbabwe	47%	35%	5%	11%
Angola	45%	21%	15%	17%
Nigeria	45%	39%	5%	10%
Madagascar	43%	17%	24%	15%
Morocco	43%	21%	15%	15%
Uganda	42%	19%	15%	24%
Rwanda	41%	21%	14%	25%
Tunisia	38%	29%	11%	17%
Chad	31%	41%	13%	15%
Ethiopia	30%	7%	29%	33%
Niger	30%	38%	8%	25%
Burkina Faso	29%	45%	8%	17%
Cameroon	29%	48%	7%	15%
Mauritania	24%	51%	10%	14%
Mali	23%	63%	7%	7%
Benin	20%	56%	9%	15%
Senegal	20%	59%	13%	8%
Guinea	19%	49%	9%	22%
Congo (Kinshasa)	18%	54%	8%	19%
Gabon	17%	62%	9%	12%
Congo (Brazzaville)	16%	54%	8%	21%
Ivory Coast	13%	49%	10%	25%

2013

GALLUP

Figure B.1 Value Africans place on education. Source: Gallup Poll (2014).

References

Abotsi, A. K., Dsane, C. F., Babah, P. A., & Kwarteng, P. (2020). Factors influencing the choice of teaching as a career: an empirical study of students in colleges of education in Ghana. *Contemporary Social Science*, *15*(4), 446–460. https://doi.org/10.1080/21582041.2019.1675092

Adorno, T. (1973). *Negative dialectics*. Seabury Press.

African Impact News. (2019). Kenyan teacher becomes first African to win global teacher prize (africanimpact.com)

African Union. (2022). *Transforming education in Africa: An evidence-based overview and recommendations for long-term improvements*. Transforming Education in Africa.pdf (unicef.org)

AIMS (African Institute for Mathematical Sciences). (2021). Celebrating World Teachers' Day. Celebrating World Teachers' Day – AIMS Ghana.

Akyeampong, K. (2017). Accountability in the education sector: The case of Ghana. UNESCO: Accountability in the education sector: The case of Ghana - UNESCO Digital Library.

Aldrup, K., Klusmann, U., & Ludtke, O. (2017). Does basic need satisfaction mediate the link between stress exposure and well-being? A diary study among beginning teachers. *Learning and Instruction*, *50*, 21–30.

Alexander, C., Wyatt-Smith, C., & Du Plessis, A. (2020). The role of motivations and perceptions on the retention of inservice teachers. *Teaching and Teacher Education*, *96*, 1–12. https://doi.org/10.1016/j.tate.2020.103186.

Allen Summer. (2018). The science of generosity. A white paper prepared for the John Templeton Foundation by the Greater Good Science Center at UC Berkeley. *Greater Good Science Center. ggsc.berkeley.edu; greatergood.berkeley.edu and organisational citizenship behaviour in Tanzanian primary and secondary schools: and Teaching*, *18*(4), 417e440. https://doi.org/10.1080/13540602.2012.696044

"Altruism, Ethical." Encyclopedia of Genocide and Crimes Against Humanity. Retrieved September 12, 2024 from Encyclopedia.com: https://www.encyclopedia.com/international/encyclopedias-almanacs-transcripts-and-maps/altruism-ethical

Amitai, A., & Van Houtte, M. (2022). Being pushed out of the career: Former teachers' reasons for leaving the profession. *Teaching and Teacher Education, 110*, 103540. https://doi.org/10.1016/j.tate.2021.103540

Andre, C., & Velasquez, M. (2014). *What is ethics? Markkula Center for Applied Ethics*. https://www.scu.edu/mcae/publications/iie/v1n1/whatis.html

Andreoni, J. (1990). Impure altruism and donations to public goods: A theory of warm-glow giving. *The Economic Journal, 100*(401), 464477. https://doi.org/10.2307/2234133.

Antonakis, J., & House, R. J. (2013). The full-range leadership theory: The way forward. *Transformational and Charismatic Leadership: The Road Ahead 10th Anniversary Edition* (*Monographs in Leadership and Management, Vol. 5*), Emerald Group Publishing Limited, Bingley, pp. 3–33. https://doi.org/10.1108/S1479-357120130000005006

APA. (2022). *Coping strategy*. https://dictionary.apa.org/coping-strategy

Aristotle. (trans. 2007). *Nicomachean ethics*. Filiquariam Publishing.

Armstrong, M. (2021). How much do countries spend on education? *Statistica*: https://www.statista.com/chart/15434/the-countries-spending-the-most-on-education/

Avolio, B. J., & Locke, E. E. (2002). Contrasting different philosophies of leader motivation: Altruism versus egoistic. *The Leadership Quarterly, 13*(4), 169–171.

Azomahou, T. T., & Yitbarek, E. (2021). Intergenerational mobility in education: Is Africa different? *Contemporary Economic Policy, 39* (3), 503–523. https://doi.org/10.1111/coep.12495

Bandura, A. (1977). *Social learning theory*. General Learning Press.

Barigaba, J. (2022). Uganda arts teachers on strike to protest unfair pay raise. *The East African*. https://www.theeastafrican.co.ke/tea/news/east-africa/uganda-arts-teachers-on-strike-to-protest-unfair-pay-raise-3859210#google_vigne.

Barnes, N. (2016). It is not easy being a teacher: My story. *Edu Research Matters*. https://www.aare.edu.au/blog/?p=1588

Batson, C. D., Lishner, D. A., & Stocks. E. L. (2014). The empathy–altruism hypothesis. In Schroeder, D. A. &William G. Graziano (ed.), *The Oxford handbook of prosocial behavior*, pp. 259–281. https://doi.org/10.1093/oxfordhb/9780195399813.013.023

BBC. (2019). (277) Sex for Grades: Undercover inside Nigerian and Ghanaian universities—BBC Africa Eye documentary—YouTube. https://www.youtube.com/watch?v=we-F0Gi0Lqs

Bilikpe, & Tengzuyele, E. (2018). Effects of teacher attrition in the Lawra district of the Upper West. *International Journal of Social Science and Humanities Research, 6*(1). https://www.researchpublish.com/papers/effects-of-teacher-attrition-in-the-lawra-district-of-the-upper-west-region-ghana

Blanc, E. (2019). *Red State Revolt: The teachers' strike wave and working-class politics*. Verso Books.

Bolman, L. G., & Deal, T. E. (2021). *Reframing organizations: Artistry, choice, and leadership* (5th ed.). Jossey-Bass.

Bolman. L. G., & Deal, T. E. (2021). *Reframing organizations. Artistry, choice, and leadership* (7th ed.). Jossey-Bass.

Bongila, J. P. (2001). *Funding strategies for institutional advancement of private universities in the United States: Applications for African/Congolese institutions of higher learning*. Dissertation.com

Bongila, J. P. (2005). *Funding strategies for institutional advancement of private universities in the United States and applications for Africa/Congolese universities*. Dissertation.com

Bongila, J. P. (2011). Identifying successful advancement approaches in four Catholic Universities: The effectiveness of the four advancement models of communication. *Journal of Catholic Higher Education, 29*(2), 195–2013.

Bretzke, J. T. (2000). Through thick and thin: Teaching ethics from a cross-cultural perspective. *Horizons. 27*(1): 63-80. doi:10.1017/S0360966900020806

Bruner, J. S. (1990). *Acts of meaning*. Harvard University Press.

Burton, N. (2020). Does true altruism exist? An analysis of altruism. *Psychology Today*. https://www.psychologytoday.com/us/blog/hide-and-seek/201203/does-true-altruism-exist

Cachero, P. (2019). Former teacher shares powerful resignation letter: 'I won't be in an abusive relationship with public education' Former teacher's powerful resignation letter goes viral (yahoo.com)

Caine, Vera. et al. (2020). *Narrative inquiry*. Ed. Paul Atkinson et al. SAGE Publications Ltd.

Caulfield, J. (2022). *How to do thematic analysis step-by-step guide & examples*. https://www.scribbr.com/methodology/thematic-analysis/

Charmaz, K. (2014). *Constructing grounded theory* (2nd ed.). Sage Publications.

Chebet, C. (2019). Peter Tabichi: World's best teacher donates 80% of his salary to the poor. *Standard Digital News*.

Cherry, K. (2022). *What is altruism? How to cultivate selfless behavior*. https://www.verywellmind.com/social-psychology-overview-4581771

Chiong, C., Menzies, L., & Parameshwaran, M. (2017). Why do long-serving teachers stay in the teaching profession? Analysing the motivations of teachers with 10 or more years' experience in England. British Educational Research Journal, *43*, 1083-1110.

Ciulla, J. B. (2005). The state of leadership ethics and the work that lies before us. *Business Ethics A European Review, 14*(4), 323–335. https://doi.org/10.1111/j.1467-8608.2005.00414.x

Ciulla, J. B. (2014). *Ethics, the heart of leadership* (3rd ed.). Praeger.

Ciulla, J. B. (2003). *The ethics of leadership*. Wadsworth/Thomson.

Clipa, O. (2017). Teacher stress and coping strategies. In O. Clipa (ed.), *Studies and current trends in Science of education* (pp. 120–128). Suceava, Romania: LUMEN Proceedings. https://doi.org/10.18662/lumproc.icsed2017.14

Cobbold, C. (2010). *Teacher retention in Ghana: Perceptions of policy and practice*. Lambert Academic Publishing. cogsys.2005.11.010

Creswell, J. & Poth, C. (2018). *Qualitative inquiry & research design: Choosing among five approaches* (4th ed.). SAGE.

Creswell, J. W., & Creswell, J. D. (2023). Research design: qualitative, quantitative, and mixed methods approaches (Sixth edition.). SAGE Publications, Inc.

Cutlip, S. M. (1965). *Fund raising in the United States: It's role in America's philanthropy.* Rutgers University Press.

da Conceição, L. (2017, September 12). Moçambique: Professores de Tete em greve por falta de salários. *DW.* Retrieved from https://www.dw.com/pt-002/mo%C3%A7ambique-professores-de-em-greve-por-falta-de-sal%C3%A1rios/a-41723964

Dal Bó, E., Finan, F., & Rossi, M. A. (2013). Strengthening State capabilities: The role of financial incentives in the call to public service. *The Quarterly Journal of Economics, 128*(3), 1169–1218.

Dalla Costa, J. (1998). *The ethical imperative: Why moral leadership is good business.* Adison-Wesley.

Danner, M. J., Pickering, J. W., & Paredes, T. M. (2018). *Using focus groups to listen, learn, and lead in higher education.* Stylus Publication.

Darling-Hammond, L. (2010). *The flat world and education. How America's commitment to equity will determine our future.* Teachers College.

Darling-Hammond, L., & Podolsky, A. (2019). Breaking the cycle of teacher shortages: What kind of policies can make a difference?. *Education Policy Analysis Archives, 27,* 34. https://doi.org/10.14507/epaa.27.4633

Darling-Hammond, L., Flook, L., Cook-Harvey, C., Barron, B., & Osher, D. (2020). Implications for educational practice of the science of learning and development. *Applied Developmental Science, 24*(2), 97–140. https://doi.org/10.1080/10888691.2018.1537791

De Frans de Waal. (2009). *Primates and philosophers: How morality evolved.* Princeton University Press.

De Neve, D., & Devos, G. (2016). Psychological states and working conditions buffer, 40(1), 6–27. https://doi.org/10.1080/02619768.2016.1246530 96. https://doi.org/10.1016/j.tate.2020.103186. Article 103186.

Deepti Mani. (2018). Education in South Korea. *World Education, News and Reviews (WENR).* Education in South Korea. https://wenr.wes.org/2018/10/education-in-south-korea *Developmental Science,* 1–44. https://doi.org/10.1080/10888691.2018.1537791

Dockrill, Peter. "Kenyan Science Teacher Who Gives 80% of His Salary Away Just Won a $1M Global Prize." *ScienceAlert* (March 25, 2019). doi.org/10.1016/j.tate.2020.103226. Article 103226.

Dolton, P. (2013). Why do some countries respect their teachers more than others? *The Guardian.* https://www.theguardian.com/teacher-network/teacher-blog/2013/oct/03/teacher-status-global-survey

Dolton, P., Marcenaro, O., DeVries, R., & Po-Wen Shi (2018). *Global Teachers Status Index.* National Institute of Economic and Social Research. Gts | PDF | Programme For International Student Assessment | Teachers (scribd.com)

Dolton, P., Marcenaro-Gutierrez, O., Pistaferri, L., & Algan, Y. (2011). If you pay peanuts do you get monkeys? A cross-country analysis of teacher pay and pupil performance. *Economic Policy, 26*(65), 5, 7–55.

Dranzoa, C. (2018). Sexual Harassment at African Higher Education Institutions. *International Higher Education,* 94, 4–6. http://dx.doi.org/10.6017/ihe.2018.94.10512

Dzeich, Billie Wright, & Linda Weiner (1990). *The lecherous professor: Sexual harassment on campus.* University of Illinois Press.

Education Endowment Foundation. (2022). https://educationendowmentfoundation.org.uk/education-evidence/teaching-learning/repeating-a-year

Education Research International. (2017). https://doi.org/10.1155/2017/7282614

Education Week (Edweek), (2022). To Make Ends Meet, 1 in 5 Teachers Have Second Jobs (edweek.org). https://www.edweek.org/leadership/to-make-ends-meet-1-in-5-teachers-have-second-jobs/2018/06

Etshim, R. (2017). Collaboration between Higher Education and labor market in Kinshasa, DR Congo. *Journal of International Education and Leadership,* 7(1). Retrieved from http://www.jielusa.org/

Evren, & Minardi, S. (2017). Warm-glow giving and freedom to be selfish. *The Economic Journal (London), 127*(603), 1381–1409. https://doi.org/10.1111/ecoj.12351

Ferraz, C., & Finan, F. (2009). *Motivating politicians: The impacts of monetary incentives on quality and performance.* NBER Working Paper No. 14906.

Flescher, A. M., & Worthen, D. (2007). *The altruistic species: scientific, philosophical, and religious perspectives of human benevolence.* Templeton Foundation Press.

Foucault, M. (1995). *Discipline and punish: The birth of the prison* (Second Vintage books edition.). Vintage Books.

Fry, R. E. (2002). *Appreciative inquiry and organizational transformation: Reports from the field.* Quorum Books,

Fullan, M. (2003). *The moral imperative of school leadership.* Corwin Press.

Fullan, M. (2018). *The Principal: Three Keys to Maximizing Impact.* Wiley.

Gallup Poll. (2014). In Africa, Parents Key to Education (gallup.com)

Ganu, J. (2018). Moral courage: The essence of ethical leadership and followership. *The Journal of Applied Christian Leadership.* Moral Courage: The Essence of Ethical Leadership and Followership—The Journal of Applied Christian Leadership (andrews.edu)

Gasparello, J., Papi, C., Zurlo, M., Cosenza, L. C., Breveglieri, G., Zuccato, C., et al. (2022) Teaching during COVID-19 pandemic in practical laboratory classes of applied biochemistry and pharmacology: A validated fast and simple protocol for detection of SARS-CoV-2 Spike sequences. *PLoS ONE,* 17(4), e0266419. https://doi.org/10.1371/journal. pone.0266419

Gat, A. (2022). *Ideological fixation: From the store age to today's culture wars.* Oxford University Press.

Gilligan, C. (1082). *In a different voice: Psychology theory and women' development.* Harvard University.

Gilligan, Carol. (1982). *In a different voice: Psychological theory and Women's development.* Harvard University Press.

Global Teacher Status Index. (2018). National Institute for Economic and Social Research. Global Teacher Status Index 2018 - NIESR

Gomba, C. (2015). Why do they stay: Factors influencing teacher retention in rural Zimbabwe. *International Journal of Instruction*, 8(2). www.e-iji.net p-ISSN: 1694-609X https://doi.org/10.12973/iji.2015.825a

Gotthelf, A. (2016). Egoism and Altruism. In *A companion to Ayn Rand* (pp. 130–156). John Wiley & Sons.

Green, T. (2019). North-South dynamics in academia. *Journal of African Cultural Studies*, *31*(3), 280–283. https://doi.org/10.1080/13696815.2019.1630263

Grunig, J. (1992). *Excellence in public relations and communication management.* Lawrence Erlbaum Associates.

Grunig, J. E., & Hunt, T. (1984). *Managing public relations.* Brace Jovanovich College Publishers.

Guirano, Santibanaz, & Daley. (2006). Teacher recruitment and retention: A review of the recent empirical literature. *Review of Educational Research, 76*, 173–208.

Habermas, J. (1991). *The Structural transformation of the public sphere: An inquiry into a category of Bourgeois Society*. MIT Press.

Habito, R. L. F., & Inada, K. (2006). *The practice of altruism. Caring and religion in global perspective.* Cambridge Scholars Press.

Haidt, J. (2021). *The happiness hypothesis: Ten ways to find happiness and meaning in life*. Random House Business Books.

Hall, E. T. (1976). *Beyond culture.* Anchor.

Hallak, J., & Poisson, M. (2009). *Corrupt schools, corrupt universities: What can be done*? UNESCO's International Institute for Educational Planning.

Hanushek, E. A. (2011). How much is a good teacher worth? www.educationnext.org

Harvard Business School online. (2022). 5 Characteristics of a Courageous Leader | HBS Online.

Hayes, A. (2022). *What is philanthropy? Examples, history, benefits and types.* https://www.investopedia.com/terms/p/philanthropy.asp

Heath, C., & Heath, D. (2010). Switch : how to change things when change is hard (1st ed.). Broadway Books.

Heatwaves Cameroon. (2022). Tribute to the teachers [Video]. YouTube. https://www.youtube.com/watch?v=IzLimJtjYIY

Henrich, J., & Henrich, N. (2006). Culture, evolution and the puzzle of human cooperation. *Cognitive Systems Research*, *7*(2–3), 220–245. https://doi.org/10.1016/j.

Hong, J. Y. (2012). Why do some beginning teachers leave the school, and others. https://doi.org/10.1016/j.tate.2015.11.010

Hu, Y.-A., & Liu, D.-Y. (2003). Altruism versus egoism in human behavior of mixed motives: An experimental study. *The American Journal of Economics and Sociology*, *62*(4), 677–705. https://doi.org/10.1111/1536

Jacksa, J. A., & Pritchard, M. S. (1988). *Communication ethics: Methods and analysis*. Wadsworth.

Jeffrey Casely-Hayford, Christina Björklund, Gunnar Bergström, Per Lindqvist, Lydia Kwak (2022). What makes teachers stay? A cross-sectional exploration of the individual and contextual factors associated with teacher retention in Sweden. *Teaching and Teacher Education,* 113:103664, ISSN 0742-051X, https://doi. org/10.1016/j.tate.2022.103664.

Jenkins, J. (2003). *Ethics and religion.* Heinemann Educational Books.

Johnson, C. E. Craig E. (2020). *Meeting the ethical challenges of leadership: casting light or shadow* (7th ed.). Sage.

Jotkoff, E. (2022). NEA survey: Massive staff shortages in schools leading to educator burnout; alarming number of educators indicating they plan to leave profession. NEA. https://www.nea.org/about-nea/media-center/press-releases/nea-survey-massive-staff-shortages-schools-leading-educator-burnout-alarming-number-educators

Kabasua, C., & Kamango, B. (2021). Au cœur des pratiques de corruption dans les universités de (Kinshasa. Actualite Cd.). https://actualite.cd/2021/06/06/au-coeur-des-pratiques-de-corruption-dans-les-universites-de-kinshasa-enquete

Kant, E. (1997). *Foundations of the metaphysis and morals.* Trans Lewis White Beck. Prentice Hall.

Kanungo, R., & Mendonca, M. (1996). *Ethical dimensions of leadership.* Sage.

Katete, S., & Nyangarika, A. (2020). Impact of teachers' delayed salaries and its effects on teaching process in public secondary schools Coast region. *International Journal of Advance Research and Innovative Ideas in Education*, *6*(4), 1291–1305.

Kelchtermans, G. (2017). "Should I stay or should I go?": Unpacking teacher attrition/ retention as an educational issue. *Teachers and Teaching: Theory and Practice*, *23*(8), 961–977. https://eric.ed.gov/?id=EJ1161945

Kellie. (2016). Queen of Katwe—The story of the African teacher. Blog: Queen of Katwe and The Story Of The African Teacher (rookie-manager.com) https://ncee.org/ https://plato.stanford.edu/cgi-bin/encyclopedia/archinfo.cgi?entry=altruism https://www.youtube.com/watch?v=IzLimJtjYIY

Kelly, K. S. (1991). *Fund raising and public relations: A critical analysis.* Lawrence Erlbaum Associates, Publishers.

Kirya, M. (2019). *Education sector corruption: How to assess it and ways to address it.* Bergen: U4 Anti-Corruption Resource Centre, Chr. Michelsen Institute (U4 Issue 2019:5)

Knafo, A., & Plomin, R. (2006). Parental discipline and affection and children's prosocial behavior: Genetic and environmental links. *Journal of Personality and Social Psychology*, *90*(1), 147–164. https://doi.org/10.1037/0022-3514.90.1.147

Konnerth, M. (2017). *The cost of altruism: A phenomenological study of teacher burnout.* ProQuest Dissertations Publishing.

Koreabridge. (2011). Teachers' Day in South Korea. https://koreabridge.net/post/teachers-day-south-korea-unloudedhope

Kramer, K. L. (2005). Children's help and the pace of reproduction: Cooperative breeding in humans. *Evolutionary*, *14*(6), 224–237. https://doi.org/10.1002/evan.20082

Kraut, R. (2020). "Altruism," *The Stanford Encyclopedia of Philosophy.* In Edward N. Zalta (ed.). https://plato.stanford.edu/archives/fall2020/entries/altruism/

Krueger, R. A., & Casey, M. A. (2009). *Focus groups. A practical guide for applied research* (4th ed.). Sage.

Kwakye, P. (2016). *Motivation and job performance: Perceptions of teachers in Kpone Katamansu District in Ghana.*

Le Goff, J. (1992). *History and memory*. Columbia University Press.

Lee, J. K. (2006). Educational fever and South Korean higher education. *Revista Electronica de Investigacion y Educativa*, *8*(1). http://redie.uabc.mx/vol8no1/contents-lee2.html

Lehrer, J. (2017, June 03). The paradox of altruism. https://www.wired.com/2012/02/the-paradox-of-altruism/

Lindqvist, P., & Nordanger, U. K. (2016). Already elsewhere e a study of (skilled) teachers' choice to leave teaching. *Teaching and Teacher Education*, *54*, 88–97.

Locatelli, R. (2018). *Education as a public and common good: Reframing the governance of education in a changing context*. Education Research and Foresight Working Papers Series, No. 22. Paris, UNESCO. https://en.unesco.org/node/268820

Luo, Z., Wang, Y., & Marnburg, E. 2013. Testing the structure and effects of full range leadership theory in the context of China's Hotel Industry. *Journal of Hospitality Marketing and Management, 22*(6), 656–677. https://doi.org/10.1080/19368623.2012.708959 https://doi.org/10.1080/13540602.2017.1379793

Macaskill, W. (2016). *Doing good better: how effective altruism can help you make a difference*. Guardian Books.

Machiavelli, N. (1961). *The Prince*. Penguin Books. [Originally published 1514].

Mangone, E. (2020). *Beyond the dichotomy between altruism and egoism: Society, relationship and responsibility*. Information Age Publishing, Inc.

Marion, R., & Gonzalez, L. D. (2013). *Leadership in education: Organizational theory for the practitioner* (2nd ed.). Waveland Pr. Inc.

Mark Ottoni-Wilhelm. (2017). Altruism and egoism/warm glow in Economics and psychology: Building a bridge between different experimental approaches. In *Social economics* (p. 79). The MIT Press. https://doi.org/10.7551/mitpress/10802.003.0008

Markley, M. (2001). Districts taking new steps to stem teacher turnover. *Houston Chronicle.com*. http://www.chron.com/cs/CDA /story.hts/topstory/1006096 on September 25

Mbiti, J. (1999). *African religions and philosophy* (2nd ed.). Heinemann Educational Publisher.

McCully, R. (2009). *Philanthropy reconsidered*. AuthorHouse.

McKay, A. B. (2019). Identifiable Factors That Influence Teacher Retention in Four Title I Middle Schools: A Multiple-Case Study. Source: https://www.semanticscholar.org/paper/Identifiable-Factors-That-Influence-Teacher-in-Four-McKay/8ba2bd955fa76f91b135b77d9bd6f06e723437ef

McKenna, A. (2010). (Ed.). *The 100 most influential leaders of all time*. The Britannica Guide to the World Most Influential People. Britannica Publishing.

Media Terre Education (2019). La RDC célèbre la Journée Mondiale des Enseignants en trois activités différentes. https://www.mediaterre.org/education/actu,20181007024612,6.html

Merriam-Webster Dictionary. (2022). *Retention*. https://www.merriam.com/dictionary/retention# *methods approaches* (5th ed.). Sage Publications.

Merriam, S. B., & Tisdell, E. J. (2016). *Qualitative research: A guide to design and implementation* (4th ed.). Jossey-Bass. Middle Schools: A Multiple-Case Study. Doctoral Dissertation. Gardner-Webb University. https://digitalcommons.gardnerhttps://digitalcommons.gardner-/webb.edu/cgi/viewcontent.cgi?article=1335&context=education_etd

Mill J. S. 1987. What utilitarianism is. In Ryan, A. (ed.), *Utilitarianism and other essays* (pp. 276–297). Penguin Books.

Miller, J. M., & Youngs, P. (2021). Person-organization fit and first-year teacher MoE (2015). Education Sector Performance Report, Ghana. Available from https://new-ndpchttps://new-ndpc-static1.s3.amazonaws.com/CACHES/PUBLICATIONS/2016/03/22/Education+Sector+Performance+Report+(ESPR)+2015_Final.pdf [Accessed 15/11/2016]. Cited by Acheampong, P. & Fosua Gyasi, J. (2019). Teacher retention: A review of policies for motivating rural basic school teachers in Ghana. *Asian Journal of Education and Training,* (1), 86–92. https://doi.org/10.20448/journal.522.2019.51.86.92

Mohr, M. (2018). *Dystopian features in "Utopia" by Thomas More and their effects on reliability and perception.* Grin Verlag Publisher.

Monroe, K. R. (1998). *The heart of altruism. Perceptions of a common humanity.* Princeton University Press.

Moore, B. D. (2022). What is Ethical Leadership? Principles & Examples. https://www.greatworklife.com/

Morris, S. G. (2005). Identifying the explanatory weakness of strong Altruism: The needle in the "Haystack Model." *Philosophy of Science*, *72*(5), 1124–1134. https://doi.org/10.1086/508121

Mulkeen, A. (2010). *Teachers in Anglophone Africa: Issues in teacher supply.* The World Bank.

Mulvahill, E. (2019). Why teachers quit? https://www.weareteachers.com/why-teachers-quit/

NEA. (2021). NEA survey finds educators back in classrooms and ready for fall Eighty-six percent of educators have had a least one shot and nearly all are back in-person. NEA survey finds educators back in classrooms and ready for fall | NEA.

Ng'ethe, J. M., Iravo, M. E., & Namusonge, G. S. (2012). Determinants of staff retention in public universities in Kenya: Empirical review. *International Journal of Humanities and Social Science*, *2*(13), 105–212.

Nguni, S., Sleegers, P., & Denessen, E. (2006). Transformational and transactional leadership effects on teachers' job satisfaction, organizational commitment, and organizational citizenship behavior in primary schools: The Tanzanian case. *School Effectiveness and School Improvement*, *17*(2), 145–177. https://doi.org/10.1080/09243450600565746

Nietzsche, F. W. (2021). *Beyond good and evil - Friedrich Wilhelm Nietzsche*. Phoenix Classics Ebooks.

Ngwale, A. A. (2021). The contribution of teachers' job satisfaction on their job performance in Northouse, P. (2021). Leadership. Theory and practice (9th ed.). Sage.

Ngwale Aziz Ayoub (2021). The contribution of teachers' job satisfaction performance in Tanzania Secondary schools. *Global Scientific Journals*, *9*(12),

1238–1244. https://www.globalscientificjournal.com/researchpaper/THE_CONTRIBUTION_OF_TEACHERS_JOB_SATISFACTION_ON_THEIR_JOB_PERFORMANCE_IN_SECONDARY_SCHOOLS_IN_TANZANIA.pdf

Nyamubi, G. J. (2017). Determinants of secondary school teachers' job satisfaction in Tanzania.

Oboko, M., & Wasswa, D. (2020). Motivation and teachers' commitment in public primary schools in Kakooge Sub-County, Nakasongola District, Uganda. *Multidisciplinary Research Academic Journal*, *5*(1), 31–39.

OECD. (2005). Teachers matter: Attracting, developing and retaining effective teachers. Attracting, Developing and Retaining Effective Teachers - Home Page - OECD

OECD. (2011). Teachers matter: Attracting, developing and retaining effective teachers. Pointers for policy development. Attracting, Developing and Retaining Effective Teachers - Home

OECD. (2018). *PISA results in focus*. https://www.oecd.org/pisa/pisa-2015-results-in-focus.pdf

OECD. (2019). *TALIS 2018 and TALIS Starting Strong 2018 User Guide,* OECD, Paris. http://www.oecd.org/education/talis/TALIS_2018 Starting_Strong_2018_User_Guide.pdf

OECD. (2019). TALIS 2018 Results (Volume I): Teachers and school leaders as lifelong learners, TALIS, OECD Publishing, Paris. https://doi.org/10.1787/1d0bc92a-en.

OECD. (2019). *TALIS 2018 Technical Report,* OECD, Paris. http://www.oecd.org/education/talis/TALIS_2018_Technical_Report.pdf

OECD. (2021). What proportion of national wealth is spent on educational institutions?. in *Education at a Glance 2021: OECD Indicators*, OECD Publishing, Paris. https://doi.org/10.1787/455a2bcc-en

OECD. (2022). *Mending the education divide: Getting strong teachers to the Schools that need them most.* TALIS. https://doi.org/10.1787/92b75874-en.

OECD. (2022). Teachers' salaries (indicator). https://doi.org/10.1787/f689fb91-en (Accessed on 14 September 2022)

Olukya, G. (2021). Teachers in Uganda despair over not being paid for over a year and bogus policies. *Andalou Agency*. Ugandan educators to mark World Teachers' Day in misery (aa.com.tr)

Opoku, M. P., Asare-Nuamah, P., Nketsia, W. Asibey, B. O., Arinaitwe, G. (2020). Exploring the factors that enhance teacher retention in rural schools in Ghana. *Cambridge Journal of Education*(2), 201–217. https://doi.org/10.1080/0305764X.2019.1661973.

Patton M. Q. (2002). *Qualitative research and evaluation method* (3rd ed.). Sage Publications.

PayScale. (2021). *The most and least meaningful jobs.* https://www.payscale.com/data-packages/most-and-least-meaningful-jobs/full-list.

Persson, B. N., & Kajonius, P. J. (2016). Empathy and universal values explicated by the empathy-altruism hypothesis. *The Journal of Social Psychology*, *156*(6), 610–619. https://doi.org/10.1080/00224545.2016.1152212

Pienaar, C., & Bester, C. L. (2008). The retention of academics in the early career phase: Empirical research. *SA Journal of Human Resource Management*, *6*(2), 32–41.

Pinkowitz, W., Moskal, J., & Green, G. (2009). *How much does your employee turnover cost?* Center for Community and Economic Development, University of Wisconsin. http://www.uwex.edu/ces/cced/economies/turn.cfm

Pisa, K. (2017). How are the world's most valued teachers? Retrieved from https://edition.cnn.com/2017/10/04/health/teacher-pay-and-status/index.html *Science Journal of Sociology and Anthropology* ISSN:2276-6359

Preston, B. (2022). Artifact. The Stanford Encyclopedia of Philosophy (Winter 2022 Edition), Edward N. Zalta & Uri Nodelman (eds.). https://plato.stanford.edu/archives/win2022/entries/artifact/

Rate, C. R., Clarke, J. A., Lindsay, D. R., & Sternberg, R. J. (2007). Implicit theories of courage. *Journal of Positive Psychology, 2,* 80–98.

Rath, T. (2007). *Strength finders 2.0.* Clifton.

Reese, L. A., & Roselfeld, R. A. (2016). *Comparative civic culture: The role of local culture in urban policy-making.* Routledge.

Ricard, M., Mandell, C., & Gordon, S. (2015). *Altruism: The power of compassion to change yourself and the world.* Translated by Charlotte Mandell and Sam Gordon. (First North American ed.). Little Brown and Company.

Rinke, R. C. (2014). *Why half of teachers leave the classroom: Understanding recruitment and retention in today's schools.* Rowman and Littlefield.

Routon, P., & Walker, J. (2017). Helping others, helping myself: Collegiate experiences and graduates' altruistic and wealth aspirations. *Nonprofit and Voluntary Sector Quarterly, 46*(3), 627–651.

Rowe, T. (2023). *Leadership chaos to clarity: Five strategic steps great leaders take to unlock their company's potential.* O'Leary Publishing.

Ruggiero, V. R. (2024). *Thinking critically about ethical issues* (11th ed.). McGraw Hill.

Ryan, A. (2020). *The virtue of selfishness. A new concept of egoism.* Meilleur.

Sandilos, L. E., Goble, P., Rimm-Kaufman, S. E., & Pianta, R. (2018). Does professional development reduce the influence of teacher stress on teacher–child interactions in pre kindergarten classrooms? *Early Childhood Research Quarterly*, 42, 280–290.

Shabe Jonas Matla, & Mgadla Ike Xaba (2020). Teachers' job satisfaction at well-performing, historically disadvantaged schools: A quantitative research in the Gauteng Province, South Africa. International Journal of Educational Management. DOI: 10.1108/IJEM-08-2019-0303 https://www.researchgate.net/

Shapiro, J. (2014). Now there's a Davos of Education and a $1 million Nobel Prize for teachers. *Forbes* (March 22, 2014).

Shapiro, J. P. & Stefkovich, J. A. (2021). *Ethical leadership and decision making in education: Applying theoretical perspectives to complex dilemmas* (5th ed). Lawrence Erlbaum.

Scherer, M. (Ed.). (2009). *Keeping good teachers.* Kindle Edition. Association for Supervision and Curriculum Development Publisher.

Schmitt, F. (2014). *Hume's epistemology in the treatise: A veritistic interpretation.* OUP Oxford.

Somaya, D., & Williamson, I. O. (2008). Rethinking the "war for talent." *MIT Sloan Management Review*, *49*(4), 29–34.

Sorokin, P. A. (1948). *The reconstruction of humanity*. The Bacon Press.

Sorokin, P. A. (1962). *Society, culture and personality: Their structure and dynamics: A system of general sociology. Teachers* Sweden. *Teaching and Teacher Education* 113 (2022) 103664 journal homepage: www.elsevier.com/locate/tate

Stahl, C. (2018). The analysis of corruption in the education sector through a behavioural lens _ IIEP UNESCO - Etico _ Platform on ethics and corruption in education: https://www.u4.no/publications/education-sector-corruption-how-to-assess-it-and-ways to-address-it.pdf

TALIS. (2020). TALIS 2018: teacher working conditions, turnover and attrition. Statistical working paper.

Tanova, C., & Holtom, B. C. (2008). Using job embeddedness factors to explain voluntary turnover in four European countries. *International Journal of Human Resource Management, 19*(9), 1553–1568. http://dx.doi.org/10.1080/09585190802294820 Tanzania secondary schools. *Global Scientific Journals*, 9(12), 1238–1244. www.globalscientificjournal.com

Tarimo, A. (2008). Politicization of ethnic identities and the common good in Kenya. http://www.scu.edu/ethics/practicing/focusareas/global_ethics/kenya.htm

The Bible. (2022). *Psalm 71*. Psalm 71 New Revised Standard Version Catholic Edition (biblehub.com)

The Decision Lab. (2022). Altruism. The Decision Lab—Behavioral Science, Applied.

The University of Massachusetts. (2022). Teacher turnover: What you need to know and how you can curb the trend. https://www.umassglobal.edu/news-and-events/blog/teacher-turnover

TISSA (Teachers Initiative in Sub-Saharan Africa). (2014). *Teacher issue in Uganda: A shared vision for an effective teachers' policy*. UNESCO: International Institute for Education Planning. www.poledakar.org Uganda arts teachers on strike to protest unfair pay raise—The East African.

Transparency International. (2019*). Corruption barometer Africa. Citizens' views and experiences of corruption*. https://www.afrobarometer.org/wp-content/uploads/2022/02/ab_r7_global_corruption_barometer_report.pdf

Transparency International. (2019). Corruption in education systems in West Africa. https://www.cislac.org/wp-content/uploads/2021/04/Policy-Paper-Corruption-in-Education-100519.docx.pdf

Trines, S. (2017). Understanding the causes and Social costs of Academic corruption. *World News and Review*. https://wenr.wes.org/2017/12/understanding-the-causes-and-social-costs-of-academic-corruption

UN (United Nations). (2022). *Academic Impact*. Education For All—United Nations.

UN (United Nations). (2021). Sustainable development goals. Education—United Nations.

UNESCO. (2016). *The world needs almost 69 million new teachers to reach the 2030 education goals*. Retrieved from http://uis.unesco.org/sites/default/files/documents/fs39-the-worldhttp://uis.unesco.org/sites/default/files/documents/fs39-the-world

-needs-almost-69-million-new-teachers-to-reach-the-2030-education-goals-2016-en.pdfneeds-almost-69-million-new-teachers-to-reach-the-2030-education-goals-2016-en.pdf

UNESCO. (2017). World Teachers' Day. World Teachers' Day—5 October 2017 (unesco.org)

UNESCO. (2020). Institute for Statistics Education Statistics. Retrieved from: http://data.uis.unesco.org/

UNESCO. (2021). Commemoration of World Teachers Day 2021 in Uganda | UNESCO.

UNESCO. (2021). Education transforms lives. Education transforms lives | UNESCO.

UNESCO. (2022). Sustainable Development Goals: Teacher attrition rate by education level. Sustainable Development Goals: 4.c.6 Teacher attrition rate by education level (unesco.org).

UNICEF (2021). *Education*. Education | UNICEF Uganda. Education | UNICEF Uganda. https://www.unicef.org/uganda/what-we-do/education

UNICEF (2022). Transforming Education in Africa. An Evidence Based Overview and Recommendations for Long-Term Improvements. https://www.unicef.org/media/106686/file/Transforming%20Education%20in%20Africa.pdf

UNICEF. United States Sentencing Commission (2022).- *Quick Facts - Sexual Abuse Offenders* FY 2017 through FY 2021 Datafiles, USSCFY17-USSCFY21. https://www.ussc.gov/sites/default/files/pdf/research-and-publications/quick-facts/Sexual_Abuse_FY21.pdf

United Nations Office on Drug and Crime (UNODC). (2022). Knowledge tools for academics and professionals Module Series on Anti-Corruption Module 9 Corruption in Education. https://grace.unodc.org/grace/uploads/documents/academics/Anti-Corruption_Module_9_Corruption_in_Education.pdf

University of Pretoria News. (2019, November 22). University of PretoriaNews.

Upadhyay, S. (2021). Sugaring: Understanding the world of sugar daddies and sugar babies. *The Journal of Sex Research, 58*(6), 775–784. https://doi.org/10.1080/00224499.2020.1867700

Van der Vyver, C. P., Kok, M. T., & Conley, L. N. (2020). The relationship between teachers' professional wellbeing and principals' leadership behaviour to improve teacher retention. *Perspectives in Education, 38*(2), 86–102. https://doi.org/10.18820/2519593X/pie.v38.i2.06

Vita-Agundu, U. C., Eseadi, C., Obasuyi, H. U., Sewagegn, A. A., & Amedu, A. N. (2022). Assessment of stress management coaching among Nigerian pre-service history teachers: A randomized controlled study. *Medicine (Baltimore), 101*(40), e30999–e30999. https://doi.org/10.1097/MD.0000000000030999

Wabule, A. (2017). Participatory approaches to unlocking negative perceptions on the choice and motivation to be a primary school teacher in Uganda. *Journal of Science and Sustainable Development, 6*(1), 77.

Wallace, C., & Sartono, A. (2010). Teacher attrition in Sub-Saharan Africa: The neglected dimension of the teacher supply challenge. A review of literature.

UNESCO International Task Force on Teachers for EFA. http://www.teachers-forefa.unesco.org

Wallnau, J. L. (2021). *Holy revolution: Finding true satisfaction in a life set apart.* Destiny Image, Incorporated.

Wayment, H. A., & Bauer, J. J. (Eds.). (2008). *Transcending self-interest: Psychological explorations of the quiet ego.* Amer Psychological Association.

Weaver-Hightower, H. B. (2019). *How to write qualitative research.* Routledge.

Wheeler, W. (2016). *Queen of Katwe* (Video). Disney Picture.

Will, M. (2020). Teacher job satisfaction hits an all-time low. *Education Week, 41*(31),15.

Wilson, D. S. (2015). *Does altruism exist?: Culture, genes, and the welfare of others.* University Press Audiobooks

Wood, L., Hoefer, L., Kammer-Kerwick, M., Parra-Cardona, J. R., & Busch-Armendariz, N, (2018). Sexual harassment at institutions of higher education: Prevalence, risk, and extent. *Journal of Interpersonal Violence,* 1–25. https://doi.org/10.1177/0886260518791228 journals.sagepub.com/home/jiv

World Bank. (2010). Africa development indicators 2010: Silent and lethal: How quiet corruption undermines Africa's development efforts: *Africa Development Indicators.* The World Bank.

World Population Review. (2022). Education ranking by country 2022. https://worldpopulationreview.com/country-rankings/education-rankings-by-country

Wu, M., Walser, J. C., Sun, L., & Kölliker, M. (2020). The genetic mechanism of selfishness and altruism in parent-offspring coadaptation. *Science Advances 6*, 1–12.

Xaba, M. I. (2003). Managing teacher turnover. *South African Journal of Education, 23*(4), 287–291.

YCharts. (2019). *South Korea public spending on education.* https://ycharts.com/indicators/south_korea_public_spending_on_education_gdp

Yin, R. K. (2017). *Case study research and applications: Design and methods (6th ed.).* Sage Publications.

Zaki, J., & Mitchell, J. P. (2011). Equitable decision making is associated with neural markers of intrinsic value. *Proceedings of the National Academy of Sciences of the United States of America, 108*(49), 19761–19766. https://doi. org/10.1073/pnas.1112324108

Zoogah, D. B., & Zoogah, R. B. (2020). Benevolence and Negative Deviant Behavior in Africa: The Moderating Role of Centralization. *Journal of Business Ethics, 161*(4), 783–813. https://doi.org/10.1007/s10551-019-04347-w

Author Index

Subject Index

About the Author

Dr. Jean-Pierre K. Bongila, Rev., is a professor of educational leadership and director of the master's program in Educational Leadership at the University of St. Thomas (MN). He also serves as a tenured member of the core doctoral faculty with expertise in educational, global, and ethical leadership. Dr. Bongila is a champion of building cultural bridges of learning and understanding. He is the recipient of the 2002 Alice L. Beeman Research Award for an outstanding doctoral dissertation in Communication for Educational Advancement, awarded by the Council for the Advancement and Support of Education (CASE). He leads a yearly course, "Leadership in the International Contexts," of such countries as South Africa, Tanzania, Cuba, Brazil, Ghana, Uganda, Egypt, and others. In 2011, the University of St. Thomas recognized him with its Global Citizen Award. He is also the recipient of the 2017 International Citizen Education Award from the International Leadership Institute (MN). He is the president of Help Diocese of Kikwit, a 501(c)3 that supports education and social activities, including the Bilingual School of Leadership project in the D.R. Congo. To learn more about this innovative school, visit www.helpkikwit.org.

www.ingramcontent.com/pod-product-compliance
Lightning Source LLC
LaVergne TN
LVHW091530200926
848483LV00002B/346
* 9 7 8 1 7 9 3 6 2 0 5 7 6 *